A NATION LIKE
NO OTHER

A NATION LIKE NO OTHER

Why American Exceptionalism Matters

NEWT GINGRICH

WITH VINCE HALEY

Since 1947
REGNERY
PUBLISHING, INC.
An Eagle Publishing Company • Washington, DC

Cataloging-in-Publication data on file with the Library of Congress
ISBN 978-1-59698-271-0

Published in the United States by
Regnery Publishing, Inc.
One Massachusetts Avenue, NW
Washington, DC 20001
www.regnery.com

Manufactured in the United States of America

10 9 8 7 6 5 4 3 2 1

Books are available in quantity for promotional or premium use. Write to Director of Special Sales, Regnery Publishing, Inc., One Massachusetts Avenue NW, Washington, DC 20001, for information on discounts and terms or call (202) 216-0600.

Distributed to the trade by:
Perseus Distribution
387 Park Avenue South
New York, NY 10016

To the first-generation Americans,
who remind us again and again that
America remains the last best hope of mankind.

CONTENTS

ON BOWLING GREEN

L ower Manhattan was in turmoil on the blazing hot afternoon of July 9, 1776. To our modern eyes, the city would seem little more than a village of thirty thousand souls, a far cry from the familiar New York of soaring skyscrapers, the Brooklyn Bridge, and the Statue of Liberty. Instead we would find two- or three-story homes, rickety wooden warehouses lining the waterfront on the East River, and little alleyways shooting off narrow cobblestone streets, the only wide street being the "broad way" that cut through the middle of the island.

The tallest building was Trinity Church (later to be shadowed, for a while, by two far taller structures, and to serve on one September morning as a makeshift hospital and morgue at the outset of another generation's great struggle). On this summer day, just up the street from that church, the defining conflict of the first generation of Americans was unfolding. A revolution was being born, and already some thought it might be dying.

After a long day of digging fortifications, drilling, and gazing with apprehension toward Staten Island, by order of Commander George Washington, a sweaty, bedraggled garrison of colonial troops halted work, picked up their muskets, formed ranks, and paraded to the City Commons, near what is now City Hall.

As they formed up, rank after rank, muskets shouldered, the soldiers understood their lives were imperiled—for just a few miles away sat an armada of more than 140 ships, theretofore the greatest transoceanic invasion force in history. It had come to force them to submit to an imperial will—and if they refused, to kill them.

The rebellion, which had started a year earlier with "the shot heard round the world" on Lexington Green, was reaching the point of no return. After winning crucial early victories, the colonists were now facing the bayonet-studded reply of the man who claimed to be their king. A 30,000-man army comprising the finest professionally trained troops in the world—an army with a century-long, nearly unbroken string of victories—was off-loading on Staten Island. The British forces included regiments both honored and feared: the Black Watch, the Coldstream Guards, and the mercenary Hessian heavy infantry and riflemen. They stepped on shore openly and defiantly, believing they had nothing to fear from this rabble-in-arms frantically digging in on the other side of the harbor.

Out on the bay, light sloops proudly flying the British Empire's royal ensign were dashing back and forth. Blockading the entrance to what had once been a thriving port, now cut off from the rest of the world, 44-gun frigates and three-decker, 70-gun ships of the line sat without fear of the assembled throng, which had no navy other than small privateers and converted merchant ships fitted with a few pieces of artillery. If provoked that day, the Brits could easily have advanced up the Hudson River with the morning tide, leveled most of the city, and annihilated the rebels. They held this "mob" in such contempt, however, that they did not even bother to venture a few gunboats up the river to disperse it. There would be plenty of time for the "fox hunt," as they called it, to finish off these "colonial bumpkins" and return home by Christmas. In fact, many British sailors expected the rebels to drop their weapons and melt away without firing a shot once the full might of Empire and King had offloaded and stood ready for battle.

Meanwhile the colonial troops, a few thousand strong, stood silent as they formed their ranks. They were men and even women who had come to Manhattan from towns throughout the colonies, fighters from as far north as New Hampshire and as far south as the Carolinas. Most were farmers, shopkeepers, fishermen, or laborers, and several hundred were hard-bitten riflemen from the distant frontier, having trekked for weeks to join this fray. Few had tasted the sting of battle other than some veterans of the fighting up around Boston the year before, or those who had faced the French and their Indian allies out on the frontier nearly twenty years prior. Most lacked uniforms, and many were barefoot after wearing out their shoes on the way to New York.

Looking out at the men, an officer stepped forward onto a hastily built dais and raised a thick sheet of paper. His audience stirred, anticipating what it was—an explanation of why they were here, why the invasion fleet was off-loading just a few miles away, and why they would be called upon to court death in the months to come.

"By orders of his Excellency, General George Washington commanding, I am to read the following!" the officer cried, his voice carrying across the park and echoing up the street of Broad Way. The chattering civilians who had gathered, most in support of the troops, some showing disdain, fell silent. The officer proclaimed, "Authored by the Continental Congress in Philadelphia this first week of July." He paused as the intense heat pushed beads of sweat down his face, and then continued:

The Declaration of Independence

When, in the course of human events, it becomes necessary for one people to dissolve the political bands which have connected them with another, and to assume among the powers of the earth, the separate and equal station to which the laws of nature and of nature's God entitle them, a decent respect to the opinions of mankind requires that they should declare the causes which impel them to the separation.

We hold these truths to be self-evident, that all men are created equal, that they are endowed by their Creator with certain unalienable rights, that among these are life, liberty and the pursuit of happiness.

That to secure these rights, governments are instituted among men, deriving their just powers from the consent of the governed.

Excited murmurs shot through the crowd. The officer continued reading:

That whenever any form of government becomes destructive to these ends, it is the right of the people to alter or to abolish it, and to institute new government, laying its foundation on such principles and organizing its powers in such form, as to them shall seem most likely to effect their safety and happiness.

Emotions rose among the listeners, but most remained silent. A nearby row of frigates, with their gun ports open so the faint, late afternoon breeze could air out their ships, was a sobering sight. For some, in the upcoming weeks the flash of fire from those guns would be the last thing they ever saw.

Step by step, grievance by grievance, the declaration outlined the American case against their British king. The listeners nodded their heads at some arguments, while other pronouncements drew excited exclamations of agreement or impassioned denunciations of King George. Finally the officer's voice shifted into a more decisive tone:

And for the support of this Declaration, with a firm reliance on the protection of Divine Providence, we mutually pledge to each other our Lives, our Fortunes, and our Sacred Honor.

The words washed over the anxious throng of cobblers, shopkeepers, tin-smiths, and farmers. When the aide finished, the regiment cheered before the officer ordered, "Battalions, dismissed!" The surrounding crowd roared in approval. The more educated among them were eager to get a copy of the Declaration, which printers were already selling for a penny a sheet. Amidst cheers and back-slapping, men held their muskets high and gave three huzzahs for General Washington and three more for the Continental Congress.

Inspired by this declaration of independence, a crowd stormed down Broad Way to the small park at Bowling Green. There, they used grappling hooks and crowbars to tear down a statue of the horse-mounted British king. They dismembered the leaden corpse with hammers and chisels, carting away the metal to use as bullets—ironically, the king's statue would now provide ammunition for the rebels to employ against his troops. The spectacle outraged the Brits, who witnessed the statue's destruction from their ships. As one of the first acts of rebellion inspired by the Declaration of Independence, the scene at Bowling Green became a symbol of the Revolution, a sign that the Declaration was not just a philosophical treatise, but a call to action.

The colonists' euphoria, however, was tempered by a sense of apprehension, especially among war veterans. This would be a hard fight that could last for years, and victory was far from certain. In fact, that night a few colonial soldiers would quietly lay down their muskets and slip away, joining the masses of civilians evacuating what was expected to soon become a bloody field of battle.

But the Declaration had struck a chord. The following dawn, the vast majority of soldiers defiantly returned for morning roll call, despite the overwhelming forces arrayed against them. They would persevere a month later through the debacle on Long Island, and after suffering months of defeats, they would brave the frozen retreat across New Jersey. On Christmas Eve, they would faithfully follow their leader back across the Delaware River to a remarkable victory at Trenton. They would withstand Valley Forge, summers of heat and disease, winters of cold and starvation, for eight blood-soaked years. They endured because they believed in a set of ideals enshrined in a document written by their fellow citizens, a declaration proclaiming that rights such as life, liberty, and the pursuit of happiness are unalienable, that we are endowed with those rights by our Creator, and that all men are created equal, as we are all made in His image.

That was worth fighting for, suffering for, and dying for. That is what made Americans unique in human history and made America, from its inception, a nation like no other.

For over four hundred years, America has cultivated a singular set of vigorous virtues and habits of liberty. We're the people whose first sovereign act was to fire our king. We did so in a classically American way, with clarity and courage.

We declared to the world who we are, explained which government actions were intolerable, and presented a clear case why King George III was a tyrant unfit to lead a free people. In proclaiming our rights as free men, we openly defied one of the greatest powers in the world. We knew this would mean invasion and war, which is why the Declaration ends with its signatories pledging to one another their lives, fortunes, and sacred honor.

The colonists fought willingly and courageously to realize the Declaration's ideals. Most were not professional soldiers but volunteers—free citizens who were willing to sacrifice everything to secure a land of freedom for their families, their children, and their grandchildren yet to be born.

★　★　★

The ideals expressed in the Declaration of Independence, and the unique American identity that arose from an American civilization that honored them, form what we call today "American Exceptionalism." This guiding ethos has always set America apart from all other nations. From its inception, our governing philosophy has been an exception to the practices of governments everywhere else in the world, as detailed by Alexis de Tocqueville and many others. Embracing freedom at a time when Europe and the rest of the world were mired in monarchies and despotism, we settled the frontier, became the world's foremost advocate of economic freedom, led the world in science and technology, vanquished fascism, won a half-century battle against worldwide Communism, and eventually emerged as the world's sole superpower.

Americans today still overwhelmingly believe in American Exceptionalism. A December 2010 Gallup poll asked, "Because of the United States' history and its Constitution, do you think the U.S. has a unique character that makes it the greatest country in the world, or don't you think so?" Eighty percent of Americans responded "yes," including 91 percent of Republicans, 77 percent of independents, and 73 percent of Democrats. Only 18 percent answered "no."

However, even while expressing support for the concept of American Exceptionalism, many Americans have forgotten the original ideals represented by that concept, ideals that have animated the ethos of American life throughout our history and have led to America's unprecedented prosperity and global preeminence. Moreover, there is a determined group of radicals in the United States who outright oppose American Exceptionalism. Often convinced America is a uniquely brutal, racist, and malevolent country, these malcontents struggle to reduce American power and transform our political and economic systems into the kind of statist, socialist model that is now failing across Europe.

You don't need to look hard today to find this radical view, especially in the mainstream media and among left-wing pundits. *Washington Post* columnist Matt Miller mocks American Exceptionalism as a symptom of declining national self-confidence, writing, "Does anyone else think there's something a little insecure about a country that requires its politicians to constantly declare how exceptional it is? A populace in need of this much reassurance may be the surest sign of looming national decline."[1] Similarly, in a *Politico* column titled "U.S. Is Not Greatest Country Ever," former *L.A. Times* editorial page editor Michael Kinsley argues that American Exceptionalism is a form of self-defeating arrogance: "The notion that America and Americans are special, among all the peoples of the earth, is sometimes called 'American exceptionalism.'... This conceit that we're the greatest country ever may be self-immolating. If people believe it's true, they won't do what's necessary to make it true."[2]

The case against American Exceptionalism was made even more boldly in a *Boston Globe* column by author and journalist Neal Gabler. The article, titled "One nation under illusion," argues:

> The hoariest and most oft-repeated cliche in American politics may be that America is the greatest country in the world. Every politician, Democrat and Republican, seems duty bound to pander to this idea of American exceptionalism, and woe unto him who hints otherwise. This country is "the last, best hope of mankind," or the "shining city on the hill," or the "great social experiment." As if this weren't enough, Jimmy Carter upped the fawning ante 30 years ago by uttering arguably the most damning words in modern American politics. He called for a "government as good as the American people," thus taking national greatness and investing it in each and every one of us.
>
> Carter was speaking when Watergate was fresh, and government had been disgraced, but still. The fact of the matter is that whenever anything really significant has been accomplished by our government, it is precisely because it was *better* than the American people.[3]

Bemoaning that "the American people are too thin-skinned and arrogant" to realize their habitual mistake of opposing benevolent government policies like ObamaCare, Gabler warns, "We've been living in a fool's paradise. The result may be a government that *is* as good as the American people, which is something that should concern everyone."

The purpose of such attacks on American Exceptionalism is clear: for those who believe Americans are generally stupid and mean-spirited, America's only hope is for an enlightened governing class to impose the "correct" policies upon its people. To these elitists, the ideals of freedom that underlie American Exceptionalism obstruct the unyielding power the government needs in order to force virtue, as they define it, on a resistant citizenry.

We must expose the agenda of these radials and fight relentlessly against their coercive, big-government policies. But it is worthwhile to consider the perspective of the larger group of people who have forgotten or just don't really understand what American Exceptionalism actually means.

President Obama, for example, simply does not understand this concept. In the past, he was outright contemptuous of American Exceptionalism, deriding Americans as "bitter" people who "cling" to guns and religion, pronouncing himself a "citizen of the world," and denouncing America's supposed past transgressions in front of foreign audiences. His speeches betrayed a strong unease with American power; at an April 2010 nuclear summit, Obama declared, "Whether we like it or not, we remain a dominant military superpower."[4] Most notably, he earned widespread condemnation when a *Financial Times* reporter asked him about American Exceptionalism point-blank, and he began his answer by asserting, "I believe in American exceptionalism, just as I suspect that the Brits believe in British exceptionalism and the Greeks believe in Greek exceptionalism."

Recent events, however, seem to have sparked a change of heart in Obama. Just over a minute into his televised speech defending his decision to intervene in Libya, he proclaimed, "For generations, the United States of America has played a unique role as an anchor of global security and as an advocate for human freedom." Throughout his remarks, he unmistakably conveyed the notion that there is indeed something special about America: "To brush aside America's responsibility as a leader and—more profoundly—our responsibilities to our fellow human beings under such circumstances would have been a betrayal of who we are. Some nations may be able to turn a blind eye to atrocities in other countries. The United States of America is different." Later, Obama invoked our founding ideals and the American Revolution:

> I believe that this movement of change cannot be turned back,
> and that we must stand alongside those who believe in the
> same core principles that have guided us through many storms:

our opposition to violence directed against one's own citizens; our support for a set of universal rights, including the freedom for people to express themselves and choose their leaders; our support for governments that are ultimately responsive to the aspirations of the people. Born, as we are, out of a revolution by those who longed to be free, we welcome the fact that history is on the move in the Middle East and North Africa, and that young people are leading the way. Because wherever people long to be free, they will find a friend in the United States. Ultimately, it is that faith—those ideals—that are the true measure of American leadership.

Many Obama supporters cited the speech as proof of his belief in American Exceptionalism; left-wing writer Glenn Greenwald agreed this was true, even as he worried that believing in American Exceptionalism may not be a good thing.[5] Nevertheless, looking past Obama's rhetoric, his policies betray a fundamental misunderstanding of what American Exceptionalism really means.

It is not enough to give a speech asserting the importance of our ideals of freedom, and insisting that governments must be "responsive to the aspirations of the people." These ideals must be manifested in actual policies. On this score, Obama's record as president comes up woefully short. Imposing a centralized, top-down healthcare system that forces all Americans to buy a private service—health insurance—does not advance or preserve freedom. Undermining school choice to sustain the failing, bureaucratic, public school system and the privileges of its powerful unions does not help children or advance or preserve freedom. Saddling our kids with ruinous debt does not advance or preserve freedom. Strangling American companies' attempts to drill for oil and natural gas, using government power to pick winners and losers among private firms, and expanding bureaucratic control over the nation's industries do not advance or preserve freedom.

In other words, belief in American Exceptionalism leads inevitably to a smaller, more effective, accountable, and limited government. The American revolutionaries did not shed their blood for the welfare state;

nor did they aim to replace the arbitrary rule of King George and his "multitude of New Offices" and "swarms of Officers," as stated in the Declaration of Independence, with their own oppressive bureaucracy. Instead, they fought for individual liberty—and that made America an exception among all other nations.

Today, American Exceptionalism is being weakened not only by the small, radical group of Americans who actively seek to undermine it, but by this larger group of people who may even vaguely support it, but don't really know what it means or where it came from. Clouded by this confusion, they acquiesce to policies that inevitably distance our nation from our founding ideals and historic values. As we slowly become more like Europe, with the attendant debt crisis, self-defeating energy policies, suffocation of private enterprise, and stifling bureaucracy that characterize that continent, they can be fooled into believing this trajectory is consistent with America's historic, exceptional nature.

The good news is that America, thanks to our founding creed, is uniquely poised to thrive in the twenty-first century. Our inherent idealism and generosity, our capitalist spirit, scientific leadership, vociferous defense of individual rights, and penchant for innovation position us to reap amazing benefits from the Information Age, in which scientific, technological, economic, and entrepreneurial dynamism—not government-led industrial planning—will increasingly determine a nation's economic strength. There is a reason why so many great innovators, from Benjamin Franklin (bifocals and the lightning rod) to the Wright Brothers (the airplane) to Steve Jobs (the iPod, iPhone, and iPad), are Americans—because American Exceptionalism cultivates and rewards the habits that made them successful.

Yet just at this moment in history, American Exceptionalism is being diminshed by growing indifference and concerted attacks against it. Instead of leveraging all our cultural advantages to excel in the new economy, the Obama administration is moving us in the opposite direction. As the government grows ever larger, ever more bureaucratic, and ever more intrusive in the economy, the ideals and habits underlying American Exceptionalism are being steadily eroded. Work, creativity, and entrepreneurship are rewarded less, while the ability to manipulate the vast bureaucracy, navigate the impenetrable thicket of regulation, and game the byzantine tax code are becoming paramount skills. Daring managers and innovative engineers become less important to companies than placing well-connected lobbyists in Washington who can directly influence the government's dispensation of favors and beneficial legislation.

For example, in March 2011 the *New York Times* reported on G.E.'s giant, 975-person strong tax department, which helped the company avoid paying any corporate income tax for 2010:

> [G.E.'s] extraordinary success is based on an aggressive strategy that mixes fierce lobbying for tax breaks and innovative accounting that enables it to concentrate its profits offshore. G.E.'s giant tax department, led by a bow-tied former Treasury official named John Samuels, is often referred to as the world's best tax law firm.... The team includes former officials not just from the Treasury, but also from the I.R.S. and virtually all the tax-writing committees in Congress.[6]

A system in which companies need an army of tax specialists, Washington insiders, and well-connected lobbyists to compete is a system in dire need of reform. This state of affairs breeds corruption as well as widespread cynicism toward both business and government. Yet too many people today accept this arrangement as our normal state of affairs, discounting the possibility that there is a better way, a system in which a smaller, more accountable and transparent government allows more freedom for people and businesses to compete honestly, a system where there is more incentive for technological breakthroughs, creative thinking, and innovative methods than there is for peddling political influence and manipulating the rules.

This is why, now more than ever, we need to restore the values and habits of American Exceptionalism. The principles of liberty that underlay America's founding point in a dramatically different direction than where we're heading now. Big Government and an increasingly centralized economy are the antitheses of liberty, which is fundamentally connected to free enterprise, local power, and smaller, more effective, limited government. Our Founding Fathers understood these ideals and fought for them, just as we, in a different way, must fight for them today.

* * *

A Nation Like No Other is dedicated to the proposition that American Exceptionalism is so central to our nation's survival that every generation must learn why being an American is a unique and precious experience.

A Nation Like No Other reflects my belief that the Left has so censored and distorted our history that too many Americans no longer understand why their country is both exceptional and an exception to the form and practice of government in all other countries.

A Nation Like No Other seeks to reaffirm and rebuild Americans' belief in their own country.

The facts are all on our side. America is simply the most extraordinary nation in history. This is not a statement of nationalist hubris. It is an historic fact. It is also proven every day by the thousands of immigrants who give up everything they had to come to our shores and realize the American Dream.

America is exceptional indeed, yet our cultural heritage, our unique habits of liberty that have made us such a successful society, are now being threatened by a combination of centralized bureaucracies, leftwing ideologies, destructive litigation, and an elite view that American Exceptionalism is no longer acceptable or even permissible.

In this book I will share with you the most important ideas of American Exceptionalism, what policies arise from it, and what we can do to sustain and strengthen our role as the singular nation of the modern world.

Our task is twofold. First, we must rediscover the meaning and vitality of American Exceptionalism. Focused on the maneuvering and horse-trading of everyday politics, many Americans on both sides of the political aisle have lost sight of the vital principles that shaped our national identity and our entire system of government. We must understand and explain the enormous energy, innovation, and wealth that have resulted from our commitment to the principles underlying American Exceptionalism. A nation that dedicated itself to protecting the right of every citizen to pursue happiness witnessed an explosion of human creativity and progress that has continued apace for more than 230 years. Abraham Lincoln eloquently described the source of this tremendous prosperity:

> All this is not the result of accident. It has a philosophical cause. Without the Constitution and the Union, we could not have attained the result; but even these, are not the primary cause of our great prosperity. There is something back of these, entwining itself more closely about the human heart. That something, is the principle of "Liberty to all"—the principle that clears the path for all—gives hope to all—and, by consequence, enterprize, and industry to all.
>
> The expression of that principle, in our Declaration of Independence, was most happy, and fortunate. Without this … we [still] could have declared our independence of Great Britain; but without it, we could not, I think, have secured our free government, and consequent prosperity. No oppressed people will fight, and endure, as our fathers did, without the promise of something better, than a mere change of masters.[7]

Recovering and reasserting American Exceptionalism will help us move toward our second goal: putting forward a program of governance that protects American liberties and offers greater opportunity and a more vibrant economic future for every American. The diminishing sphere of liberty today, particularly economic liberty, demands redress. The tools to do so are already at our disposal. The principles of American Exceptionalism point to a clear, proven alternative to the corrupting, insider-dominated, government-centric system that inevitably leads to the replacement of genuine free enterprise with crony capitalism.

Our Founding Fathers got it right. Now it's time we did, too.

PART I

REMEMBERING WHO WE ARE

A civilization without memory ceases to be civilized. A civilization without history ceases to have identity. Without identity there is no purpose; without purpose civilization will wither.

—Michael Kammen[1]

CHAPTER ONE

THE AMERICAN CREED

The fundamental ideas of American Exceptionalism are found in the Declaration of Independence read to General Washington's troops near Bowling Green. The Declaration was drafted by the Continental Congress in Philadelphia, where the Founders sought to affirm their common beliefs in a clear, straightforward manner. The Congress, led by the Declaration's fifty-six signers, ordered that the document be distributed widely across the new nation.

The Declaration sets forth an American Creed, a unifying body of beliefs to which the Founders and their countrymen subscribed. It is this creed, not Europe's historic conception of blood and soil, that defines membership in the American nation. A creed is open to everyone who shares the beliefs, and immigrants become Americans through affirming it. The creed set America apart, an exception to the beliefs other countries have about organizing government and society.

The American Creed is the source of American Exceptionalism to this day. It is both universal and timeless—relevant and accessible to the present generation and to future ones. Spiritual and political leaders throughout our history have called on us to reaffirm our creed and renew our civilization. Martin Luther King Jr. did this explicitly when he declared, "I have a dream that one day this nation will rise up and live out the true meaning of its creed."

The action announced in the Declaration—a severing of political ties with the world's most powerful empire—was radical, but its ideas were not new. Instead, the Declaration of Independence was a succinct summation of beliefs—what the Founders called "truths"—already deeply ingrained in the American psyche. That is why the Second Continental Congress voted unanimously that these truths were "self-evident."

Years later, in an 1825 letter to Henry Lee, Thomas Jefferson wrote that the Declaration's purpose was

> not to find out new principles, or new arguments, never before thought of, not merely to say things which had never been said before; but to place before mankind the common sense of the subject, in terms so plain and firm as to command their assent, and to justify ourselves in the independent stand we are compelled to take. Neither aiming at originality of principle or sentiment, nor yet copied from any particular and previous writing, it was intended to be an expression of the American mind.

If the ideas in the Declaration were not new or particularly radical, then why did this single document fundamentally alter world history? The answer is this: no nation had ever before embraced human equality and God-given individual rights as its fundamental organizing principle. America was the exception, because never before had a nation recognized sovereignty in the citizen rather than the government. And never before had a nation been brought forth that was dedicated first and foremost to identifying the source and nature of the individual's rights and defending those rights, and only secondarily to defining the scope of governmental power—and then only in relation to, and limited by, the individual's unalienable rights.

At the time of the American Revolution, many of the world's rulers justified their authority on the divine right of monarchs, while others didn't bother with any justification other than their ability to wield brute force against their populations. But in America, the individual—not the government—has always mattered above all. Unalienable rights are vested in the individual, not the government, to which we temporarily and conditionally give limited power for the purpose of maintaining social order, the public good, and national defense.

In sum, America's founding document contradicted the prevailing theory and practice in the rest of the world that prioritized government rights over individual rights. In America, the government was designed as the servant of the people, not their master.

AN APPLE OF GOLD
AND A PICTURE OF SILVER

During the "Miracle in Philadelphia" in the summer of 1787, delegates to the Constitutional Convention translated the ideas of the Declaration of Independence into a supple, sophisticated, and unique expression of Enlightenment governing philosophy. Their work ultimately produced the United States Constitution, and shortly thereafter, its first ten amendments that comprise the Bill of Rights.

Two of the amendments, the ninth and tenth, state clearly where ultimate power lies—not with a dictatorial central power, but with the various states and their people. In the great debate leading up to the Constitution's ratification, many states conditioned their acceptance of the Constitution on the promise that the first order of business after its ratification would be passing those amendments, a promise the Founders kept.

Abraham Lincoln employed a vivid analogy to explain the connection between the Declaration and the Constitution. He said the Declaration was like an "apple of gold," and he likened the Constitution to a "picture of silver, subsequently framed around it." He continued, "The picture was made, not to conceal, or destroy the apple; but to adorn, and preserve it. The picture was made for the apple—not the apple for the picture. So let us act, that neither picture, or apple shall ever be blurred, or bruised or broken. That we may so act, we must study, and understand the points of danger."

Undeniably, the Declaration's commitment to unalienable rights had a profound impact on the drafting of the Constitution and the Bill of Rights, resulting in the following features:

- Religious liberty is the first liberty protected by our Bill of Rights, contributing to a free, flourishing religious life in the United States unlike that found in any other country.
- Private property is protected and contracts are upheld, so that people will be rewarded for their work and realize the fruits of their labor and their innovations.
- People can freely assemble and associate with whomever they want without interference from the government.
- People have a right to know the laws; these laws are followed by the government and are not applied arbitrarily; and people can petition to change the laws or government decisions.
- Government must protect the physical safety of the people in their homes and communities, and the safety and sovereignty of the nation itself—a precondition for securing all other rights.

The Constitution was not Americans' first written commitment to these and other rights; as described below, the colonists had long been enacting their own written compacts and constitutions. But with the establishment of a new nation, distinctly American habits of liberty thrived in the new constitutional order and became the surest support for an individual's rights and his ability to pursue happiness.

In a country of unique natural bounty, the protection of each of these rights through the rule of law led to extraordinary individual creativity and economic prosperity. These indisputably exceptional results originated from a unique set of historical and cultural circumstances. But exceptional results and exceptional circumstances should not be confused with the wellspring of American Exceptionalism expressed in the Declaration—the idea that the individual has unalienable rights from God that no government can abridge.

A HIGHER INSPIRATION

The Declaration's writers understood there was a force in the universe greater than themselves, and they incorporated this humbling recognition in their work. One of the Declaration's most famous passages proclaims, "We hold these truths to be self-evident, that all men are created equal, that they are endowed by their Creator with certain unalienable Rights, that among these are Life, Liberty and the pursuit of Happiness." This assertion makes some key assumptions about the relationship between man and God:

- It assumes that God created man.
- It assumes that God is sovereign over the universe.
- It assumes that man must obey an order of justice that God has instituted.

That order of justice requires all men and women to honor each other's natural rights, because these rights are an unalienable endowment from the Almighty. When someone violates another's rights, he is not merely breaking the law, he is violating God's grant of protection.

This points to two additional assumptions underlying the Declaration: first, that if our rights are given by a divine Creator, then there is a divine plan for humanity; and second, that since all men are equal before God, they should be legally and politically equal as well. The equality of men was fundamental to the teachings of "New Light" preachers like Jonathan Edwards and George Whitefield, which permeated all the colonies during the Great Awakening of the 1730s and '40s.

The Declaration acknowledges that our Creator endows all men with unalienable rights, and that to secure those rights men organize governments. Thus the source of authority for both instituting government and deposing it lies with the people. Indeed, the Declaration's opening paragraph asserts the people's sovereign authority from God to determine their own government:

> When in the Course of human events it becomes necessary for one people to dissolve the political bands which have connected them with another and to assume among the powers of the earth, the separate and equal station **to which the Laws of Nature and of Nature's God entitle them,** a decent respect to the opinions of mankind requires that they should declare the causes which impel them to the separation. (Emphasis added)

With every individual receiving sovereign authority directly from God, the Founders argued that individuals then have the power to loan some of this sovereign authority to government to organize its powers in such a way as to advance their own safety and happiness.

Acceptance of this simple hierarchy—God, then the individual, then government—set America apart, an exception from all nations that came before it.

A NATION FORGED IN EQUALITY

The Declaration of Independence was clear on the issue of equality—"All men are created equal." There would be no hereditary monarch ruling over his subjects, nor would the people be made subservient to a privileged aristocracy. First expressed in the Mayflower Compact more than 150 years earlier, the concept of legal equality was the only logical outcome of the Declaration's proclamation of liberty, unalienable rights, and government being rooted in the consent of the governed. The perpetuation of slavery blatantly violated both the letter and the spirit of our founding document.

The great American nation that arose from our forefathers' revolution was ripped asunder by the Civil War. The war initially centered around constitutional questions, but two years into that terrible conflict, on the field at Gettysburg, Lincoln fundamentally redefined the struggle by harkening back to the Declaration at the beginning of his historic address: "Four Score and seven years ago, our fathers brought forth on this continent a new nation, conceived in liberty and dedicated to the proposition that all men are created equal." Lincoln was saying the war was no longer being fought over a narrow disagreement over constitutional interpretation, but had become a far more fundamental dispute over the nature of human freedom and equality.

Indeed, America is perhaps the only nation on earth to fight a civil war over the nature of equality. Lincoln understood the wider ramifications of this struggle, repeatedly declaring that the United States was the "last best hope of earth," and warning that the entire world would suffer if we failed to hold together a Union based on freedom.

During the twentieth century, America emerged triumphant from terrible struggles in which we spent trillions of dollars and lost hundreds of thousands of lives. Recall our various enemies: Germany under both the Kaiser and Hitler, Imperial Japan, worldwide Communism, Saddam Hussein's Iraq, and currently, radical Islamism. Now consider this: did any of our foes engage in war to secure equality and individual rights? They might declare the superiority of their race or social class, or demand that all must submit to their religion. But never did one of our foes fight for the simple, self-evident truth that all men are created equal. It was for this principle that so many Americans made the ultimate sacrifice. And it is our duty to honor and remember them—and the ideals for which they fought.

AMERICAN CITIZENS
OF BRITISH LIBERTY

The Declaration encapsulated the Founders' ideas about politics, history, and philosophy, all of which were highly influenced by British thinkers. Most of the Founders were born in Britain's North American colonies, though a few hailed from Britain itself or its other colonies. They considered themselves British, but emphasized their status as free and equal citizens and as beneficiaries of a British tradition of liberty, rather than as subjects of monarchical authority. As Bernard Bailyn writes, "The colonists' attitude to the whole world of politics and government was fundamentally shaped by the root assumption that they, as Britishers, shared in a unique inheritance of liberty."[2]

This inheritance was a special source of pride for most Englishmen, as historian Gordon Wood observes:

> Englishmen everywhere of every social rank and of every political persuasion could not celebrate [the British Constitution] enough. Every cause, even repression itself, was wrapped in the language of English liberty. No people in the history of the world had ever made so much of it. Unlike the poor enslaved French, the English had no standing army, no lettres de cachet; they had their habeas corpus, their trials by jury, their freedom of speech and conscience, and their right to trade and travel; they were free from arbitrary arrest and punishment; their homes were their castles.[3]

The "liberties of Englishmen" were bedrock for the colonists, but they were keenly aware these rights were hard-won, unevenly applied, and if history was any guide, impermanent.

In Britain, natural rights were assumed to be an integral part of the unwritten English constitution. Beginning with the Magna Carta (Great Charter) in 1215, Britain had slowly and steadily limited the government's powers and expanded the rights of its citizens. At Runnymede, in return for monetary payments from his barons, King John conceded that the barons had certain rights that he would not violate—an early step toward recognizing the principle of no taxation without representation. The Stuarts rolled back many of those ancient liberties, but the ensuing English Civil War in the mid-seventeenth century, as well as the Glorious Revolution of 1688, revived Britain's tradition of gradually limiting monarchical power.

By the seventeenth and eighteenth centuries, a new doctrine was forming out of the British Common Law and the essays of political thinkers who chipped away at the legitimacy of absolute monarchs by proposing that citizens held permanent rights transcending those of governments. Though emerging in Britain, this new model reached full bloom first in the Scottish Enlightenment and then in the American colonies, where the reach of government was weaker and the lure of freedom was stronger.

Americans increasingly believed they had the right to resist oppressive government, even if it was as powerful as the British Empire. This transformation from a government-centric model to a citizen-centric model was an intellectual revolution that formed the philosophical basis of the American Revolution that followed.

A NATION WITH THE SOUL OF A CHURCH

The Founders were undeniably religious, and their faith found expression in the Declaration's assertion that man's unalienable rights come from God. As John Adams declared in 1813, "The *general principles* on which the fathers achieved independence, were ... the general principles of Christianity, in which all those sects were united, and ... that those general principles of Christianity are as eternal and immutable as the existence and attributes of God; and that those principles of liberty are as unalterable as human nature and our terrestrial, mundane system."[4]

However, most of the Founders' religiosity broke with the traditional bounds of Christian thought in Europe. They were particularly critical of the trappings of official, state-sponsored religion across the old continent and especially in England. Although the Glorious Revolution had resulted in a measure of tolerance for religious dissent in Britain, the Church of England remained a privileged, state-sponsored faith, and religious minorities faced various forms of official discrimination, causing hundreds of thousands of Scottish and Scotts-Irish Presbyterians to migrate to America.

By the time of America's founding, by contrast, religious pluralism was flourishing in the colonies, which provided a welcome home for religious refugees. In America, citizens were free to select the church they attended without government interference. As a result of this "American voluntarism," the colonies' churches enjoyed much higher attendance rates and more committed congregations than was the case on the continent.

Freedom of religion, absent the stifling bureaucracy and hierarchy that characterized Europe's official churches, democratized the practice of faith in the American colonies, giving rise to a vibrant, pluralistic religious community. A British bureaucrat observed that the colonies had "no distinctions of Bishops, Priests or Deacons, no Rule or Order, no Dean Chapters or Archdeacons. All were Priests and nothing more."[5] With God as the only recognized higher authority, the individual was made directly accountable to Him. America's flourishing religious tradition stood in stark contrast to Europe's rigid, conflict-ridden religious life, encouraging the Founders to believe that a country founded on liberty could not only survive, but thrive.

NATURAL LAW AND THE NATURAL RIGHTS OF MAN

Aside from its religious influences, the Declaration was impacted by European thinking on the issue of liberty. The document confirmed natural rights stemming from the identification of man as an inherently sovereign and dignified being—a proposition the Founders confirmed through both reason and experience.

These ideas had developed over centuries. Drawing on Greek classical thinkers, Thomas Aquinas and other medieval theologians identified man's ability to reason and act autonomously as evidence of his personal sovereignty. Renaissance thinkers later stressed man's self-awareness (Descartes' "I think therefore I am") as proof of personal sovereignty, which could be expressed outwardly in violence or benevolence, in horror or genius. Great individual accomplishments in arts and sciences reinforced this notion—from Da Vinci to Shakespeare, from Galileo to Newton, individuals demonstrated the power to remake the world around them.

Other thinkers developed a parallel belief in the inviolate dignity of man. Citing Judeo-Christian texts, medieval scholars identified the inherent dignity of man as a gift from God. Because the universality of God's gift required the same responsibility of everyone, this reasoning implied all men were equal in God's eyes—a revolutionary doctrine that inspired challenges to the authority of Church prelates and state officials alike.

Drawing on these currents, the English philosopher John Locke devised theories that would strongly influence America's Founders. Locke argued against the ideas of fellow Englishman Thomas Hobbes, who insisted it was man's natural instinct to reject the dignity of his fellow man. This instinct, Hobbes argued, reduced life to a brutish, anarchic "state of nature" that can only be avoided by ceding individual rights to an immensely powerful central authority—a so-called "Leviathan." For Locke, however, individuals in the "state of nature" were sovereign and equal under God, and therefore dignified. Locke observes:

> People in this state do not have to ask permission to act or depend on the will of others to arrange matters on their behalf. The natural state is also one of equality in which all power and jurisdiction is reciprocal and no one has more than another. It is evident that all human beings—as creatures belonging to the same species and rank and born indiscriminately with all the same natural advantages and faculties—are equal amongst themselves. They have no relationship of subordination or subjection unless God (the lord and master of them all) had clearly set one person above another and conferred on him an undoubted right to dominion and sovereignty.

Locke believed man's inherent reason forestalled the onset of a Hobbesian "war of all against all," yet he acknowledged that reason, by leaving man free to do good or ill, made an individual's "life, liberty, and property" insecure. To correct for that insecurity, individuals can willingly band together to create a society that secures rights for mutual benefit.

According to Locke's doctrine of consent, the transfer of power from individuals to a state or society is conditional and incomplete. Man's natural freedom, and his right to life and liberty, are God-given and cannot be ceded even willingly because they are not his to give—in other words, these rights are "unalienable." Locke argued,

> The natural liberty of man is to be free from any superior power on earth, and not to be under the will or legislative authority of man, but to have only the law of nature for his

rule. The liberty of man, in society, is to be under no other legislative power, but that established, by consent, in the commonwealth; nor under the dominion of any will, or restraint of any law, but what that legislative shall enact, according to the trust put in it.

Crucially, Locke maintained that the social contract, as it was formed willingly, can be dissolved freely when the government no longer abides by its terms.

When any one, or more, shall take upon them to make laws, whom the people have not appointed so to do, they make laws without authority, which the people are not therefore bound to obey; by which means they come again to be out of subjection, and may constitute to themselves a new legislative, as they think best, being in full liberty to resist the force of those, who without authority would impose any thing upon them. Every one is at the disposure of his own will, when those who had, by the delegation of the society, the declaring of the public will, are excluded from it, and others usurp the place, who have no such authority or delegation.

French philosophes such as Montesquieu, Diderot, and Voltaire further refined the notion of personal sovereignty and popular sovereignty, as did the thinkers of the Scottish Enlightenment. The Founders distilled all these disparate influences into a "liberal philosophy" that emphasized the personal sovereignty and dignity of the individual. As Bailyn explains, "Borrowing from more original thinkers, they were often, in their own time and after, dismissed as mere popularizers. Their key concepts— natural rights, the contractual basis of society and government, the uniqueness of England's liberty preserving 'mixed' constitution—were commonplace of liberal thought at the time."[6]

Though commonplace at the time, these ideas were expressed in the Declaration of Independence with such clarity and conviction that the document would give birth not only to a country, but to an ethos that, to this very day, resonates throughout the world.

ENGLAND'S FIRST VENTURES IN AMERICA

Though they regarded themselves as British, the Founders were conscious of their special status in the New World. They were the progeny of refugees, immigrants, utopians, and frontiersmen, living free from many of the ancient artifices and institutions of Europe, with the opportunity to import social structures or invent their own. For them, the intuitive claims of history could be reasoned and tested against rival notions before being accepted. America in effect became a great laboratory for experimentation.

The initial colonists' successes and failures gave rise to an American way of thinking about how to confront challenges, adapt, survive, and thrive. Alongside its European philosophical influences, the Declaration of Independence also reflected the colonists' unique struggles and the resulting worldview that affirmed self-reliance and individual responsibility in the face of utterly new circumstances.

The first English settlement in the American colonies was an abject failure, providing a valuable lesson for future efforts. The settlement at Roanoke under Sir Walter Raleigh in the 1580s had confused aims, feuding leaders, and unprepared participants. Furthermore, as historian Paul Johnson notes, Roanoke "had no religious dimension … [no] God-fearing, prayerful men"[7]—a crucial quality that infused other, successful settlements with a common purpose. Amidst debilitating infighting, the expedition's fleet simply sailed off without the colonists. War with Spain and the invasion of the Spanish Armada prevented their re-supply, and the colonists vanished before a return expedition arrived.

The Founding Fathers took inspiration from the hard-won success of the two subsequent English colonies in the New World, at Jamestown and Plymouth Plantation. Although the two colonies had different aims, comprising capitalist adventurers and Christian idealists, respectively, both groups were convinced that England, like Biblical Israel, was endowed with a special destiny by God—and as new Israelites, the settlers sought out their own land of milk and honey. Moreover, both settlements overcame initial misdirection from London and developed similar traditions and values emphasizing industriousness, self-reliance, and Godliness. These traits grew into a new, American worldview that found expression in America's founding documents.

JAMESTOWN

The Virginia Company of London founded the colony of Jamestown on the James River in Virginia in 1607. The initial financing was entirely from private investors, with settlers promised freehold land in return for seven years of communal labor for the colony. When the first settlers landed, they quickly built a church, signaling their common purpose.

The harsh environment and dwindling supplies took a heavy toll on the settlers, who became increasingly listless and undisciplined. Unprepared for the physical hardships and demotivated by the requirement for communal labor, many of them moved elsewhere. The deteriorating situation was first reversed when John Smith, who had been elected by popular vote to head the Jamestown Council, announced new work rules. Smith decreed:

> You must obey this now for a Law, that he that will not worke shall not eate (except by sickness he be disabled:) for the labors of thirtie or fortie honest and industrious men shall not be consumed to maintaine an hundred and fiftie idle loyterers.[8]

Smith's order, alluding to the Biblical passage 2 Thessalonians 3:10, repudiated the colony's initial feudal structure under which "high-born" colonists had refused to perform much manual labor. It was a profoundly democratic directive and a dramatic breakthrough for equality, as each man was expected to contribute or perish.

But John Smith was injured and had to return to England in 1609, after only eighteen months in Virginia. Once he departed, conflict with the local Indians combined with demotivating work rules led to a "starving time" during the winter of 1609–1610 that took the lives of all but sixty of the 500 colonists.

The colony was revived when a new "high marshal," Sir Thomas Dale, arrived in 1611 and encouraged individual initiative by establishing private property rights to individual plots of land. Several years later another settler, John Rolfe, pioneered tobacco cultivation, setting the colony on the road to prosperity. In 1619, Jamestown adopted governance on republican principles with a representative and responsible "House of Burgesses" that met in the Jamestown church. Emphasizing the rule of law and a self-governing ethic, the colony affirmed unique principles of liberal governance that dramatically differentiated it from Europe.

PLYMOUTH

As the Jamestown settlers struggled against the elements, the Pilgrims—a congregation of dissenters and separatists from the Church of England—received a charter to establish their own foothold in America. In 1620, the Pilgrim fathers penned an early draft of the American Creed while en route to the New World on the *Mayflower*. Having veered off-course from their destination in Virginia, some of the would-be colonists asserted the change-of-course had voided the king's charter, necessitating a new contract. In the Mayflower Compact, the Pilgrims mutually agreed to a social contract binding themselves together under God. Plymouth Colony's governor, William Bradford, preserved the pledge:

> In the name of God, Amen. Having undertaken, for the Glory of God and advancement of the Christian Faith and Honour of our King and Country, a Voyage to plant the First Colony in the Northern Parts of Virginia, do by these presents solemnly and mutually in the presence of God and one of another, Covenant and Combine ourselves together into a Civil Body Politic, for our better ordering and preservation and furtherance of the ends aforesaid; and by virtue hereof to enact, constitute and frame such just and equal Laws, Ordinances, Acts, Constitutions and Offices, from time to

time, as shall be thought most meet and convenient for the
general good of the Colony, unto which we promise all due
submission and obedience.[9]

Wholly independent of the Jamestown colony, the Pilgrims established
their settlement in Plymouth, Massachusetts, on democratic and egali-
tarian principles and the rule of law. Their framework set a precedent
for future frontier agreements and was a radical departure from the
European model, as no institutions but God and king preceded their
compact.

The Plymouth Pilgrims had much in common with the settlers in
Virginia, but they departed from the Jamestown model in a crucial
respect: their efforts would be dedicated to glorifying God. To the Plymouth settlers, the colony would represent an uncorrupted ideal, serving
as an example to the decadent, fallen, and unreformed. Their compact
and ensuing laws were modeled not on the principles of English liberties,
but on the covenant between God and the Israelites.

The radical principles of governance based on consent and equality
boded well for the colony. But as in Jamestown, the Pilgrims learned the
hard way that without the proper incentives for work even a project
comprised of godly men was doomed. Amidst poor harvests and spreading unrest, William Bradford scrapped the communal living and work
rules, which had been imposed by the Virginia Company in London, and
granted private freehold title to land directly to family units. The colonists' natural industriousness and ingenuity quickly re-emerged.

The leader of the follow-on Massachusetts Bay Colony, John
Winthrop, also saw his project as a fundamentally redemptive one, an
opportunity to start the world anew in the unspoiled wilderness. Plymouth
Plantation, like Jamestown, enjoyed de facto self-government through
distance and circumstance,[10] but the colony's founders managed to get a
charter approved in 1629 that required no oversight meetings in London,
giving the Massachusetts Bay Colony great legal flexibility. The self-
governing principle, along republican and religious lines, clearly imbued the
Bay Colony, which Winthrop, drawing from Jesus' Sermon on the Mount,

proclaimed to be "as a City upon a Hill," adding "The eyes of all people are upon us." In Winthrop's terms, America was an exemplar burdened with history's judgment. The American Creed was coming into focus as a principled exception to European models of governance.

Despite their democratic procedures, neither Plymouth Plantation nor the Bay Colony in Boston were bastions of liberty. Pilgrim leaders governed Plymouth like a theocratic dictatorship, and the Bay Colony banished Quakers and other religious dissenters.

One dissenter expelled from the Bay Colony was the Baptist Roger Williams, who later established a separate colony in Rhode Island that affirmed the radical precept of religious liberty. Along the Williams model, more colonies based on religious tolerance emerged in British North America, such as Lord Baltimore's Catholic haven in Maryland (founded in 1634) and William Penn's Quaker-led colony in Pennsylvania (founded in 1682). All the while, the frontier beckoned liberty-seeking pioneers, offering a new social contract along less rigid lines of religious or political control. The space of the New World, as much as political and religious doctrine, made America home to liberty.

Notably, these experiments in self-government preceded the high-minded theories of Rousseau, Locke, and Hobbes. Locke, whose ideas would ring through the Declaration of Independence, was himself strongly influenced by the American colonial experience in crafting his ideas on the social contract and natural liberty.[11] Remarkably, America helped to spread ideas of liberty far before its independence.

UNITY UNDER GOD

Though the various American colonies had similar governing principles based on man's equality and personal sovereignty, by the close of the seventeenth century the colonies featured highly diverse political structures and economies. From British Army general James Oglethorpe's debtors' haven in Georgia to Virginia's plantation culture to New York's commercial hub, the colonies developed their own traditions and modes of life. Religious practice was particularly diverse; though a fraction of Britain's size, the combined colonies had hundreds of faiths evangelizing and growing aggressively in the spiritual free market of America, in stark contrast to Britain's thirty socially proscribed "non-conformist" sects.[12]

The transformation of the disparate colonial cultures into a common American identity occurred through a massive religious revival that began in the 1730s. As John Adams noted, "But what do we mean by the American Revolution? Do we mean the American war? The Revolution was effected before the war commenced. The Revolution was in the minds and hearts of the people: a change in their religious sentiments of their duties and obligations."[13]

Adams was referring to the Great Awakening, which swept from small New England towns through the mid-Atlantic ports and southern agrarian outposts. The movement, which de-emphasized religious cere-mony and stressed an intense, emotional, and individual relationship with God, further democratized religion, as independent sects flourished, religious education became personalized, and crucially, "New Light" believers abandoned the government-established Church of England in droves. A key leader of the Awakening was the revivalist George White-field, who visited every colony in English North America, delivering an estimated 18,000 spellbinding sermons from the 1730s until his death in 1770. Whitefield's efforts were assisted by Benjamin Franklin, who became a friend of Whitefield's, though not a convert, and reprinted at great profit Whitefield's sermons in his newspaper.

True liberty had come to mean freedom of faith and conscience, while religion was deemed necessary to support liberty, a gift of God. The purpose of liberty was to give glory to God. If God was forsaken, liberty's purpose would be destroyed, and liberty itself would give way to tyranny. In the words of Gouverneur Morris, a key contributor to the U.S. Con-stitution, "Religion is the only solid Base of morals and Morals the only possible Support for free governments."[14]

The Great Awakening had a deep, unifying effect on the American colonists. As Paul Johnson writes, the Awakening "taught different colo-nies, tidewaters and piedmonts, coast and up-country, to grasp and appreciate what they had in common, which was a very great deal."[15]

With their common experiences, values, and beliefs, the colonists were transforming into a nation.

* * *

The New World, though created by men of the Old World, birthed wholly new expressions of ancient ideas. The American experience taught the Founders that self-government was not only possible, but effectual and just—that God's gifts of life and liberty were universal and good. These ideas had been bandied about in European universities and salons for centuries, being refined and debated by high-minded scholars, but they were made real by the citizens of the primitive townships of colonial America. The New World, as much as the Old, wrote the American Creed.

By the time that creed was codified in the Declaration of Independence, it was already widely known and understood, from Boston to Savannah. For the tinkers, farmers, soldiers, and cobblers in New York who heard it read aloud as the British Navy lurked off Staten Island, the source of their rights *was* self-evident. They were free and godly men, equal in God's eyes and self-sufficient in life. The natural rights of the Englishmen, derived from the Reformation, Enlightenment, and constitutional settlements, had now passed on to the colonists.

The Declaration of Independence was not radical in thought but in action. It took bold steps to enshrine these sacred principles as the basis of a new country. With the Declaration, America set itself apart, an exception from the ways of the other nations of the world, and embarked on a radically new course in history, in pursuit of neither wealth, nor power, nor racial or ethnic purity, but an idea: God-given liberty for all.

CHAPTER TWO

HABITS OF LIBERTY

THE SHIELD OF
THE AMERICAN REVOLUTION

A s the delegates to the Constitutional Convention were completing their work, Benjamin Franklin reportedly walked outside and encountered a woman who asked him, "Well, Dr. Franklin, what have you done for us?" Franklin responded, "My dear lady, we have given to you a republic—if you can keep it."[1]

In a single sentence, Dr. Franklin summed up the extraordinary drama that would play out for all of American history between the two vital forces that sustain American Exceptionalism: freedom and responsibility.

In 1787, the American people created a government that maximized individual freedoms. In order to guard against the growth of unchecked federal power, the Founders carefully designed a republic that divided this power among three separate but co-equal branches of a central government of limited powers, with each having the authority to check and balance the powers of the others.

Moreover, the Founders recognized that the effectiveness of these safeguards, and of the nation's overall governmental structures, would ultimately depend upon the character of the American people. The people would have to exercise responsibility, both for themselves and for their neighbors, if they were to keep a republican form of government and the freedoms it was designed to protect.

THE REPUBLIC WE WERE GIVEN

Notably, the Founding Fathers created a republic instead of a direct democracy. In a direct democracy, legislation is passed by a direct majority vote of all the people, whereas in a republic the people elect representatives who then pass legislation. In a direct democracy, the source of authority is the people. In a republic, the source of authority is the rule of law, which is typically codified in a constitution.

Understanding both the flawed nature of man and historical precedent, the Founders were adamantly opposed to direct democracy, fearing such a system would fail to protect true liberty and would allow for the "tyranny of the majority"—the scenario in which a majority can adopt unjust policies and oppress a minority of voters solely on the basis of their numbers. James Madison argued that "democracies have ever been spectacles of turbulence and contention; have ever been found incompatible with personal security, or the rights of property; and have, in general, been as short in their lives as they have been violent in their deaths."[2] According to John Adams, "[D]emocracy never lasts long. It soon wastes, exhausts, and murders itself. There never was a democracy yet that did not commit suicide."[3]

The Founders, however, were also aware of the shortcomings of republics—especially their historical tendency to decay into aristocratic and tyrannical government, as was the case with the ancient Roman republic and with the English Parliamentary Commonwealth under Oliver Cromwell. They understood that previous republics had failed due to man's susceptibility to the intoxicating temptations of power. As Sam Adams remarked, "The depravity of mankind [is] that ambition and lust of power above the law are ... predominant passions in the breasts of most men."[4]

Acknowledging this inherent weakness in man, the Founders sought to diffuse governmental power so that no single person, group, or governing branch could accumulate enough to encroach on the people's unalienable rights. In Federalist no. 51 James Madison wrote,

> [W]hat is government itself, but the greatest of all reflections on human nature? If men were angels, no government would be necessary. If angels were to govern men, neither external nor internal controls on government would be necessary. In framing a government which is to be administered by men over men, the great difficulty lies in this: you must first enable the government to control the governed; and in the next place oblige it to control itself. A dependence on the people is, no doubt, the primary control on the government; but experience has taught mankind the necessity of auxiliary precautions.

Similarly, in his presidential farewell address, George Washington stressed that the American people needed to develop the "habits of thinking" that would preserve limited government:

> It is important, likewise, that the habits of thinking in a free country should inspire caution in those entrusted with its administration, to confine themselves within their respective constitutional spheres, avoiding in the exercise of the powers of one department to encroach upon another. The spirit of encroachment tends to consolidate the powers of all the departments in one, and thus to create, whatever the form of government, a real despotism.
>
> A just estimate of that love of power, and proneness to abuse it, which predominates in the human heart, is sufficient to satisfy us of the truth of this position.
>
> The necessity of reciprocal checks in the exercise of political power, by dividing and distributing it into different

depositaries, and constituting each the guardian of the public weal against invasions by the others, has been evinced by experiments ancient and modern; some of them in our country and under our own eyes.

To preserve them must be as necessary as to institute them.

If, in the opinion of the people, the distribution or modification of the constitutional powers be in any particular wrong, let it be corrected by an amendment in the way which the Constitution designates.

But let there be no change by usurpation; for though this, in one instance, may be the instrument of good, it is the customary weapon by which free governments are destroyed. The precedent must always greatly overbalance in permanent evil any partial or transient benefit, which the use can at any time yield.

Controlling the federal government through checks and balances, and arraying the governing branches' power against each other, was a crucial innovation by the Founders to keep man's natural corruptibility from consuming the people's liberties.

Nevertheless, Madison candidly acknowledged that these constitutional safeguards were only "parchment barriers" to man's desire to accumulate power. Despite all its innovative bulwarks, the republic would still be administered by imperfect men whose vulnerability to corruption had to be tempered by a culture of virtue and responsibility.

FIVE AMERICAN HABITS OF LIBERTY

The Founding Fathers understood that governmental safeguards were not enough to defend the people's natural rights—the republic's survival ultimately depended upon the good character of its citizens. The preservation of liberty in a republic would require personal responsibility, a vital quality they called "virtue." John Adams maintained that "religion and virtue are the only Foundations, not only of Republicanism and of all free Government, but of social felicity under all Governments and in all Combinations of human society."[5]

Another signer of the Declaration of Independence, Benjamin Rush, declared that "the only foundation for a useful education in a republic is to be laid in religion. Without this there can be no virtue, and without virtue there can be no liberty, and liberty is the object and life of all republican governments."

Likewise, Alexander White, a Virginia delegate to the Constitutional Convention, wondered whether the American people had the qualities demanded by republican governance: "Have we that Industry, Frugality, Economy, that Virtue which is necessary to constitute it?"[6]

Virtuous, responsible citizens are indeed indispensable for sustaining a free republic. They not only take responsibility for their own lives, but also are concerned for the welfare of their families, friends, and community, especially for those in need and those who have difficulty taking care of themselves.

In terms of politics, virtuous citizens become knowledgeable about the issues of the day so they can make informed decisions at election time, and so they will know how and when to hold their government officials accountable. When holding office, virtuous citizens exercise authority responsibly, recognizing and abiding by the proscribed limits of their power.

Crucially, since virtue is instrumental to our republic's survival, the Founders believed the people must develop and maintain institutions that cultivate virtue and responsibility in its citizenry. George Washington spoke of the need for sources outside of government that nurture these qualities. In his farewell address, he cited religion and morality as vital buttresses of liberty:

> Of all the dispositions and habits which lead to political prosperity, religion and morality are indispensable supports.
>
> In vain would that man claim the tribute of patriotism, who should labor to subvert these great pillars of human happiness, these firmest props of the duties of men and citizens.
>
> The mere politician, equally with the pious man, ought to respect and to cherish them. A volume could not trace all

their connections with private and public felicity. Let it simply be asked: Where is the security for property, for reputation, for life, if the sense of religious obligation deserts the oaths which are the instruments of investigation in courts of justice?

And let us with caution indulge the supposition that morality can be maintained without religion. Whatever may be conceded to the influence of refined education on minds of peculiar structure, reason and experience both forbid us to expect that national morality can prevail in exclusion of religious principle.

It is substantially true that virtue or morality is a necessary spring of popular government. The rule, indeed, extends with more or less force to every species of free government. Who that is a sincere friend to it can look with indifference upon attempts to shake the foundation of the fabric?

Washington clearly understood the importance of religion and morality, but what are the "dispositions and habits" to which he referred? Looking through four hundred years of American history, back to the first colonists' arrival at Jamestown, we find five habits of liberty that have been crucial to sustaining American Exceptionalism. They are:

- faith and family
- work
- civil society
- rule of law
- safety and peace

Tempering man's worst impulses, these distinctly American habits are vital to cultivating an engaged, informed citizenry, which is needed to sustain a free republic and secure the unalienable rights asserted in the Declaration of Independence. The emphasis on these habits set America apart from its European counterparts, where monarchs were intent on cultivating passive, obedient subjects unlikely to challenge their rulers' claim to power.

EXEMPLARS OF LIBERTY

The Founders encouraged these habits of liberty both through policy and by personal example. Recognizing that a virtuous republic must be based on a virtuous citizenry, they assumed the American nation would not prosper, regardless of its governing structures, unless the people vigorously practiced these habits and inculcated them in future generations. We can see these habits in action through the lives of five members of America's founding generation.

JOHN ADAMS AND THE HABIT
OF FAITH AND FAMILY

As God endowed man with rights, the Creator also gave man the first and most durable of human institutions: the family. God repeatedly affirmed the family as the best means to secure a happy, just, and moral life. Faith and family grew up in tandem as the twin pillars of Judeo-Christian civilization.

Faith gave the Founders context and meaning in their lives; families gave them an outlet for expressing their understanding of the world, and the obligation and privilege to love and be loved in return. The Founders laid their greatest hopes for the American republic on a commitment of free men to faith and family, since these two pillars defend liberty against licentiousness and tyranny.

John Adams, a signer of the Declaration of Independence and later vice president and president of the United States, was a devoted husband of Abigail and father of six children. The couple had known each other since childhood, basing their marriage upon mutual respect and admiration. As they witnessed the birth of a new republic and experienced the fatigue and separation of war, John and Abigail continually looked to each other for emotional, spiritual, and intellectual support.

The struggle for American independence kept Adams away from his family for long periods, sometimes years at a time. But the couple maintained an extensive correspondence, particularly during his time in Philadelphia during the Continental Congress. Their letters reveal an unshakeable commitment and devoted love for one another. They shared a mutual appreciation for philosophy, poetry, and politics, and their letters show how much John valued Abigail's counsel on matters of government and public life.

The Adams also understood the importance of education in the lives of their children, and their own responsibility to instill in them the virtues and values vital to the new nation's success. Early in his legal career, John wrote about the importance of the proper education of youth:

> It should be your care, therefore, and mine, to elevate the minds of our children and exalt their courage; to accelerate and animate their industry and activity; to excite in them an habitual contempt of meanness, abhorrence of injustice and inhumanity, and an ambition to excel in every capacity, faculty, and virtue. If we suffer their minds to grovel and creep in infancy, they will grovel all their lives.

In a letter to Abigail in 1780, he likewise explained why he supported the armed struggle to secure the nation's independence:

> I must study politics and war that my sons may have liberty to study mathematics and philosophy. My sons ought to study mathematics and philosophy, geography, natural history and naval architecture, navigation, commerce and agriculture, in order to give their children a right to study painting, poetry, music, architecture, statuary, tapestry, and porcelain.

Adams' love of family compelled him not only to study politics and war, but to engage in both, to ensure that his children could enjoy the blessings of liberty. He believed that the education of children was central to the maintenance of liberty, and he hoped a free republic would provide an environment where his children could study the greatest expressions of human culture and man's God-given creativity—painting, poetry, music, architecture, and other arts. Both John and Abigail understood that the cultivation and protection of these virtues all begin in the family.

Indeed, above their status as citizens, workers, or statesmen, the Founders cherished their role in their families. The family was prized as the best incubator for love, charity, religion, work, and safety, and a model for all other social relations. As John Adams wrote in a letter to Thomas Jefferson in 1814, "As long as Property exists, it will accumulate in Individuals and Families. As long as Marriage exists, Knowledge, Property and Influence will accumulate in Families." Once again, Adams demonstrated that he saw the institution of family as the cornerstone of a free society, and marriage as the fundamental building block of the family. He also believed that the family was inextricably linked to economic prosperity.

Family is the most basic social unit, and for the Founders, the model for all society and the locus of work, education, religion, love, discipline, and national memory. The Pilgrim settlers described the family as "a little commonwealth" whose constituent members had deep and abiding obligations to themselves and to each other for their mutual prosperity, safety, and happiness. These values, developed in the home, extended to society at large. According to Adams, "The foundation of national morality must be laid in private families."

Strong and healthy families created strong and healthy citizens and taught those citizens their responsibilities to society. A mid-eighteenth-century Protestant preacher explained, "As the Civil State, as well as the Churches of Christ, is furnished with members from private families: if the governors of these little communities, were faithful to the great trust reposed in them, and family-religion and discipline were thoroughly, prudently and strictly, maintained and exercised ... the Civil State would prosper and flourish from Generation to Generation."[7] The preacher's assertion implied that if the family ever faltered, the colonists' virtues could be erased in one generation.

Experience had taught the colonists the value of extended families as a stabilizing force in society. After the disaster at Roanoke and early stumbling at Jamestown, the colonies were settled not by individuals, but almost exclusively by family units that were stable, productive, and self-sustaining.[8] The division of responsibilities among family members created mutual dependence within the family but independence from the outside community, allowing families to raise children to be free and self-sufficient citizens.

Both liberty and family life derived from something greater than their constituent parts. In 1813, looking back on his life, Thomas Jefferson observed, "The happiness of the domestic fireside is the first boon of Heaven; and it is well it is so, since it is that which is the lot of the mass of mankind."

The Founders viewed liberty as a special privilege from God that was inextricably tied to their family and their faith. George Whitefield, the renowned preacher of the Great Awakening and close friend of Benjamin Franklin, summed up why Americans should be thankful: "Your situation in life, every one must confess, is one of great blessing: the providence of God has given you a wonderful heritage, above many of your fellow-creatures."[9] Faith and family both secured and gave meaning to the blessings of liberty.

BENJAMIN FRANKLIN AND THE HABIT OF WORK

The colonies' first settlers were adventurers and frontiersmen who established an American tradition of pursing fortune and knowledge through work. Labor, whether manual or intellectual, increased man's dignity and liberty as he became self-sufficient and availed himself of self-made opportunities. Ever since John Smith introduced the "Law of Work" at Jamestown, a strong work ethic was more than a moral maxim—it was a necessity for survival and a route to prosperity.

Benjamin Franklin stands out among the Founders as the embodiment of this ethic of work, industry, and innovation. For Franklin, the key to prosperity lay in his Thirteen Virtues, among them Industry and Frugality. Industry, as Franklin defined it, was to "lose not time; be always employed in something useful; cut off all unnecessary actions."[10]

Franklin lived that ethic of work and encouraged his countrymen to do the same. As a young man, he became a successful printer and author, writing *Poor Richard's Almanack* at the age of twenty-six. He became the celebrated inventor of bifocals and the Franklin stove, as well as an authoritative scientist on subjects such as lightning, ocean currents, and meteorology. In his distinguished career as a diplomat and statesmen, Franklin guided the colonies toward revolution and unity, navigating them through the treacherous waters of European diplomacy.

Franklin's greatest legacy, though, is the ethos of self-made success that he advocated and exemplified. To him, the pursuit of happiness was best understood as an unalienable right to pursue property; and consequently he understood the accumulation of wealth as evidence of a "moral striving" that benefitted society.[11] This notion was fundamentally democratic; a man was to be judged solely by what he produces, not by his social class or some other artificial criteria. As Franklin advised immigrants, "People do not inquire concerning a Stranger, What is he? but, What can he do?"[12]

Franklin suggested the government's rightful role was to defend liberty and opportunity, allowing man to improve his condition through his own initiative: "I think the best way of doing good to the poor, is not making them easy in poverty, but leading or driving them out of it.... The less was done for them, the more they did for themselves, and became richer."[13]

Ingenuity and discovery, as Franklin showed by example, were part and parcel of this American work ethic. The relentless quest for scientific discovery and economic opportunity also provided an animating force for exploring and settling America, from the Northwest Ordinance to Jefferson's Louisiana Purchase to the Lewis and Clark expedition.

The Founders considered innovation and invention so important that they wrote protections for inventors into the Constitution—the document that articulated our society's most precious and protected liberties. The Patent and Copyright Clause reads, "To promote the Progress of Science and useful Arts, by securing for limited Times to Authors and Inventors the exclusive Right to their respective Writings and Discoveries."

The American republic was conceived as a commercial republic in which hard work and innovation would create a level of prosperity unrivaled in history. As Alexander Hamilton observed in Federalist no. 12, "The prosperity of commerce is now perceived and acknowledged by all enlightened statesmen to be the most useful as well as the most productive source of national wealth, and has accordingly become a primary object of their political cares."

The Founders, especially Benjamin Franklin, revered work as a moral virtue and a great habit of liberty. With industry and ingenuity, work was the great means by which the American people could achieve independence and pursue happiness.

BENJAMIN RUSH AND THE HABIT OF CIVIL SOCIETY

The Founders recognized that citizens of a free republic would have to accept extraordinary responsibilities. In European monarchies, the people were subjects who owed loyalty and obedience to their superiors, while the Court and the aristocrats were duty bound, at least in theory, to guard the best interests of commoners and of society as a whole. A republic, by contrast, required that each man, serving as his own sovereign, act not only in his own best interest but also in the interest of his fellow countrymen.

Benjamin Rush, a physician and signer of the Declaration of Independence, exemplified a commitment to his fellow citizens in his own life. In Philadelphia, he helped lead The Sons of Liberty, a society that arose in all the colonies dedicated to educating and organizing the people to champion liberty. The Sons of Liberty played a vital role as a meeting place for like-minded patriots to develop the ideals of the Revolution. The group also engaged in collective actions—its members staged the famous Boston Tea Party, and some of its adherents helped tear down the statue of King George III on Bowling Green. Later in life, Dr. Rush dedicated himself to public health and helped to contain a yellow fever outbreak in Philadelphia in 1793. Though most other doctors fled the epidemic, Rush stayed, risking his own life and saving thousands.

The Founders believed this kind of private virtue, manifested through philanthropy, charity, and participation in civic life, was crucial to America. And indeed, myriad popular associations dedicated to helping the poor, often based around churches and immigrant groups, spread throughout the colonies and the early republic.[14] To facilitate their work, local and state governments gave these groups tax exemptions and other privileges. Land grants and endowments flourished in colonial America and afterward, transforming the nation into a great educational and philanthropic society.

After America's founding, associations dedicated to philanthropy, science, philosophy, and politics sprung up across the new nation. In the early 1800s, Alexis de Tocqueville observed how widespread these civic groups had become: "In no country in the world has the principle of association been more successfully used or applied to a greater multitude of objects than in America.... A vast number of others are formed and maintained by the agency of private individuals."[15] As Tocqueville noted, the societies ranged from political parties and public safety commissions to religious groups and commercial associations.

These groups expanded the bounds of civil society and provided a bulwark against tyranny, as volunteers worked to achieve common aims outside of government. They cultivated a vibrant civic life in America, an exception to this day from the life of all other nations.

JAMES MADISON AND
THE HABIT OF THE RULE OF LAW

The Declaration of Independence tasks the government with securing natural rights, not granting or creating them; life, liberty, and the pursuit of happiness are gifts from our Creator, not from government. In order to secure these rights, the government is obligated to institute the rule of law. Crucially, the rule of law requires that government officials abide by the same laws they enact and enforce, and refrain from taking arbitrary action against the people—in other words, the government is bound by its commitments to exercise power in predictable and even-handed ways.

The Founders were convinced that the rule of men, as opposed to the rule of law, leads to tyranny. This was evident in the "abuses and usurpations" of the Crown listed in the Declaration of Independence. The king had consistently and impudently flouted the law, holding men without trial, refusing to enact laws for the general welfare, undermining judicial independence, and committing many other abuses that put his will above the law and above the good of the people. To the Founders, this arbitrary authority infringed on both the natural liberty of men and their equality, for no man stands above another in the eyes of God.

For James Madison, the problem lay in the uncertain status of the British constitution, which was an unwritten accumulation of traditions. The king could ignore or arbitrarily enforce acts of Parliament, since there was no higher authority to provide redress. To remedy this tendency toward tyranny, the law had to be codified, transparent, and universal.[16]

Initially, the Founders established the Articles of Confederation to accomplish this goal and to tie the states together in a union. But the powers of the various states were in conflict, and citizens risked the same arbitrary application of laws as under the British Crown. Eventually, the Constitution became the ultimate basis of the rule of law in America, with clear delineation and limitation of the federal government's powers. The Constitution also expressly prohibited certain types of inherently arbitrary laws such as ex post facto laws (allowing people to be prosecuted for crimes that had been legal when they committed them) and bills of attainder (allowing for convictions without a court trial).

While he was helping to devise the Constitution, Madison was also worried by the specter of the tyranny of the majority—which might use its power in the democratic process to undermine a minority's rights—and by the prospect of an overly powerful judiciary. The Constitution implemented various checks and balances to guard against these threats, including a bicameral legislature, a strong executive with veto power over legislation, judicial independence, and the legislature's power to impeach executive and judicial officials. Madison noted, "The great difficulty lies in this: you must first enable the government to control the governed; and in the next place oblige it to control itself."[17]

Though he did not see the need for a separate bill of rights, Madison acknowledged concerns of Anti-Federalists that the proposed Constitution would not adequately protect individual rights. To assuage their fears, he and other Founders promised to codify the people's fundamental rights in amendments to be drafted after the Constitution was ratified. With the Constitution's approval in 1789, Madison took charge personally of compiling those amendments, sending his proposals to the first Congress of the United States, which passed them. After being ratified by the states in 1791, the first ten amendments—the Bill of Rights—became part of the Constitution.

The Founders believed that preserving the rule of law would require eternal vigilance. In Federalist no. 57, Madison asserted that "a dependence on the people is, no doubt, the primary control on the government." The people, having organized a government, had to guard their own liberty and insist that government restrain itself.

The Founders based the Constitution on a realistic assessment of human nature and provided sophisticated safeguards to counter the natural temptations of power. The debate over this charter was informed, deep, and thorough, and the ratification process assured that it gained the true consent of the people who would live under its authority.

GEORGE WASHINGTON AND
THE HABIT OF SAFETY AND PEACE

In order to secure life, liberty, and the pursuit of happiness as unalienable rights, a society must provide for the safety of its members. John Jay noted the primacy of this consideration in Federalist no. 3: "Among the many objects to which a wise and free people find it necessary to direct their attention, that of providing for their safety seems to be the first." Without security, liberty is temporary and ultimately meaningless.

Both the safety and the liberty of the American people had a special guardian in George Washington. A seasoned veteran of the French and Indian War, a noted patriot, and a recognized leader in his native Virginia, Washington was selected by a unanimous vote of the Continental Congress as commander in chief of the continental armies.

Washington led the revolutionary armies with dedication, courage, humility, and skill, transcending the lack of provisions from Congress and the paucity of professional soldiers in his armies. Waging war against the most powerful army in the world, Washington held his forces together in the field for eight years amidst a series of demoralizing defeats. He repeatedly helped to deliver strategic, morale-boosting blows against the British, and eventually, with the help of France, he secured America's independence by capturing an entire British army at Yorktown.[18]

Washington's decision to relinquish power after the Revolutionary War, in stark contrast to the power-grabs common to victorious generals throughout history, added to his stature. When he agreed to preside over the Constitutional Convention in 1787, his presence lent credibility to a contentious process whose outcome was far from certain. Throughout that hot summer in Philadelphia, the delegates took comfort in the willingness of the great man presiding over their debates to serve as the country's initial chief executive. Washington's ensuing presidency, along with his character and probity in setting hundreds of precedents for all subsequent presidents, were instrumental to the successful launch of the new republic.

As America's commander in chief, Washington prioritized the safety and security of the American people. He sent an army in 1793 to defeat hostile Indian tribes that were attacking settlers on the frontier in the Ohio River Valley, and the following year he personally led a military force that disbursed the Whiskey Rebellion in western Pennsylvania without firing a shot.

Washington recognized that peace and safety required vigilance and military readiness. In addition to building up America's coastal and frontier defenses, he ensured the militias were well-equipped and pre-pared for battle. As the Anglo-French wars came perilously close to American waters and threatened America's trade, Washington recom-missioned the navy.

However, Washington undertook these and other military prepara-tions with the aim of forestalling war, not provoking it; his hope was that a well-armed, well-defended America would force other powers to leave the young nation alone to grow and prosper in peace. Striving to keep the United States neutral in the Anglo-French wars of the early 1790s, he warned his countrymen in his 1796 presidential farewell address of the danger of foreign entanglements.

Subsequent presidents heeded Washington's caution to prepare for war while seeking to avoid it. When the Barbary States of North Africa began capturing U.S. merchant ships in the Atlantic and Mediterranean, holding American sailors for ransom and even enslaving them, our earli-est diplomats, notably New York's John Jay, first tried to find a diplo-matic solution. When those efforts failed, the war-weary federal government adopted the European practice of paying the Barbary States an annual tribute to prevent further attacks.

By 1801 the situation had become intolerable. The bribes paid to the pirate states exacted a heavy toll on the federal budget and enraged the American people while failing to end the pirates' maritime terrorism.

Refusing Tripoli's demand for further tribute, newly elected president Thomas Jefferson sent a group of American frigates to the Mediterranean to protect the merchant fleet. After skirmishes with enemy ships, Congress authorized the president in 1802 to "employ such of the armed vessels of the United States as may be judged requisite ... for protecting effectually the commerce and seamen thereof on the Atlantic Ocean, the Mediterranean and adjoining seas."

Although the conflict only comprised a few short battles and a successful blockade, the campaign against Barbary piracy—the United States' biggest military engagement since the Revolutionary War—secured a treaty ending the pirates' depredations. Preferring armed action over the continued payment of tribute, America showed the world that, though it did not seek war, it would defend itself from foreign attack and would protect its citizens' God-given rights to life and property.

* * *

American Exceptionalism is the remarkable and dynamic result of the American nation, sustained by the moral convictions of the American people, living out its freedoms through the people's habits of liberty. Such a dynamic society cultivates extraordinary creativity, courage, and allegiance, implanting the optimistic belief that any person can succeed who works hard and plays by the rules.

Five habits of liberty—faith and family, work, civil society, rule of law, and safety and peace—have been practiced by the American people as both public and private virtues. As responsibilities of a free people, these habits support and protect the unalienable rights of liberty and allow Americans to pursue happiness. The Founders appealed to these habits and, through word and deed, showed their countrymen their importance for the preservation of the new republic.

As the beneficiaries of the Founders' genius and sacrifice, American citizens are still responsible for cultivating and preserving these habits today. As Dr. Joseph Warren charged his fellow countrymen in 1776 before he gave his life for his country in the Battle of Bunker Hill, "On you depend the fortunes of America. You are to decide the important question, on which rest the happiness and liberty of millions yet unborn. Act worthy of yourselves."

Parts II and III of this book will explore how these five habits of liberty evolved, how they helped to make America exceptional, how they are being dangerously undermined, and how we can revitalize them and restore American Exceptionalism. But before we begin that discussion, let's step away from our study of history and briefly consider, through the words of some notable witnesses, how powerful—and how crucial to our future—American Exceptionalism really is.

CHAPTER THREE

WHO WE ARE

IN THE WORDS OF NEW AMERICANS
AND THOSE WHO LOVE AMERICA

Much of this book will discuss American Exceptionalism as it relates to history and to America's political institutions. But we need to acknowledge that American Exceptionalism is something deeper than that—it's also a visceral, emotional attachment to America and to the common destiny we Americans share.

This feeling tends to be particularly strong in recent immigrants. Attracted to America by the prospect of freedom and opportunity, and often fleeing wars or oppressive governments, new Americans instinctively embrace the tenets of American Exceptionalism. There are many accounts from the early twentieth century of the awe felt by ship-bound immigrants upon seeing the Statue of Liberty, a sight that reduced many voyagers to tears. Talking to new immigrants today, we find the same deeply felt connection to America and the same conviction that something special sets America apart from all other nations.

More people from more countries speaking more languages and with more diverse ethnic and cultural backgrounds come to the United States than to any other country in history. Every year the United States accepts more legal immigrants than all the other countries in the world combined.

People find opportunity in America that they can only dream of in their home countries. If Arnold Schwarzenegger had remained in a small town in Austria, he would never have become a multimillionaire businessman, a worldwide movie star, and a renowned politician. If Hakeem Olajuwon had stayed in Nigeria, he could not have grown into an internationally acclaimed basketball star. If Andrew Carnegie remained in Scotland, he would not have risen from being a factory worker to become a steel magnate and world famous philanthropist. If Levi Strauss had settled down in his native Bavaria, he would not have made his first name synonymous with an article of clothing now worn in every country in the world.

You don't need to live in America to be struck by the grandeur of American Exceptionalism; foreign observers of our nation have long admired Americans' adventurous, entrepreneurial spirit. Indeed, the American Dream is understood far and wide, enticing tens of thousands of people every year to give up everything they have to create a new life of opportunity in America.

The following passages are testaments, offered by new immigrants to America as well as foreign observers, to the American character and the unique promise of this land. Ranging from world leaders to war refugees, these speakers offer a heartening reminder of the unique passion that America inspires.

ALEXIS DE TOCQUEVILLE
FRENCH POLITICAL PHILOSOPHER, *DEMOCRACY IN AMERICA*, VOL. I, 1835

The chief circumstance which has favored the establishment and the maintenance of a democratic republic in the United States is the nature of the territory which the Americans inhabit. Their ancestors gave them the love of equality and of freedom, but God himself gave them the means of remaining equal and free, by placing them upon a boundless continent, which is open to their exertions. General prosperity is favorable to the stability of all governments, but more particularly of a democratic constitution, which depends upon the dispositions of the majority, and more particularly of that portion of the community which is most exposed to feel the pressure of want. When the people rules, it must be rendered happy, or it will overturn the State, and misery is apt to stimulate it to those excesses to which ambition rouses kings. The physical causes, independent of the laws, which contribute to promote general prosperity, are more numerous in America than they have ever been in any other country in the world, at any other period of history. In the United States not only is legislation democratic, but nature herself favors the cause of the people.

... In Europe we are wont to look upon a restless disposition, an unbounded desire of riches, and an excessive love of independence, as propensities very formidable to society. Yet these are the very elements which ensure a long and peaceful duration to the republics of America. Without these unquiet passions the population would collect in certain spots, and would soon be subject to wants like those of the Old World, which it is difficult to satisfy; for such is the present good fortune of the New World, that the vices of its inhabitants are scarcely less favorable to society than their virtues. These circumstances exercise a great influence on the estimation in which human actions are held in the two hemispheres. The Americans frequently term what we should call cupidity a laudable industry; and they blame as faint-heartedness what we consider to be the virtue of moderate desires.

NICOLAS SARKOZY
PRESIDENT OF FRANCE, ADDRESS BEFORE A JOINT SESSION OF THE U.S. CONGRESS, NOVEMBER 7, 2007[1]

From the very beginning, the American dream meant putting into practice the dreams of the Old World.

From the very beginning, the American dream meant proving to all mankind that freedom, justice, human rights and democracy were no utopia but were rather the most realistic policy there is and the most likely to improve the fate of each and every person.

America did not tell the millions of men and women who came from every country in the world and who—with their hands, their intelligence and their heart—built the greatest nation in the world: "Come, and everything will be given to you." She said: "Come, and the only limits to what you'll be able to achieve will be your own courage and your own talent." America embodies this extraordinary ability to grant each and every person a second chance.

Here, both the humblest and most illustrious citizens alike know that nothing is owed to them and that everything has to be earned. That's what constitutes the moral value of America. America did not teach men the idea of freedom; she taught them how to practice it.

And she fought for this freedom whenever she felt it to be threatened somewhere in the world. It was by watching America grow that men and women understood that freedom was possible.

What made America great was her ability to transform her own dream into hope for all mankind.

ALP GURPINAR

TURKISH IMMIGRANT, *REAL AMERICAN STORIES*[2]

Why I came here? The main reason is: America is the land of opportunity. You can achieve whatever you want. I am a student of mathematics at Hunter College. In Europe or in Turkey, to be a student at 43 years old is very difficult—there are a lot of barriers there. But, here you can. Here you could be an artist even if you are 80 years old. To be able to go back to university to study what you want, to be able to do what you want in the future, makes you feel happy. Freedom is a big concept. For me, America is a place with no barriers. This is a great country with big opportunities. I love America!

JULIA GILLARD

PRIME MINISTER OF AUSTRALIA, ADDRESS BEFORE A JOINT SESSION OF THE U.S. CONGRESS, MARCH 10, 2011[3]

For my parents' generation, the defining image of America was the landing at Normandy. Your "boys of Point-du-Hoc" … risking everything to help free the world. For my own generation, the defining image of America was the landing on the moon. My classmates and I were sent home from school to watch the great moment on television. I'll always remember thinking that day: Americans can do anything. Americans helped free the world of my parents' generation. Americans inspired the world of my own youth. I stand here and I see the same brave and free people today. I believe you can do anything still. There is a reason the world always looks to America. Your great dream—life, liberty and the pursuit of happiness—inspires us all.

. . . You have a friend in Australia. And you have an ally. And we know what that means. In both our countries, true friends stick together. . . . [I]n both our countries, real mates talk straight. So as a friend I urge you only this: be worthy to your own best traditions. Be bold. In 1942, John Curtin—my predecessor, my country's great wartime leader— looked to America. I still do. This year you have marked the centenary of President Reagan's birth. He remains a great symbol of American optimism. The only greater symbol of American optimism is America itself. The eyes of the world are still upon you. Your city on a hill cannot be hidden. Your brave and free people have made you the masters of recovery and reinvention. As I stand in this cradle of democracy I see a nation that has changed the world and known remarkable days. I firmly believe you are the same people who amazed me when I was a small girl by landing on the moon. On that great day I believed Americans could do anything. I believe that still. You can do anything today.

IGOR FINKLER
RUSSIAN IMMIGRANT, ON CBS REALITY SHOW
UNDERCOVER BOSS, FEBRUARY 21, 2010

I am living an American Dream now. America is the best country in the world. You guys just do not really know how blessed you are, because you take it for granted. I came to the U.S. with little English, no knowledge of any culture, $50 in my pocket—and I survived. That's a story about America. That's not a story about me. I am blessed, I am really blessed. And now you ask me why I am so motivated? Because I am so thankful for this country which allowed me to survive and be happy.

FAROOZ

IRANIAN IMMIGRANT, "CITIZENSHIP: THE PURSUIT OF HAPPINESS," REASON.TV, JUNE 30, 2010[4]

If you have an idea, you have the freedom to do it or pursue it. Whether you achieve it or not, that's another question. I am Farooz … from Iran. I drive a taxi cab.…My passion from childhood was art. So I got my BA and Masters in fine arts. I am a painter.…New ideas and new trends in everything—whether it is in politics, or art, or movies, whatever—starts here in the United States and spreads across the world. This is because of the freedom that exists in this country, in every respect. And each person in their own field are free to do whatever they like.

SUDANESE IMMIGRANT

"CITIZENSHIP: THE PURSUIT OF HAPPINESS," REASON.TV, JUNE 30, 2010[5]

I was born Christian. And this is my religion. I am not going to give it up because my government doesn't want me to be Christian.…I think this is the country where people can speak up. Everyone has rights. And nobody would deny your rights.

TONY BLAIR

FORMER PRIME MINISTER OF THE UNITED KINGDOM, *TIME* MAGAZINE, SEPTEMBER 2, 2010[6]

Americans can be all that the rest of the world sometimes accuses them of: brash, loud, insular, obsessive and heavy-handed. But America is great for a reason. It is looked up to, despite all the criticism, for a reason. There is a nobility in the American character that has been developed over the centuries, derived in part, no doubt, from the frontier spirit, from the waves of migration that form the stock, from the circumstances of independence, from the Civil War, from a myriad of historical facts and coincidences. But it is there.

That nobility isn't about being nicer, better, or more successful than anyone else. It is a feeling about the country. It is a devotion to the American ideal that at a certain point transcends class, race, religion, or upbringing. That ideal is about values: freedom, the rule of law, democracy. It is also about the way you achieve: on merit, by your own efforts and hard work. But it is most of all that in striving for and protecting that ideal, you as an individual take second place to the interests of the nation as a whole. It is what makes the country determined to overcome its challenges. It is what makes its soldiers give their lives in sacrifice. It is what brings every variety of American, from the lowest to the highest, to their feet when "The Star-Spangled Banner" is played. Of course the ideal is not always met—that is obvious. But it is always striven for.

The next years will test the American character. America won't be loved in this presidency any more than in previous ones. But America should have confidence. That ideal, which produces the optimism that generates the achievement, is worth all the striving. It is the most precious gift a nation can have. The world is changing. New powers are emerging. But this does not diminish the need for that American ideal. It reaffirms it, renews it, gives it added relevance. There is always one, more prosaic, test of a nation's position: Are people trying to get into it, or to get out of it? I think we know the answer to that in America's case, and that ideal is the reason.

A friend of mine whose parents were immigrants, Jews from Europe who came to America in search of safety, told me this story. His parents lived and worked in New York. They were not well off. His father died when he was young. His mother lived on, and in time my friend succeeded and became wealthy. He often used to offer his mother the chance to travel outside America. She never did. When eventually she died, they went back to recover the safety box where she kept her jewelry. They found there was another box. There was no key. So they had to drill it open. They wondered what precious jewel must be in it. They lifted the lid. There was wrapping and more wrapping and finally an envelope. Intrigued, they opened it. In the envelope were her U.S. citizenship papers. Nothing more. That was the jewel, more precious to her than any other possession. That was what she treasured most. So should America today.

UTKARSH SATA

INDIAN IMMIGRANT CURRENTLY APPLYING FOR CITIZENSHIP, *REAL AMERICAN STORIES*[7]

I was doing my chemical engineering in India, and during my sophomore year, I always thought that I wanted to specialize in petro chemicals, and I was always watching Westerns and Hollywood movies in India, and always imagined Texas as a big state with a lot of space and big cars and big hats and everything big. So I came to Texas to get a degree in Masters of Petroleum and Tech Engineering.

I make chemical warfare protective clothing for U.S. Army soldiers. Right now we are trying to come up with material that is better protective and has less logistic burden so that it saves lives. I was in the United States during 9/11. I was very sad that morning, so I chose this research area so that we can do something to protect the freedom of the United States and protect the people and the soldiers who are fighting for that freedom of the U.S., of which I want to become a citizen.

It is very important for me to become a U.S. citizen. It gives me an opportunity to choose in elections people who share the true democratic values which I believe in. It really means a lot to me to become a citizen of the United States—I am in the process—because then I can consider myself as an American. I am really proud to wear any colors that are red, white, and blue.

POPE BENEDICT XVI

APOSTOLIC JOURNEY TO THE U.S., WELCOMING CEREMONY AT THE WHITE HOUSE, APRIL 16, 2008[8]

From the dawn of the Republic, America's quest for freedom has been guided by the conviction that the principles governing political and social life are intimately linked to a moral order based on the dominion of God the Creator. The framers of this nation's founding documents drew upon this conviction when they proclaimed the "self-evident truth" that all men are created equal and endowed with inalienable rights grounded in the laws of nature and of nature's God. The course of American history demonstrates the difficulties, the struggles, and the great intellectual and moral resolve which were demanded to shape a society which faithfully embodied these noble principles. In that process, which forged the soul of the nation, religious beliefs were a constant inspiration and driving force, as for example in the struggle against slavery and in the civil rights movement. In our time too, particularly in moments of crisis, Americans continue to find their strength in a commitment to this patrimony of shared ideals and aspirations.

... Freedom is not only a gift, but also a summons to personal responsibility. Americans know this from experience—almost every town in this country has its monuments honoring those who sacrificed their lives in defense of freedom, both at home and abroad. The preservation of freedom calls for the cultivation of virtue, self-discipline, sacrifice for the common good and a sense of responsibility towards the less fortunate. It also demands the courage to engage in civic life and to bring one's deepest beliefs and values to reasoned public debate. In a word, freedom is ever new. It is a challenge held out to each generation, and it must constantly be won over for the cause of good.

JEFFREY KOFMAN
CANADIAN IMMIGRANT AND ABC NEWS CORRESPONDENT, FROM HIS KEYNOTE ADDRESS AT HIS OWN NATURALIZATION CEREMONY, FEBRUARY 25, 2010[9]

When the interview was over the immigration officer reached to the far side of her desk and grabbed a bulky rubber stamp. I watched as it hit the paper. When she lifted it, it left behind a big red imprint. In the middle, the single word "APPROVED." As I looked at my application and at the bright red stamp, it hit me.

I am now an American.

And at that very moment I wondered how many people before all of us have put so much of their future on that red stamp and that single word: APPROVED....I know that at least some of you came from lives of hardship to realize this day and this dream. But think for a moment about the people of previous generations who achieved this day. For them U.S. citizenship in a significant way marked the end to nightmares and violations of dignity that we can only begin to imagine.

I think it is fair to say that what drew you and me and all of those before us to this country and this moment is a simple concept that we can all understand and share. It is summarized in a single word: FREEDOM.

Perhaps it was to escape a state of oppression, or extreme poverty, corruption, or violations of human rights. Or perhaps, as in my case, you simply came here to pursue a dream.

What we all share is a thirst for Freedom: a desire to live as we want, without unreasonable interference, without unfair obstacles. A dream that through determination and hard work we can rise to a level we deserve.

CHRISTOPHER HITCHENS
BRITISH IMMIGRANT, AUTHOR, AND COLUMNIST, INTERVIEW WITH BRIAN LAMB, C-SPAN, APRIL 26, 2009[10]

The American Revolution, the one that says build your republic on individual rights not group rights; have a Bill of Rights that inscribes these and makes them available and legible to everybody; separate the church from the state; separate the executive, the judicial, and the political branch. Do all these things. It doesn't sound like much, but it is really a very revolutionary idea. There is hardly a country in the world that would not benefit from adopting those principles. I think that gives the United States a really good claim to be a revolutionary country, as well as of course, paradoxically, it's a very conservative one. So, it makes me very glad, very proud to become a citizen of it.

ANTONY KIM
KOREAN IMMIGRANT AND PROFESSIONAL GOLFER[11]

What is the American dream? I am the American dream....My mom told me that she came over here with $300 in her pocket and knew absolutely nobody. So, it's an amazing story....I know that one of [my father's] goals was to have a son that could maybe play professional golf....They did everything they could, they sold the house, they maybe overextended and gave me the opportunity to go out to La Quinta [to live near a golf course]....The fact that a kid that really wasn't supposed to be doing what I'm doing right now, is playing on the Ryder cup team and has won two tournaments by the time I'm 23, those are accomplishments I am very proud of. I would say I am the American dream right now. I am living it.

ANONYMOUS VIETNAMESE IMMIGRANTS;
HASSAN ASMAN ALI, IRAQI IMMIGRANT; JASMINE GRACE EMAD, SUDANESE IMMIGRANT, "I AM AN AMERICAN," *NEBRASKA STORIES* (SWEARING IN OF NEW AMERICANS FROM ACROSS THE GLOBE)[12]

Vietnamese immigrants: The whole family comes together, because he [a newly naturalized American] was in the military for South Vietnam and was in a prison camp for five years....In Vietnam, you work hard, but you do not see the results. That's one nice thing in America. If you work hard and believe in whatever you believe in, you can get it....She [another newly naturalized American] now has the benefits of life. She can vote, and she feels like she is an American now.

Hassan Asman Ali: We are thankful they gave us a home, food, and everything. We are very thankful for everything. We are very thankful to be in America.

Jasmine Grace Emad: I feel special. Free to be you and just get the best out of it.

GIULIANA RANCIC
ITALIAN IMMIGRANT, HOST ON THE E! TV NETWORK AND STAR OF REALITY TV SHOW "GIULIANA AND BILL," *REAL AMERICAN STORIES*[13]

I was born in Naples, Italy, and I moved to America when I was about six or seven years old. At a young age, I realized just how much my parents had done for us. They left their life behind. They left all their friends and a huge family to come to America, a country of complete strangers, just for us. I was an Italian kid who moved to America and didn't speak a lick of English. We didn't really look like a lot of other people. We had no money and to come to this country with no connections to the entertainment business, and the fact that I was able to become a journalist and actually make a living from being on TV and speaking English and giving people news—it's incredible. So, now when my parents see me on TV it makes them so happy.

We are so lucky to live in this country. I think that when you're from somewhere else you really appreciate America even more and you don't take it for granted, because you know what it's like to live somewhere else. This country is incredible. There are no walls that you can't break down. One of the things that definitely unites us is freedom and the fact that we are free to do pretty much whatever we want to do. I am free to express myself, and I am free to advance in my career and not be held down. And, you can't say that for every other country. I love this country more than anything. Yeah, you know there are bumps in the road, but for the most part, the citizens of this country do a pretty darn good job living in harmony. We are all so different. This is a country based on people who are different living together. That's what makes it so great.

TEUTA DEDVUKAJ
ALBANIAN IMMIGRANT, *REAL AMERICAN STORIES*[14]

I was born in Shkoder, Albania, we moved here when I was just about eight years old. When I was younger, as I sat down with my father, I said, "Dad, what is the one thing that actually made you move here?" And he said to live in a country where you don't have freedom of religion, freedom of press, freedom of opportunity, and you're told what to do, was certainly not a place he wanted to raise his own family. He just wanted us to be able to achieve so much more. He knew that America would be the only place to do that. And they left everything behind. They left their families, their work, everything that they had ever achieved, and just started from scratch—not speaking a word of English, not having anything to them.

So when I graduated college with a political science degree, just being there and just seeing the tears in my parents' eyes, and just seeing the joy—was the greatest thing that's ever happened in my life. To be an American, for my whole entire family, is truly a blessing. We may have many differences and different things that we do, but at the end of the day, we all as Americans come together as one. We all unify as one.

MAE JOO
KOREAN IMMIGRANT, FOX NEWS PRODUCER AND FORMER AIDE TO THE BUSH WHITE HOUSE, "A PERFECT FIT," *REAL AMERICAN STORIES*[15]

My mom was a hairdresser [before coming to America] and my dad owned his own business as a plumber in Seoul. My first impression [of America] was, "Wow it's huge," and it was a little scary. I was holding onto my parents because I did not speak the language....When my parents first decided to purchase this [dry cleaning] store, it was actually going out of business. There wasn't a lot of customers, so it was a big risk, but it was also one of those things where they really believed in the area, and they thought it would develop, but I remember for a couple of months it was really hard. I think my mom just usually kind of prayed that things would get better and the customers would notice, because it was a big investment. It was their life savings, and it was for us.

...When I was 12, I was always interested in social studies and government, and I thought, "Wow, this is really fascinating," and I said to my parents, "I really want to work at the White House." My parents said, "Just know that if you believe you can and work hard, you can." And so I said, "You know, I think I will."...The biggest joy and the biggest emotion that I've experienced is seeing my mom and dad when I brought them over to the White House for the first time. Just seeing their emotions and how proud they are of what I've done so far—that just means the world to me....As a first-generation immigrant, this is the greatest country in the world and you can achieve anything that you set your mind to. I feel as though my parents enabled me to achieve my American dream.

GEORGE PATDAVIL
INDIAN IMMIGRANT, *REAL AMERICAN STORIES*[16]

I became a citizen in 1984, and since then, I feel that this is my country, and I love this country. I liked living in other places but never felt a sense of belonging. When you come to the United States, you feel that you are a part of this country. I am accepted and included as one of this great nation. In America, everybody came from somewhere, and so, we are all immigrants.

OLEG HASKEL
RUSSIAN IMMIGRANT, *REAL AMERICAN STORIES*[17]

I came here when I was 10 years old. My parents brought me over from Russia. We were among the wave of immigration in the early '90s that came over here. I think the main reason why my parents brought me and my brother here is for us to grow up and have a better life, to know that their child can go through life without having the hardships that they had to go through—being told what to do and what you can think and what you can't think. Freedom. You're perfectly free to go out and make your own decisions. You're free to practice whatever religion you want.

In Russia I don't even know if they allowed any religions—definitely not the Jewish religion. I was able to come out and not be afraid about what my future is going to bring for me, and knowing that my brother and my parents are here and they'll make their future whatever they want it to be, and I'll make it whatever I want it to be. If you ask me what this country means to me: it means home. This is the place for me. This is where I grew up. This is where I built my life. This is where I see my future.

TOVA FRIEDMAN
HOLOCAUST SURVIVOR, *REAL AMERICAN STORIES*[18]

This country has always been a symbol of democracy, a symbol of letting people be who they wanted to be. We came with nothing. We came literally with a tiny suitcase. I love what is inscribed in the statue of liberty, "Give me your tired, your poor, your hungry masses yearning to be free." It's still true. You feel like you can be who you are, can be who you want to be—there is no shame. When we talk about diversity, I don't think you can find diversity in any other country as you can find in America. Because it's part of our nature to accept people from all over.

DERRECK KAYONGO
UGANDAN REFUGEE, "GLOBAL SOAP PROJECT," *REAL AMERICAN STORIES*[19]

Americans are constantly creating, constantly innovating, so as a new immigrant, as a new American, I have no excuse to come here and not do remarkable stuff....The ultimate dream is that we will all stop saying we don't have enough resources to solve problems. We do have the resources; all we need is a little bit of creativity....What did JFK say: ask what *you—me—*can do for your country. That line has come to define my whole life in the U.S.

PART II

DEFINING AMERICAN EXCEPTIONALISM

Freedom is a fragile thing and is never more than one generation away from extinction. It is not ours by inheritance; it must be fought for and defended constantly by each generation, for it comes only once to a people. Those who have known freedom and then lost it have never known it again.

—Ronald Reagan

CHAPTER FOUR

FAITH AND FAMILY

WHY BOTH ARE UNDER ATTACK

*I*n his book Remember Why You Play, *sports columnist and author David Thomas chronicles a season of high school football played by the Grapevine Faith Christian Lions. At one point during the season, Coach Kris Hogan saw an opportunity to teach his team something much more important than how to win a football game.*

The Lions were preparing to play against Gainesville State, which was a maximum-security juvenile detention facility housing kids who had been convicted of everything from drugs to armed assault, and whose parents had long ago disowned them. Every game played by the Gainesville State Tornadoes ended with uniformed officers escorting the players to their bus in groups of five, handcuffs at the ready.

Before the game, Coach Hogan sent an email asking his team and their friends and family to do something unusual: he asked for half the Faith Christian fans to "switch sides" and to cheer for the other team's players, by name. When asked by his own team members why he was making this surprising request, Hogan responded, "Imagine if you didn't have a home life. Imagine if everybody had pretty much given up on you. Now imagine what it would mean for hundreds of people to suddenly believe in you."

Well, the Gainesville Tornadoes soon learned. On game night, they entered the field to find a line of Faith fans who were cheering for <u>them</u>. Confused at first, the Tornadoes soon realized that hundreds of Faith fans and even cheerleaders were not mistakenly cheering for the wrong team; they heard their own names being shouted from the stands. After that, they played better than they had played all season, and even though they still lost, they gave their head coach a sideline Gatorade shower as if they had just won the state championship. More important, they left the field that night forever changed.

Following the game, both teams came together to pray. A Gainesville player intoned, "Lord, I don't know how this happened, so I don't know how to say thank you, but I never would've known there was so many people in the world that cared about us."

As the Gainesville coach left the field, he grabbed Hogan and said, "You'll never know what your people did for these kids tonight. You'll never, ever know."

Coach Hogan described the message he intended to send to the youth of Gainesville State that night: "We love you. Jesus Christ loves you. You are just as valuable as any other person on planet Earth."

Perhaps the most revolutionary concept espoused by America's Founders and enshrined in our Declaration and Constitution was that *every* life has equal value and worth. It is the same ideal that motivated the Founders to go to unprecedented lengths to protect religious liberty.

Indeed, our entire American system of government is premised upon a deeply religious ideal. The proposition that "all men are created equal" expresses a profound religious principle that recognizes God as the ultimate authority over any government. Men are only equal if they are, in fact, *created*. Only if we assume we have a Creator can we assert that our rights have been "endowed" to us by God—and only then are those rights "unalienable."

While these concepts may seem commonplace features of our government today, constituting a government based upon them was radical for the Founders' generation.

If all men are created equal, then not even the most powerful man, group, or government on earth has the power to infringe or trample upon your rights.

If all men are created equal, then all human beings are equally flawed and equally susceptible to the appeal of power and to the inherent temptation to dictate how others should live their lives. Thus, the best government is a limited one; one that restricts the rule of man by instituting the rule of law, which applies to everyone from presidents to parking lot attendants.

If all men are created equal, then every person is equally accountable to God and to his fellow man to live a life of virtue, productivity, and personal responsibility. This life can only be realized in a society in which each person has the freedom to choose between right and wrong. For freedom to endure, it is vital to cultivate the values that make it possible to sustain such freedoms.

If all men are created equal, then each and every individual has equal dignity and inherent worth, regardless of his or her station in life, ethnic background, political beliefs, or personal failures or achievements.

If all men are created equal, then every life is, in fact, as valuable as any other person on planet Earth—whether youths from the Gainesville State detention facility or the family of Faith Christian fans who cared enough to cheer for someone else's child and to call them by name.

The story of Coach Hogan illustrates two key truths about American Exceptionalism: the dignity of the individual—the idea that every person does indeed matter—and the centrality of God and faith in American families and communities.

An America that openly rejects faith and the faithful will undermine the surest supports of human dignity in American life. That anti-religious America would soon cultivate a utilitarian culture that elevates the powerful and crushes the weak. But an America that continues to welcome faith and the faithful as integral to American public life will transmit to the poorest and most forgotten segments of society the hope that they too have a right to the American Dream.

ONE OUT OF MANY: THE REVOLUTIONARY AMERICAN MODEL OF RELIGIOUS PLURALISM

The Founders knew that religious vibrancy in a free society is the surest bulwark against government corruption. And yet their method of promoting and protecting religious vibrancy was an exception to historical precedent. To understand why, one must first recall just how deeply and fervently committed the Founders were not to an abstract notion of faith, but to a faith that was explicitly Christian. Consider the following quotes by some of our most notable Founders, who not only openly articulated their own commitment to Christianity, but their belief that it was *only* a moral and religious people who could sustain a government of, by, and for the people:

- John Quincy Adams said that the Declaration of Independence "laid the cornerstone of human government upon the first precepts of Christianity."[1]
- The same Patrick Henry who proclaimed, "Give me liberty or give me death" also said, "It cannot be emphasized too strongly or too often that this great nation was founded not by religionists, but by Christians, not on religions, but on the Gospel of Jesus Christ."[2]
- John Adams said, "The highest glory of the American Revolution was this: it connected in one indissoluble bond the principles of civil government with the principles of Christianity."[3] He also declared, "We have no government armed with power capable of contending with human passions unbridled by morality and religion. Avarice, ambition, revenge or gallantry would break the strongest cords of our Constitution as a whale goes through a net. Our Constitution was made only for a moral and

religious people. It is wholly inadequate to the government of any other."[4]

The Founders' distinctively Christian faith is well documented, as is their conviction that government must be infused with Christian principles. But they resisted the inclination to establish a Christian sect as the official church of the new nation or to impose religious tests to enforce an established church.

Why would men who believed the truths of Christianity were essential to living a moral life and were indispensable to a healthy civil society go to such great pains to ensure the institutions of religion remained *separate* from government?

History reveals two reasons. First, Christianity, particularly as understood in the post-Reformation era, teaches that every individual is endowed with the solemn dignity and free will to choose either to believe or not to believe. To the Christian, God "stands at the door and knocks";[5] He does not break the door down and forcibly enter. Truth is something that is offered to man and made available for him to voluntarily seek and discover. It is never something he is compelled to accept. It follows that a human government should aspire to do nothing more or less.

Thus our Founders believed that a government is not legitimate unless it is grounded in the principles of individual sovereignty and free will, which begin with freedom of conscience and religious liberty. Only a society that protects the dignity of every person—his ability to believe or not to believe, to speak freely about his beliefs or to remain silent; his right to act according to the dictates of conscience; and ultimately, his prerogative to remain personally accountable to his Creator in each of those areas—could be considered just or morally legitimate.

Second, the Founders knew that whenever there is a state-sponsored religion, the government tends to encroach upon, to increasingly regulate, and finally to dictate religious belief and expression. The government may do this directly, by usurping the right to conscience belonging solely to the individual, church, or religious institution, or indirectly, by gradually eroding the pillars of religious life that generate and strengthen the social vibrancy and moral commitments of a self-governing republic.

Government control over religion historically resulted in a system of "crony clericalism" in which professional clergy fell prey to the temptations of unchecked power and personal greed. This typically led to tyranny, the suffocation of religious liberty, and the snuffing out of every other freedom, as the Founders understood. Paul Johnson described how the first Americans utterly rejected this model:

> If there was one characteristic which distinguished [America] from the start—which made it quite unlike any part of Europe and constituted its uniqueness in fact—it was the absence of any kind of clericalism. Clergymen there were, and often very good ones, who enjoyed the esteem and respect of their congregations by virtue of their piety and preachfulness. But whatever nuance of Protestantism they served, and including Catholic priests when they in due course arrived, none of them enjoyed a special status, in law or anything else, by virtue of their clerical rank. Clergy spoke with authority from their altars and pulpits, but their power ended at the churchyard gate.[6]

Instead of looking to entrenched clergy to define religious doctrine, early Americans studied the Bible themselves to learn spiritual truth first-hand. To defend this tradition, they needed a political system that protected the right to discover truth, to openly exchange ideas, and to dissent. This is the foundation of freedom of conscience, which protects believers and non-believers alike.

For this reason, more than any other American habit of liberty, religious liberty is the cornerstone of American freedom and the guiding force that makes America exceptional. The freedom to know and pursue God is not a Republican or Democratic value; neither is it liberal or conservative. It is a universal thirst written into the heart of every person.

Only when a government is firmly committed to the defense of this liberty can religious vibrancy and moral strength be cultivated in a nation. A government that fails to respect the dignity of every person, beginning first and foremost with their freedom of conscience and religious liberty, surrenders its rightful authority to govern, if it ever had it in the first place.

It bears noting that a commitment to religious pluralism—or affording every individual's religious beliefs the equal protection of the law—is not the same as saying all beliefs are equal. Tolerating a differing opinion does not make that opinion true, but it does respect the right of the individual to possess it, and it trusts in the equal ability and right of every person to discern truth for himself.

Radical secularists often seek to undermine the moral legitimacy of America's religious heritage by pointing to occasions in our history when we Americans have failed to live up to our own ideals—whether in the case of slavery, the denial of civil rights, or other instances in which our historic commitment to liberty for all was radically compromised by other political agendas and pursuits.

But in each of these instances, it was our very commitment to moral and religious principle, to an authority and law higher than our own, that impelled us to self-correct and to use our greatest mistakes as the greatest opportunities to reassert the dignity of every human being and the cause of human freedom.

America has indeed endured moments that tested our commitment to freedom and individual dignity, and other moments when we abandoned those core principles in exchange for a more expedient or utilitarian course. But much of what makes America an exceptional nation is that it was in some of those darkest times that America reclaimed its self-evident truths and redeemed, sometimes at great cost, the principle that *all* people are indeed created equal and endowed with equal dignity and worth.

AMERICA AWAKENS

Almost every middle school student receives at least a tacit introduction to American history, often beginning with the Revolutionary War. But few students are taught to appreciate the religious convictions that motivated those first Americans to risk everything, and often to pay the ultimate price, to secure that freedom. And fewer still are taught the actual origins of so many of the ideas that produced the American Revolution.

Beginning in the earlier part of the eighteenth century, more than four decades before the Revolution, a moral, spiritual, and cultural renewal spread throughout America. Like small brushfires flaring up throughout a vast, parched land, sparks of renewed religious fervency began to catch fire in the minds of first hundreds, then thousands of colonial settlers. Galvanized by the fiery sermons of George Whitefield, Jonathan Edwards, and others, these revivals—which held no name or label at the time—tended to begin not in a church or city center, but in the open air of the countryside, eventually evolving into the camp-meetings that were a prominent feature of American frontier life for the following two centuries.

As touched upon in chapter one, the Great Awakening democratized and personalized religion. Such open-aired meetings were accessible not only to the wealthier, long-established patrons of traditional churches, but also to the most humble laborers, farmers, and pioneers, many of whom had no other opportunity to access spiritual teaching. Itinerant preachers recited a Gospel that was deeply individualized, centered on a personal knowledge of truth and a personal relationship with God. Crucially, they encouraged individuals to read the Bible and discern these principles for themselves.

Though occasionally referring to worldly affairs, the preachers' message was not inherently political. Yet their declaration of personal salvation, personal knowledge and study of Scripture, and man's equality before God had enormous political ramifications that are still evident in the American character today, especially in the commitment to personal responsibility over every aspect of one's religious, family, and social life—that is, to self-government.

It was this notion, not merely indignation at the price of tea, that was at the core of the Revolutionaries' cry for liberty. The Great Awakening had cemented a deep and immoveable belief that ultimate authority rested with God alone, that God—not government—gave man his rights, and that a government that usurped the sovereign authority of God or the right of man to govern himself had lost its legitimacy.

It was through a renewed commitment to these religious truths that Americans gleaned the moral strength to endure a long, costly, but ultimately victorious war for their independence.

SLAVERY AND THE CIVIL WAR

At the beginning of the nineteenth century, America was swept by the Second Great Awakening—another movement of profound spiritual renewal that emphasized God's accessibility to every person. Though historians often fail to make the connection, this deeply religious movement, and its emphasis on the equal dignity of all men, strongly impacted prevailing beliefs about the issue of slavery, as witnessed in the writings and speeches of America's foremost opponent of human bondage.

Years before the Civil War began, Abraham Lincoln argued that the practice of degrading and abusing human beings made in the image of God was incompatible with America's foundational principles. He described the inescapable conflict between the forces of freedom and slavery in a speech in 1854: "Near eighty years ago we began by declaring that all men are created equal; but now from that beginning we have run down to the other declaration, that for SOME men to enslave OTHERS is a 'sacred right of self-government.'"[7]

Lincoln repeatedly appealed to the conscience of America to reject slavery, not on pragmatic or economic grounds, but by reasserting the moral and religious truths that animated the Founders and the eighteenth-century revivalists. In a speech on August 17, 1858, in Lewistown, Illinois, he declared,

> These communities, by their representatives in old Independence Hall, said to the whole world of men: "We hold these truths to be self-evident: that all men are created equal; that they are endowed by their Creator with certain unalienable rights; that among these are life, liberty and the pursuit of happiness." This was their majestic interpretation of the economy of the Universe. This was their lofty, and wise, and noble understanding of the justice of the Creator to His creatures. Yes, gentlemen, to *all* His creatures, to the whole great

family of man. In their enlightened belief, nothing stamped
with the Divine image and likeness was sent into the world to
be trodden on, and degraded, and imbruted by its fellows.[8]

The belief that the "Divine image" had been stamped upon every person, slave or free, sustained Lincoln through the dark and horrible
crucible of a civil war that cost the lives of more than 600,000 Americans. It was by reminding Americans of this truth that Lincoln continually rekindled the moral will of a free people. It was the knowledge
that they fought for a cause not merely political, but deeply spiritual
and eternally significant, that inspired the Union to press on to victory
despite the devastating cost.

THE EUGENICS MOVEMENT AND THE REPUDIATION OF LIBERTY

Charles Davenport, one of the first American eugenicists, called
eugenics the science of "the improvement of the human race by better
breeding."[9] Essentially, eugenicists believed in advancing society by selec-
tively breeding the most talented or beautiful or intelligent people, while
preventing the reproduction of the disabled, the poor, or the so-called
"feebleminded." Eugenicists drew widespread attention with their warn-
ings that "defective" people were reproducing at a much higher rate than
were "normal" people, threatening all of society.

These repugnant theories took root in American academia in the early
twentieth century and from there began to permeate the wider American
culture.

Eugenics was especially aimed against immigrants. When immigrant
populations were given IQ tests that were largely vocabulary-based,
eugenicist Henry Goddard unsurprisingly discovered that over 80 percent
of immigrant test-takers—whether Hungarian, Polish, Italian, or Russian—were mentally defective.[10] He then concluded that feebleminded-
ness was inherited through genetic traits, a standard argument among a
large group of eugenicists who believed certain races or ethnicities were
more likely to be "defective," and were therefore less useful to society,
than other races.

Odious ideas have consequences. Elected leaders looked to science for solutions to social ills, and eugenicists offered a seemingly scientific answer to what was deemed a scientific problem.

By 1940, more than thirty states had enacted compulsory sterilization laws, and by 1941, tens of thousands—at least 60,000 according to one source—of eugenic sterilizations had been performed in the United States.[11]

This brief history should be seen as a stark warning against diminishing or ending an innocent human life simply because "society" deems that life to be burdensome; in doing so, we compromise every ideal and belief in human dignity that has made America great, and we tear at the very fabric that holds our exceptional society together. The history of the eugenics movement in America will always blight the nation's soul, demonstrating the danger of straying from our foundational principles. But this history also shows that when we renew our commitment to the self-evident truths of the Declaration of Independence, even the largest ship of state can be righted and set on course again.

THE CIVIL RIGHTS MOVEMENT

Like the issue of slavery, the 1960s-era struggle for civil rights forced America to confront deep, long-standing injustices.

The most prominent leader of the civil rights movement, Martin Luther King Jr., was a Baptist minister who believed that the effort to end racial discrimination and segregation was premised on the same religious truths that our Founders had proclaimed. Indeed, he understood that no objective claim can be made to civil or legal rights without the assumption that there are God-given moral rights and principles of justice. It was only by appealing to these unchangeable laws of justice—especially the natural law that *all* men are equal and endowed with dignity from their Creator—that King believed the case for civil rights could retain its moral legitimacy. King clearly articulated these beliefs in his "Letter from a Birmingham Jail":

An unjust law is a human law this is not rooted in eternal law and natural law. Any law that uplifts human personality is just. Any law that degrades human personality is unjust. All segregation statutes are unjust because segregation distorts the soul and damages the personality. It gives the segregator a false sense of superiority and the segregated a false sense of inferiority....Hence segregation is not only politically, economically and sociologically unsound, it is morally wrong and sinful.[12]

Moreover, King knew that by reasserting these core truths, civil rights activists were, in his words, "standing up for what is best in the American dream and for the most sacred values in our Judaeo-Christian heritage, thereby bringing our nation back to those great wells of democracy which were dug deep by the founding fathers in their formulation of the Constitution and the Declaration of Independence."[13]

REAGAN SHINES A LIGHT

In autumn 1989, the most potent symbol of totalitarian evil, the Berlin Wall, was ripped apart by the people it had imprisoned for nearly thirty years. Two years later, the Soviet Union officially dissolved, on Christmas Day 1991. The fall of the Wall and the dissolution of the Soviet Union transpired in relative calm, but they followed decades of repression, cruelty, and murder by the Soviet regime and its satellite governments.

The Wall fell due to a mix of political, economic, diplomatic, and military events. But spiritual factors were decisive, as President Ronald Reagan did his part to rally the West to defend religious freedom and human dignity. Most people know of Reagan's demand, issued in June 1987 at the Brandenburg Gate, next to the Berlin Wall, that Soviet leader Mikhail Gorbachev "tear down this wall." Unfortunately, this iconic statement has overshadowed the rest of his speech, in which Reagan described the "fundamental distinction between East and West." Said Reagan, "The totalitarian world produces backwardness because it does such violence to the spirit, thwarting the human impulse to create, to enjoy, to worship."[14]

Reagan then ridiculed how the "totalitarian world finds even symbols of love and of worship an affront." He pointed to the frantic attempts by the Communist East German government to correct with paints and chemicals what they found to be a major flaw in the glass sphere of the massive communications tower they built in 1969. Reagan noted that their attempted fixes had failed, since "even today when the sun strikes that sphere—that sphere that towers over all Berlin—the light makes the sign of the cross."[15]

This theme was nothing new to Reagan; he had been stressing the primacy of the spiritual struggle against Communism since he had taken office. In his 1981 Notre Dame commencement address, four months into his presidency, Reagan issued this rallying cry: "For the West, for America, the time has come to dare to show to the world that our civilized ideas, our traditions, our values, are not—like the ideology and war machine of totalitarian societies—just a facade of strength. It is time for the world to know our intellectual and spiritual values are rooted in the source of all strength, a belief in a Supreme Being, and a law higher than our own."[16]

Similarly, in his "Evil Empire" speech in 1983, Reagan declared, "The source of our strength in the quest for human freedom is not material, but spiritual. And because it knows no limitation, it must terrify and ultimately triumph over those who would enslave their fellow man."[17]

When human freedom and dignity were under assault during the Cold War, Reagan knew that the spiritual nature of man and the freedom to know God were central to defining humanity and decisive in defeating tyranny.

THE WAR ON FAITH

In his dissenting opinion in *Wallace v. Jaffree* (1985), Supreme Court Justice William Rehnquist stated, "The 'wall of separation between church and state' is a metaphor based on bad history, a metaphor which has proved useless as a guide to judging. It should be frankly and explicitly abandoned."[18]

His declaration was a blunt reminder that no attack on American culture is more historically dishonest or socially destructive than the relentless effort of radical secularists to drive God out of America's public square.

While radical secularists claim to support religious neutrality in the public realm, in fact they focus almost exclusively on attacking expressions of Judeo-Christian morality, revealing that their real agenda is to banish our Judeo-Christian heritage from public life altogether. Their campaign is waged on two main fronts: the classroom and the courtroom. Additionally, they have recently extended their attacks to the family, and to the rights of parents to direct the upbringing of their children.

In June 2002, the Ninth Circuit Court of Appeals shocked Americans nationwide by ruling the phrase "under God" in the Pledge of Allegiance to be unconstitutional. The ruling brazenly trampled upon centuries of American religious heritage, disregarded countless judicial precedents, and flouted the explicit will of the American people as asserted by Congress and President Eisenhower when they formally adopted the phrase in 1954.

With that ruling, many Americans realized just how hostile our elites have become to the public expression of our traditional religious precepts. But in fact, the Pledge of Allegiance decision was only the latest effort in a decades-long campaign to eliminate not only the words but the very concept that America is "under God." Consider the following Supreme Court decisions:

- In 1962, the Court banned prayer from public schools.[19]
- In 1963, the Court found that reading the Bible in public schools was unconstitutional.[20]
- In 1980, the Court invalidated a state law requiring the Ten Commandments to be displayed in public school classrooms.[21]
- In 1985, the Court struck down a state law requiring a moment of silence for private prayer or meditation in public schools.[22]

- In 1989, the Court found the display of a nativity scene at a county courthouse to be unconstitutional.[23]
- In 1992, religious figures were prohibited from offering prayer during public school graduation ceremonies.[24]
- In 1993, the Court ruled that it was unconstitutional for a Christian club to meet on the campus of a public school.[25]
- In 2004, a student who earned a state scholarship to college was denied the right to use the funding to pursue a degree in theology.[26]
- In 2005, a display of the Ten Commandments in two Kentucky county courthouses was ruled unconstitutional.[27]

The campaign against public prayer and the display of religious symbols is only the tip of the iceberg.[28] Consider the following examples:

- In New Jersey, a second-grade public school student was prohibited from singing "Awesome God" in an after-school talent show.[29]
- In January 2004, in Balch Spring, Texas, senior citizens meeting at a community senior center were prohibited from praying over their meals.[30]
- In October 2004, in St. Louis, Missouri, an elementary student caught praying over his lunch by a school official was lifted from his seat, reprimanded in front of the other students, and taken to the principal, who ordered him to stop praying.[31]
- In October 2006, the president of William and Mary College removed a cross from the historic Wren Chapel, implying it was an unwelcoming religious symbol.[32]
- In November 2006, a student at Missouri State University studying to be a social worker was interrogated by school faculty and subsequently threatened with expulsion when, after being required to lobby state legislators in favor of same-sex couple adoptions, she asked for an

alternative assignment that did not violate her Christian beliefs.[33]

- In May 2009, a pro-life nurse at a New York hospital was forced to participate in a late-term abortion, even though the hospital had agreed in writing to honor her religious convictions.[34]
- In October 2009, Congress passed a "hate speech" law subjecting pastors and other faith leaders to prosecution for preaching aspects of their faith that the state decides are "hate speech."[35]
- In January 2010, a Baptist minister was sentenced to thirty days in jail for peacefully protesting outside a Planned Parenthood abortion clinic in Oakland, California.[36]
- In February 2010, five men were threatened with arrest for preaching Christianity on a public sidewalk in Virginia.[37]
- A Methodist camp meeting association in New Jersey now faces civil rights charges after refusing a request to host a same-sex couple's "civil union ceremony" in its worship space.[38]
- A young Christian photographer was fined nearly $7,000 in attorneys' fees after she refused to photograph the "commitment ceremony" of a same-sex couple.[39]
- A student at Tomah High School in Wisconsin received a grade of zero, a formal reprimand, and two days of detention after drawing a picture containing a cross and Scripture reference in art class.[40]
- Members of a Christian club in an Arizona high school were disallowed from sharing information during morning announcements simply because their announcement contained the word "prayer."[41]

The Founders would have regarded such efforts to remove God from public life as a fundamental threat to liberty. They saw no contradiction between the First Amendment, which was designed to *protect* religious liberty, and the need for a free people to remember that their liberties come from God. Indeed, when George Washington spoke of the "sacred fire of liberty," he implored the people to safeguard liberty by acknowledging God's providence and seeking His blessing on behalf of the nation.[42]

FAMILY: THE INCUBATOR OF LIBERTY

The most fundamental institution for preserving liberty arose before any other social arrangement, and has existed under every political system in history. The family is the cornerstone of society, and is the surest means by which the most cherished values of any culture are transmitted to the next generation.

The family can accomplish what no government institution can. No organization or association is better suited to imparting the values and principles of a free society. No department of welfare, department of health, or department of education can accomplish what the family does.

It is at the family hearth that children learn the essential truths about God and human existence, and are provided the foundational worldview that in turn shapes and informs their beliefs and interactions.

No government agency can teach children the value of personal responsibility and work; it is in the family that children gain their deepest sense of patriotism, their sense of self-worth and dignity, and their sense of justice and their commitment to freedom. It is the family that is most capable of inculcating the hearts and minds of children with the honesty, character, and virtue that is necessary to preserve a free republic.

Consider the words of former United States education secretary Bill Bennett. In his book *The De-Valuing of America*, Bennett writes,

> Nothing more powerfully determines a child's behavior than his internal compass, his beliefs, his sense of right and wrong. If a child firmly believes, if he has been taught and guided to believe, that drugs, promiscuity, and assaulting other people are wrong things to do, this will contribute to his own well-being and to the well-being of others. And if this lesson is multiplied a million times—that is, taught a million times—we

have greater and broader well-being, fewer personal catastrophes, less social violence, and fewer wasted and lost lives. The character of a society is determined by how well it transmits true and time-honored values from generation to generation. Cultural matters, then, are not simply an add-on or an afterthought to the quality of life of a country; they determine the character and essence of the country itself. Private belief is a condition of public spirit; personal responsibility a condition of public well-being. The investment in private belief must be constantly renewed.[43]

A society that depends on family-instilled virtues must both protect the family as an institution and respect the rights of parents to raise their children according to the dictates of their own conscience. It is no surprise, then, that those who strive to socially reengineer American culture and replace it with radical, anti-religious secularism are seeking to undermine both the family and the timeless right of parental sovereignty within that institution.

As George Weigel has stated, at the heart of the word culture is *cult*, or religion. Religion is the primary means by which the deepest values and moral virtues are imparted to the next generation of leaders, businessmen, teachers, and history-makers. Since family is the main instrument for instilling and transmitting these ideals, it is families that radical secularists target in so many of their contemporary assaults on liberty.

The weakening or devaluation of the family creates debilitating societal costs. For instance, the success of our economy undoubtedly depends upon the virtue of those individuals who operate within it. While a successful business depends upon the quality, accuracy, timeliness, and reliability of the products and services in which the business trades, it depends far more upon the honesty, integrity, forthrightness, and reliability of those who work within and manage that business—virtues that are first cultivated within the family. If families fail to transmit these virtues, businesses will not be run capably and honestly, and the whole economy will suffer.

Strong virtues can also be cultivated in the workplace for the benefit of families and society. Millions of Americans have learned the value and rewards of hard work as employees of honest, well-run businesses. Such work opportunities have helped countless Americans pursue their God-given potential and strengthened family and community life. A nation committed to promoting economic growth and defending free enterprise therefore invariably promotes the strengthening of family life.

These reinforcing ties between economic freedom and the family make economic conservatives and social conservatives natural allies: those who seek to preserve economic freedom in America should be especially concerned with the defense of family life, and those who care about the dignity and purpose of every life should defend free enterprise. Both groups share common opponents, who typically attack both economic freedom and the institution of family.

Consider the drama that has played out in recent years in California. In November 2008, a majority of California voters approved a ballot initiative called the California Marriage Protection Act, or "Proposition 8." The measure would amend the California state constitution to define marriage as being between one man and one woman.

The law was immediately challenged before the state Supreme Court as well as the federal district court. While California's high court upheld the measure, U.S. District Chief Judge Vaughn R. Walker overturned the proposition and suspended its implementation, with the Ninth Circuit Court of Appeals later extending the stay indefinitely pending appeal. As of this writing, the measure's fate remains in the hands of the courts.[44]

Whether in the effort by radical activists to cancel Proposition 8, or by the court's constitutionally insupportable decision to overturn it, or by the refusal of the state of California to defend it, we see the willingness of government elites, many unelected, to run roughshod over the principles of self-government in an effort to radically redefine an institution that has served as the bedrock of American society since colonial times.

Meanwhile, the California government's inability to produce a balanced budget, its adoption of job-killing business regulations and some of the nation's highest tax rates, and its refusal to rein in spending that is often ideologically driven, have all brought the world's eighth largest economy to the brink of financial insolvency.

It should be no surprise that threats to family life and threats to free enterprise are interrelated. To counter these threats, social and economic conservatives should unite, recognizing their common interest in defending the principle that underlies both their causes: the dignity of the individual.

CHILDREN AND THE FUTURE OF FREEDOM

Just as abolitionists understood that slavery could not coexist with human freedom; just as Americans came to understand that eugenics is appalling and dehumanizing; and just as the civil rights movement demonstrated that liberty is unfulfilled unless the law guarantees equal protection to *all* people; so must Americans eventually realize that without the unalienable right to life for every human being, including the unborn, every other right we possess is devalued and weakened.

Abortion is perhaps the most contentious public issue today, testing the professed American principle that every human life is precious and entitled to constitutional protection. With the advent of increasingly sophisticated ultrasound technology, public opinion on abortion has shifted, with a majority of Americans now identifying themselves as pro-life.

As with any public policy, the more strongly public opinion is swayed in defense of unborn life, the more our laws should and will change as a result. For example, the federal government can immediately cease appropriating public funds to abortion providers. Planned Parenthood, the country's largest abortion provider, has been receiving more than $330 million in federal, state, and local government funding every year. In 2009 Planned Parenthood performed 332,000 abortions and fewer than 1,000 adoption referrals. A mother was 340 times more likely to have her child aborted rather than adopted if she went to Planned Parenthood for advice.[45]

It is logically and ethically indefensible for our representative government to continue allocating taxpayer funds to a practice that the majority of Americans find morally abhorrent.

Whether in the cases of slavery, eugenics, or the denial of civil rights, history has proven the willingness of the American people to reject even the most entrenched policies once it becomes clear that those policies conflict with our most deeply held values and principles. While government has usually been slow to respond to these shifting sentiments, respond it has and respond it must.

A separate issue pertaining to the family is the need to protect parents' time-honored right to direct the upbringing of their own children, and specifically to choose the type of education that is best fitted to the needs of their children.

In 1922, Oregon voters passed a referendum to amend the Oregon Compulsory Education Act and require all children between the ages of eight and sixteen to attend public schools. In its 1925 decision in *Pierce v. Society of Sisters*, the Supreme Court struck down the Oregon statute as unconstitutional, affirming the right of parents to direct the upbringing and choose the best form of education for their children:

> The fundamental theory of liberty upon which all governments in this Union repose excludes any general power of the State to standardize its children by forcing them to accept instruction from public teachers only. The child is not the mere creature of the State; those who nurture him and direct his destiny have the right, coupled with the high duty, to recognize and prepare him for additional obligations.[46]

The Court's ruling became a landmark case affirming parental rights over their children's education. Almost fifty years later, in the 1972 case *Wisconsin v. Yoder*, the Court reaffirmed this fundamental principle by stating, "The primary role of the parents in the upbringing of their children is now established beyond debate as an enduring American tradition."[47]

Despite these clear rulings, the case law is becoming increasingly conflicted as parental rights are once again coming under serious threat. Consider the following cases:

- In 2007, a West Virginia mother was ordered by a family court judge and a local circuit judge to share custody of her four-year-old daughter with two of the girl's babysitters whom the judges referred to as "psychological co-parents."[48]
- In Washington state, a thirteen-year-old boy was encouraged by his school counselors to complain to Child Protective Services that his parents took him to church too often. He was removed from his family, placed in foster care, and only returned to his family after his parents agreed to take him to church less frequently.[49]
- In 1980 the parents of a young teenage girl in Washington state sought to place their daughter in a receiving home after she began running away from home and indulging in drug abuse. The girl filed a complaint with Child Protective Services, citing conflict between parent and child. She was removed from her parents' home and placed in foster care. Despite the judge finding that the girl's parents had acted within their rightful authority, state law upheld the authorities' right to remove her from her family.[50]

Such cases reveal an effort to radically change the long-established authority structure between families and government by forcibly inserting the state between parent and child. The issue is especially relevant today, as our public school system is increasingly geared toward serving the needs of government employee unions and other special interest groups instead of the educational, moral, and emotional needs of our children.

With public schools becoming increasingly bureaucratic, hostile to religious expression, and unresponsive to parental input, American families are increasingly choosing alternative education methods for their children such as private schools, charter schools, and homeschooling. Such options allow parents to customize their child's curriculum and learning environment, provide a safe environment free of drugs and violence, and impart strong religious values.

More than two million students are currently being educated at home, and that number is increasing by as much as 8 percent every year, reaping significant social benefits. Home-educated students score an average of fifteen to thirty points higher than public-school students on standardized tests, including the SAT and ACT, regardless of their parents' level of formal education or the level of family income.[51] Because families who homeschool do not depend on taxpayer-funded resources, taxpayers save an estimated $16 billion each year thanks to homeschooling.[52]

The point is not to demonize the public school system; many of America's (and indeed the world's) greatest leaders, scientists, educators, and businessmen have been products of that very system. Rather, the point is to reinforce the time-honored principle that the authority and responsibility to raise children, direct their education, and instill in them the values that make a free society flourish, all reside with the child's parents, not the state. Except in cases of demonstrable neglect or abuse, lawmakers and judges must enact and enforce policies that support the right of parents to direct the upbringing of their children and choose the educational model that best suits the child's needs, whether public school, private or parochial school, or homeschooling.

A society that trusts and empowers parents to act in their kids' best interest will inevitably cultivate a responsible and virtuous citizenry, one that recognizes the value and dignity of every human life and encourages every individual to achieve his maximum potential.

★ ★ ★

Every time America has strayed from the proposition that all men are created by God, and that they are therefore equal, great suffering and turmoil has ensued.

Likewise, every time government oversteps its bounds and exerts control over an individual's right to religious freedom, or otherwise attempts to usurp his ability to discover truth for himself, it must lie to do so.

A government that enacts or enforces policies that diminish the value of one category of human life is telling the lie that every person is not created equal.

A government that prohibits an individual from praying or reading the Bible or displaying religious symbols in public is telling the lie that our Founders intended only certain types of religious expression to be protected.

A government that usurps the role of a parent by arbitrarily inserting itself between the parent and child, that says it alone knows best what kind of education, what kind of family life or structure, what kind of upbringing is best for a child, is telling the lie that the child's parents are incapable of discovering the strengths of their own child, incapable of cultivating those strengths, and incapable of lovingly guiding their child toward a future that is productive, moral, and fulfilling.

A government that systematically removes the people's ability to make laws based on moral or religious judgment is lying about American history, the rule of law, and the American practice of self-government.

A government that tries to eliminate the concept "under God" from our Pledge of Allegiance as well as our entire political philosophy is lying not only about America's religious heritage but about the nature of human freedom itself.

Freedom is indeed the most fragile of human possessions, and in every generation it has faced some form of these threats. Consider the words of Joseph Story, a former Supreme Court justice, renowned writer on the Constitution, and the first dean of Harvard Law School:

> Let the American youth never forget, that they possess a noble inheritance, bought by the toils, and sufferings, and blood of their ancestors; and capable, if wisely improved and faithfully guarded, of transmitting to their latest posterity all the substantial blessings of life, the peaceful enjoyment of liberty, of property, of religion and of independence.... It may, nevertheless, perish in an hour, by the folly, or corruption, or negligence of its only keepers, THE PEOPLE.[53]

Today, a clique of radical secularists is striving to remove the constitutional protections of faith and the faithful from our system of government, and to eliminate any public acknowledgment that these liberties come from God. No one should be fooled into believing that this was the intention of our Founding Fathers, nor that doing so will yield anything but a corrupt, despotic government.

The choice before us is whether to accept such a society, or to reassert the truth within our families, our workplaces, and our communities that the cause of human freedom can only be realized in a society that protects the institution of family and supports and defends the fundamental rights of religious liberty and freedom of conscience.

CHAPTER FIVE

WORK

IN AMERICA, IT'S CALLED "OPPORTUNITY"

*I*n *her best-selling 2004 book* Hello Laziness: Why Hard Work Doesn't Pay, *author Corrine Maier offered her fellow French citizens a how-to guide for avoiding work. Unlike Horatio Alger, whose stories preached the benefits of hard work, honesty, and diligence, Maier argued that "doing the least possible" is the true key to success.*[1]

But she does have one exception to her rule: America.

When asked in a 2005 interview with CBS' 60 Minutes whether she thought Americans were insane for their work habits, Maier replied, "No, because Americans, I think, believe more in future than French people. We, French people, right now don't believe that the future will be better than now. We think that the future will be worse than now, so we don't have any reason to work."[2]

Like Thomas Paine, who celebrated the American Revolution as an opportunity to start the world anew, Americans have always anticipated a better future. This forward-looking worldview has been essential to fueling America's exceptional work ethic and extraordinary system of wealth creation.

From the settlers at Jamestown to the immigrants who land on our shores today, Americans have believed hard work provides the opportunity to pursue happiness and enjoy the fruits of one's labor. Faith in the future and faith in a just reward for work are, as Corrine Maier intimated, still vibrant sources of American Exceptionalism.

THE LORD'S WORK

America's exceptional attitude toward work is based on our Judeo-Christian tradition and was further developed in the writings of philosophers such as John Locke.

In his book *The Spirit of Democratic Capitalism*, philosopher and author Michael Novak explains that "Judaism and Christianity are distinctive among the world religions because they understand salvation as a vocation in history. It is the religious task of Jews and Christians to change the world as well as to purify their own souls; to build up 'the Kingdom of God' in their own hearts and through the work of their hands."[3]

Novak later explains the theological implications of John Locke's insights into work and creation:

> It may have been John Locke (1632–1704) who first articulated the new possibility for economic organization. Locke observed that a field of, say, strawberries, highly favored by nature, left to itself, might produce what seemed to be an abundance of strawberries. Subject to cultivation and care by practical intelligence, however, such a field might be made to produce not simply twice but tenfold as many strawberries. In short, Locke concluded, nature is far wealthier in possibility than human beings had ever drawn attention to before.
>
> Permit me to put Locke's point in theological terms. Creation left to itself is incomplete, and humans are called to be

co-creators with God, bringing forth the potentialities the
Creator has hidden. Creation is full of secrets waiting to be
discovered, riddles which human intelligence is expected by
the Creator to unlock.

... After Locke ... [n]o longer were humans to imagine
their lot as passive, long-suffering, submissive. They were
called upon to be inventive, prudent, farseeing, hardworking—in order to realize by their obedience to God's call the
building up and perfecting of God's Kingdom on earth.[4]

America provided the perfect laboratory and proving ground where this
moral vision of work could be put into practice.

Work is one of our most significant sources of personal identity. From
the time of the Apostles, Christians everywhere have sought to reconcile
their identity and their work with the will of God. They have placed the
highest priority on discerning and obeying God's call in their lives. The
famous opening of Augustine's *Confessions* (397–98 AD) summarizes
this yearning beautifully, as Augustine prays to God, "You have made us
for yourself, and our hearts are restless until they find their rest in you."

Throughout American history, we find the religious-tinged view that
work is a moral good in and of itself. "The man who builds a factory builds
a temple," President Coolidge declared, adding, "The man who works
there worships there." Henry Ford was even more adamant: "Work is the
salvation of the human race, morally, physically, socially."[5] At the turn of
the twentieth century, the sociologist Max Weber memorably described
this kind of industriousness as "the Protestant work ethic."

Alexis de Tocqueville found that a "kind of spiritual energy coursed
through America's mechanics and artisans, farmers and carpenters, men
and women of every station who felt charged to make their own world."[6]
Ken Burns' documentary on building the Brooklyn Bridge describes this
same American energy and work ethic: "People in every country in
Europe received letters back from recent emigrants to America, all making the same point: 'Well, it is true you can make yourself rich in this new
country, but if we had ever worked *this* hard back home, we could have
gotten rich there too!'"[7]

AN AMERICAN MERITOCRACY

As Benjamin Franklin observed, in America merit has always determined a man's worth. Merit serves as the great leveler, as even those born into difficult circumstances can—and do—succeed through hard work and intelligence. As George Washington asserted in 1784, "A people ... who are possessed of the spirit of commerce, who see, and who will pursue their advantages, may achieve almost anything."[8]

To achieve "almost anything," the American people needed a system that rewarded work and risk-taking, incentivized discovery, and encouraged commerce. God's gifts were not to be hidden away, but illuminated by work and enterprise enabled by the flame of liberty. Such a system requires secure property rights, minimal government interference in trade, and an outlet for innovation and experimentation. It rewards knowledge and understanding with success, and in the process it affirms the dignity of the individual and his unique talents.

In colonial America, with its abundance of free land and relatively small population, labor was always in short supply. American wage levels and job opportunities could not be matched in Europe, providing powerful incentives for migration to the New World, especially among refugees from Europe's religious wars.

The vast majority of colonists were middle- and lower-income Protestants. The colonies grew wealthy producing crops for export to European and Caribbean markets. Virginia quickly became solvent through the tobacco trade, while other colonies exported grain, hides, lumber, and later, rice, indigo, and cotton to European manufacturers, mainly in Britain.

America's system of free enterprise contrasted sharply with the mercantilist system—a state-controlled economy of cartels and monopolies—that stunted the European economies. State-run consortiums and legal restrictions hindered the formation of European companies, diminished wealth creation, and suppressed economic dynamism, as the economies were designed to funnel as much state revenue as possible through a few favored hands.

In colonial America there was no entrenched, ruling elite that could steer the nation's economy to their own ends. Americans thus enjoyed unrivaled freedom to innovate and to reap the rewards of their own enterprise. Under these circumstances, the American colonies became the world's richest nation per capita and the undisputed leader in innovation and social mobility.

PRIVATE PROPERTY:
THE LINCHPIN OF A FREE ECONOMY

John Locke proclaimed the unalienable rights of life, liberty, and "property," rather than the "pursuit of happiness." For Locke, man's ability to keep the fruits of his own labors—his property—was a matter of justice. The term "property" also referred to private property, or land, which Locke believed should be protected by government from the insecurity of the "state of nature."

America's earliest settlers learned the importance of private property the hard way; as historian Daniel Boorstin noted, "America began as a sobering experience. The colonies were a disproving ground for utopias."[9] Whimsical "planners" of the Virginia Company of London initially required settlers at both Jamestown and Plymouth to agree to work collectively for seven years before they would receive private plots of land. The policy led to starvation in both colonies, which only recovered after settlers received private land titles. The practical lesson was clear: if a man owned his own land and was responsible for his own family, he was far more productive than if he was expected to contribute to a communal account, with no direct reward for working harder, more productively, or more creatively.

This lesson was applicable beyond those two settlements; it held true throughout colonial America and has been confirmed countless times across the world, from the Soviet Union's famine-inducing collectivization of agriculture to the food shortages, inflation, and blackouts that have plagued Venezuela since property rights became a casualty of Hugo Chavez's socialist "revolution."

Secure property rights also promote essential capital investment, which makes available the tools and equipment that make workers more productive. The resulting rise in productivity boosts wages over time and raises a nation's standard of living. With property rights secure, investors know that the capital they develop and accumulate will not be stolen from them. That encourages more savings and investment, which promotes increasing prosperity.

The patriots at Lexington and Concord were farmers defending their land and their rights against the British invaders. Subsequent generations pushed ever westward into new lands. In 1787 the Founders agreed to incorporate the old North-West Territory—the land between the Allegheny Mountains and the Mississippi—into the new nation. Then in 1803 President Thomas Jefferson nearly doubled America's land mass by purchasing the Louisiana Territory, stretching roughly from the Mississippi to the Rocky Mountains, from Napoleon for $15 million. Thousands of adventurers, frontiersmen, and farmers followed Lewis and Clark into the territory, and eventually the country was settled all the way to the Pacific coast. Property was a tangible asset enabling men of the most modest means to achieve financial independence and secure a direct stake in their own futures and in America's as well.

It took nearly a century for American historians to realize that the process of exploring, settling, and developing all that territory had fundamentally impacted the character of the American people. In 1893, a young professor from the University of Wisconsin, Frederick Jackson Turner, delivered a short paper on American history at the World's Columbian Exposition in Chicago.

Turner stated his thesis in a single sentence: "The existence of an area of free land, its continuous recession, and the advance of American settlement westward explain American development."[10]

He elaborated on the connection between the frontier and the American character:

> To the frontier the American intellect owes its striking characteristics. That coarseness and strength combined with acuteness and inquisitiveness; that practical, inventive turn of mind, quick to find expedients; that masterful grasp of material things, lacking in the artistic but powerful to effect great ends; that restless nervous energy; that dominant individualism, working for good or evil, and withal that buoyancy and

exuberance which comes with freedom—these are traits of the frontier. Since the days when the fleet of Columbus sailed into the waters of the New World, America has been another name for opportunity.[11]

Turner's "Frontier Thesis" became one of the most influential explanations of American Exceptionalism ever written, deeply affecting the teaching of history and spawning a popular genre—the Western—that would encompass literature, film, and television. Situating land, work, and property rights at the core of the American character, the thesis explained the unique circumstances and habits that still define our nation today.

THANK HAMILTON

The United States transformed from an agricultural country into the world's preeminent commercial and industrial power thanks to policies developed by Alexander Hamilton and embraced by George Washington. The two men worked together in a remarkable partnership from the end of the Revolution to the Constitutional Convention and then through Washington's two terms of office.

Washington and Hamilton had endured eight years of war with the British Empire. They knew that the lack of American industry and financial strength had lengthened the war and made Americans dependent on foreigners for the equipment and finances needed to win freedom. They also knew that national security required a national economy and national finances.

As chronicled in Ron Chernow's superb biography, Alexander Hamilton understood that a complex, efficient economy has to be underpinned by a specific set of rights: property rights (including protection for intellectual property through patents and copyrights), freedom of contract, and the rule of law (including an independent judiciary for settling disputes). When these rights are secure, producers can focus on areas where they have the greatest comparative advantage.[12] According to *The Wealth of Nations*, Adam Smith's seminal work on free enterprise, such a division of labor is the foundation of modern prosperity.

Hamilton also identified other crucial ingredients for a nation's economic success: minimum taxation and minimum regulatory barriers (a condition that incentivizes increased production), and sound money tethered to real world values (which provides a stable medium of exchange and a stable medium for savings and investment). Overall, Hamilton understood that nations rise or fall over seemingly mundane issues like the rate of interest required to secure foreign loans, the availability of foreign capital, and implementing the policies that most effectively encourage work. As Daniel Defoe wrote, "It is not the longest sword that conquers, but the longest purse."

In his *Report on Public Credit*, Hamilton presented a detailed blueprint of the government's fiscal machinery, wrapped in a broad political and economic vision. In this renowned study, Hamilton maintained that the government's debt, largely incurred from fighting the Revolutionary War, was the "price of liberty" and had to be paid off, both for economic reasons and as a matter of simple morality. Hamilton's advice, of course, has some resonance today, when the United States is burdened by a $14 trillion national debt—a figure the Founders surely would have regarded as not only economically harmful, but immoral.

Later, in his *Report on Manufactures*, Hamilton laid the policy foundation for the great American industrial boom. Arguing against advocates of the agrarian idyll like Thomas Jefferson, Hamilton claimed America's focus on agriculture was not a natural by-product of geography and culture, but the result of overt protectionism by European manufacturers who hoped to keep the American economy subservient to their industries. Hamilton cited the colonies' inability to manufacture essential goods during the Revolution to explain the importance of increasing America's manufacturing capability. He then correctly predicted that both manufacturers and industrial workers would flock to a country with rich natural resources, low taxes, and the rule of law.

The Constitution's ratification firmly implanted the rule of law in America, while the government's assumption of the states' war debts—a move advocated by Hamilton—increased investor confidence in the new country. But these events and policies merely created the framework for economic success. The actual transformation of America's agricultural economy into the world's primary industrial powerhouse was enacted, first and foremost, through the hard work of the American people.

The United States had been essentially bankrupt as the Constitution took effect, but thanks to Hamilton's foresight and the American work ethic, just two years later George Washington was able to write, "The United States enjoy a scene of prosperity and tranquility under the new government that could hardly have been hoped for.... Our public credit stands on that [high] ground which three years ago it would have been considered as a species of madness to have foretold."

A SAFE HARBOR FOR INNOVATION

In 2005, *Popular Mechanics* magazine conducted a survey to determine the world's top fifty inventions of the last half-century. The experts considered everything from the polio vaccine to ATMs to digital music as they weighed in on which innovations had the biggest impact on the world. When the results were released, thirty-seven of the top fifty—almost 75 percent—were developed by American scientists, American firms, or American universities.[13]

This is no coincidence.

The rights and freedoms guaranteed by our Constitution have provided the invaluable tools for America to become the most innovative and productive society in history. The government provides the framework, and curious and courageous Americans—sometimes from the least likely places—do the rest.

Recall that it was a pair of bicycle mechanics from Dayton, Ohio, the Wright brothers, who experimented on their own for years until they invented the airplane and revolutionized the way we travel. And it was a telegraph operator with a lifelong love of tinkering who became one of history's most prolific inventors—among other things, Thomas Edison made the first commercially viable light bulb, the first phonograph, and the first major electricity distribution network.

The Founders knew that for the United States to become the creative and technological center of the world, Americans would need the opportunity to innovate without fear of anyone, including government officials, stealing their discovery, idea, or invention. With the Constitution's property protections, including the explicit protection of intellectual property, these guarantees are secure. The government has no right to confiscate a person's property without due process, and in fact the government is obligated to protect property against those who would encroach upon it.

At the core of American Exceptionalism is the notion that one does not need to be from a wealthy background, or possess a fancy degree, or have the support of the government, in order to develop and pursue a great idea. By creating a free-enterprise system that embodies this notion, America has not only cultivated its own great thinkers and innovators, but has attracted the best and brightest immigrants to lend their talents to the American project.

Alexander Graham Bell, the Scottish-born inventor of the telephone, and Nikola Tesla, the Austria-born father of electric power systems, both immigrated to America and eventually became U.S. citizens. Each was drawn by the strong property rights, free markets, and access to capital that only America provided. Later, in the 1930s, some of Europe's most brilliant minds, including Albert Einstein, fled tyrannical governments and settled in America, where they found personal and academic freedom. More recently, new Americans from East and South Asia have been crucial to the technological innovation in the Silicon Valley since the 1960s, and to this day, tens of thousands of gifted foreigners seek out the limited number of U.S. student and high-skilled visas.

What makes America so unique? Our markets and institutions reward talent and hard work. Our Constitution and rule of law guarantee one's right to the fruits of their labor. And our government plays a limited but critical role in ensuring that anyone can take risks, knowing their property and innovations will be well protected.

A LOST WAR

For the Founders, work was endowed with moral value. More than a necessity for physical survival, work contributed purpose and meaning to life.[14] These values helped Americans to endure countless hardships and sacrifices during the Great Depression and World War II.

After the war, America's estimated poverty rate fell from 32 percent in 1950, to 22.4 percent in 1959, to 12.1 percent in 1969. But in 1965,

President Lyndon Johnson famously announced the War on Poverty. Robert Rector of the Heritage Foundation reports that from 1965 to 2008, total spending on this "war" reached nearly $16 trillion in 2008 dollars, more than twice the cost of all military conflicts from the American Revolution to today.[15] And what did we get in return? Soon after the War on Poverty programs were adopted, the years-long decline in American poverty suddenly stopped.

From 1978 to 1982, the poverty rate rose by almost a third to 15 percent. By 2009 the poverty rate stood at 14.3 percent—about where it was when the War on Poverty began. As Peter Ferrara explains in *America's Ticking Bankruptcy Bomb,* after the War on Poverty commenced, work among low-income Americans collapsed.[16] In 1960, nearly two-thirds of low-income households were headed by persons who worked,[17] but by 1991, the proportion had fallen to one-third, with only 11 percent working full time, year round.[18] With the government providing so much in free welfare, many people chose not to work.

Once caught in the web of the welfare state, the poor face grave difficulties in trying to break free, a problem Art Laffer has called the "poverty trap." Simply put, welfare recipients who go to work lose their benefits as their income rises. This is effectively an extra tax on work that must be paid on top of the usual array of federal, state, and local taxes. Laffer and others have shown that the effective tax rate on those trying to work to get off of welfare can even exceed 100 percent.

Once free of welfare, those trying to remain productive face the burdens and disincentives of welfare state tax rates. Despite the popularity among politicians of one-time tax rebates, these are largely political gimmicks. With regard to work incentives, the most important metric is the tax rate—the lower the rate, the greater the incentive to work, save, invest, start businesses, expand businesses, create jobs, and produce, because the producer is free to keep a higher percentage of what he or she produces. The higher the tax rate, the bigger the disincentive to work.

HOW TO LIBERATE WORK

In 1996, when I served as Speaker of the House of Representatives, the Republican majority enacted the most successful national welfare reform in history, which restructured the failed New Deal-era Aid to Families with Dependent Children (AFDC) program. More than a legislative reform, it was a cultural reform that valued work and restored the dignity that welfare had destroyed for millions trapped in the system.

The reform returned the share of federal spending on the program to each state in the form of a "block grant" to be used in a new welfare program redesigned by the state based on mandatory work or education for the able-bodied. Federal funding for AFDC previously was based on a matching formula, with the federal government giving more to each state the more it spent on the program, effectively paying the states to expand welfare. The key to the 1996 reforms was that the new block grants to each state were finite, not matching, so federal funding did not vary with the amount the state spent. If a state's new program cost more, the state had to pay the extra costs itself. If the program cost less, the state could keep the savings.

To give the states broad flexibility in designing the new replacement program, the AFDC's status as an entitlement was ended. The reasoning was simple: states would not be free to redesign their programs if their citizens were entitled to coverage and benefits as specified in federal standards. The reformed program was renamed Temporary Assistance to Needy Families (TANF).

The reform was opposed bitterly by the liberal welfare establishment, with Senator Daniel Patrick Moynihan, the Urban Institute, and others predicting the reforms would create a "race to the bottom" among the states and would produce a million starving children within a year.

But quite to the contrary, the reform was immensely successful, exceeding even the predictions of its most ardent supporters. The old AFDC rolls were reduced by two-thirds nationwide, even more in states that pushed work most aggressively. "As a result, in real dollars total federal and state spending on TANF by 2006 was down 31 percent from AFDC spending in 1995, and down by more than half of what it would have been under prior trends," according to *Forbes* magazine.[19]

At the same time, because of the resulting increased work by former welfare dependents, child poverty declined every year, falling by 2000 to levels not seen since 1978. Ron Haskins of the Brookings Institution reports that by 2000 the poverty rate for black children was "the lowest it had ever been."[20] Because of their renewed work effort, the total income of these low-income families formerly on welfare increased by about 25 percent.

There was just one problem with the 1996 reforms: they only reformed one federal program.

The federal government sponsors another 184 means tested welfare programs, including Medicaid, Food Stamps, twenty-seven low-income housing programs, thirty employment and training programs, thirty-four social services programs, another dozen food and nutrition programs, another twenty-two low-income health programs, and twenty-four low-income child care programs, among others.

All these programs could and should be block granted back to the states just as AFDC was in 1996, effectively shedding the federal government of responsibility for welfare. With the states in charge, each one could structure its welfare system to suit its own particular needs and circumstances. State control would also allow states to experiment with different reforms, as real-world results would prove what works and what doesn't. Economic and political competition among the states would lead them to adopt what has proven to work best.

To restore the traditional American incentives to work, save, invest, start and expand businesses, create jobs and produce, America also needs broad based tax reform—namely, an optional 15 percent flat tax, where every taxpayer could choose to file under the new flat rate tax or under the old tax code.

America's traditional work ethic still permeates this country, but it is being undermined by government disincentives. Whether these programs and policies are well-intentioned efforts to help the poor or socialist acts of class warfare, they hurt those they purport to help by devaluing the work ethic. The Founders understood what kind of policies promote a productive citizenry—low taxes, low debt, low regulation, maximum freedom. We could learn profoundly from their example.

THE BETRAYAL OF THE PRIVATE SECTOR

America has risen to become the richest, most powerful country in the world. It owes that achievement to its longstanding belief in the tremendous capacity of individuals to accomplish great things. Our nation's amazing contributions to science, industry, finance, and medicine were not the product of government initiative and bureaucratic control. They came from the genius and labor of individual men and women—many of whom, like Benjamin Franklin, Andrew Carnegie, and John D. Rockefeller, started with practically nothing.

The Founders of this great nation envisioned an economic system comprising a wide variety of energetic private interests, all pursuing their own enlightened self-interests under a carefully constructed system of federalism. The government they created was charged with creating a legal and policy environment that would allow the American economy and civil society to flourish.

That government was *not* authorized to become the producer and director of the great drama that is America. And yet the Progressive movement, strongly influenced by the purported "efficiency" of nineteenth-century Prussian "planning," and later of Soviet "planning," has embraced a top-down director's role for the government over the lives of the American people.   .

One of the two great political parties in the United States has essentially abandoned its responsibility to represent the private sector. It is now focused almost entirely on the demands of the public sector—state and federal government employees, their unions, and to the extent the Democrats listen to the private sector at all, the crony capitalists who profit from influencing government.

Government employee unions have become the largest contributors to the Democratic Party's election campaigns and its candidates, followed by a string of other government-related special interest groups. As a result of this fixation on the public sector, for the past several years, state and federal government employee payrolls have been expanding rapidly, even while job creation and incomes remain stalled among the private-sector workers who pay their salaries.

The political power of this party depends on increasing the percentage of the population that depends on Big Government and that votes to keep it in power. It is now imperative that the American people, who value and honor the legacy of freedom they have received from the Founders, step forward and restore the traditional American commitment to work and independence—or settle for a life of dependency on Hayek's road to serfdom.

CHAPTER SIX

CIVIL SOCIETY

THE UNITED CITIZENS OF AMERICA

W*hen flood waters from Iowa's Cedar River drowned 1,300 city blocks and 4,000 homes in more than four feet of water in June 2008, Christian Fong—the son of a Chinese immigrant and a Nebraska farm girl—acted. A native-born Iowan, Mr. Fong began to organize volunteers in a broad, faith-based initiative to evacuate and care for flood victims.*

Fong and the faith-based group Serve the City worked alongside the police and National Guard to save lives and property in the flood-ravaged area. After the emergency ended, Christian Fong knew his work had only just begun. He launched a new group, Corridor Recovery, devoted to getting the community back on its feet. With 5,000 volunteers, Fong's organization brought together dozens of local civic groups including churches, businesses, and charities to assist in delivering flood assistance to the needy.

Corridor Recovery, bolstered by Boy Scout volunteers, restored 100 houses per week that summer and fall, and even delivered services to government agencies, shattering the expectations of the federal bureaucrats who had been sent to handle the recovery. The group also served as an information hub for redevelopment grants and aid, and engaged in various other initiatives geared toward the area's long-term recovery.

FEMA predicted the flood would permanently shutter 40 percent of Cedar Rapids' businesses, but through the efforts of Corridor Recovery, half of those supposedly doomed enterprises are now open for business. Cedar Rapids is back on its feet today because its citizens stepped up when their community needed them. For his efforts, Fong, a successful business executive before the floods, was lauded as the "Hero of Cedar Rapids."

Christian Fong is an everyday American hero. He does not have a cape or a fancy title; he is just a citizen who takes his responsibilities to his community seriously. He showed extraordinary leadership during the Iowa flood, but he could not have done it alone. He tapped into America's greatest resource—individuals voluntarily gathering together within the framework of civil society. With such efforts, the entire community united to save the lives and property of friends, family, neighbors, and strangers.

The community's response in Cedar Rapids is not unique—it's rather common for ordinary Americans to band together to achieve a common purpose. A few years before the Cedar Rapids flood, Hurricane Katrina had struck the Gulf Coast with unprecedented ferocity. In Mississippi, ordinary citizens and civic groups met that challenge head-on and jump-started the region's recovery. Disaster victims were assisted by nearly a million volunteers who donated 10 million man-hours (worth $143 million in labor costs) and $400 million in financial assistance.[1] From Catholic Charities USA, the Salvation Army, and the Red Cross to small church congregations and independent volunteers like Compassion First, Americans came together to help those in need. The civic activism in Iowa and the Gulf Coast reflect the kind of energetic civil society that the

Founders believed was a critical component of early American civilization.

The Declaration of Independence does not catalog acceptable and unacceptable pursuits of happiness and does not instruct people on how to live out their freedoms. This was not the concern of the Founders, who focused on limiting government's power to infringe on individual freedom, especially the right of individuals to live their lives as they see fit, including through associations.

Thanks to the Founders' successes and sacrifices, successive generations of Americans have enjoyed the freedom to pursue the good and virtuous life. A brief history of American civil society will show how our dedication to neighbor, community, and country became a hallmark of American Exceptionalism.

CIVIL SOCIETY IN ACTION

America's frontier settlers knew firsthand the value of mutual assistance through informal institutions. As they moved west, pioneers assembled into makeshift communities of wagon trains. Individuals and families created communities by binding their fates together, combining their labors and resources for their mutual defense against the elements and hostile Indian tribes. Notably along the Oregon Trail, pioneers aided each other and provided common defense in the absence of government. When the pioneers set down roots, they created organic communities, with individuals cooperating with each other to erect homes, barns, churches, schools, civic buildings, roads, and bridges.[2]

Before a formal local government was established in an area, civil society—individuals pursuing a common goal either through an organization or through an informal group—accomplished myriad individual and mutual aims. In the movie *Witness*, the Amish community barn-raising vividly illustrates what had once been a common American experience—dozens of families coming together to build a barn for their neighbor and to share a meal and socialize after the work was done.

The settlers' interdependence did not conflict with the tradition of American individualism. Rather, civil society married the two through a system of interdependent free institutions and associations. As author Michael Novak notes, the settlers "took pride in being free persons, independent, and self-reliant; but the texture of their lives was cooperative and fraternal."[3]

Such associations were often geared toward ensuring the settlers' physical survival, but others served Americans' intellectual needs, giving rise to scores of schools and educational institutions across the colonies. Benjamin Franklin was energetically involved in such efforts, founding the Junto, an association dedicated to self-improvement and doing social good, and later establishing the American Philosophical Association and the school that would become the University of Pennsylvania.[4]

Likewise, churches relied on the private generosity of their congregations and the public. St. Patrick's Cathedral, an icon of American Catholicism and New York City architecture, raised much of the funds for its construction through appeals to local Catholics, mostly impoverished Irish immigrants who scrimped and saved their nickels and dimes to help build the majestic church.[5] Throughout America, similar instances of collective generosity enabled the creation of museums, hospitals, zoos, charities, and countless other civic-minded institutions.

CIVIL SOCIETY: AN AMERICAN INNOVATION

From its inception, the United States has featured a dynamic civil society comprising a multiplicity of private associations and organic structures. This was one of the most striking and unique features of American life according to Frenchman Alexis de Tocqueville. He observed, "In the United States associations are established to promote the public safety, commerce, industry, morality, and religion. There is no end which the human will despairs of attaining through the combined power of individuals united into a society."[6]

The Founders' insistence on limited government created the space for this flourishing civic life. In turn, to this day, civic groups check and balance government power by fulfilling roles that government is tempted to assume, and by cultivating habits of personal responsibility that make individuals more capable of challenging government encroachments in their affairs.

In the eighteenth century, governments throughout the world suppressed civic groups as threats to their power. But America was different from the start. As historian Gordon Wood observes, after the American Revolution "newly independent American men and women came together to form hundreds and thousands of new voluntary associations expressive of a wide array of benevolent goals," including "mechanics societies ... orphans' asylums ... societies for the promotion of industry, indeed societies for just about anything and everything that was good and humanitarian." Wood further notes, "There was nothing in the Western world quite like these hundreds of thousands of people assembling annually in their different voluntary associations and debating about everything."[7]

Edmund Burke, the great defender of the American cause in the British Parliament, argued that such private associations were the foundation of a strong, stable society:

> To be attached to the subdivision, to love the little platoon we belong to in society, is the first principle (the germ as it were) of public affections. It is the first link in the series by which we proceed towards a love to our country, and to mankind. The interest of that portion of social arrangement is a trust in the hands of all those who compose it; and as none but bad men would justify it in abuse, none but traitors would barter it away for their own personal advantage.[8]

Burke's "little platoons"—voluntary associations acting independent of government—bind us to our communities and country in unions that promote individuals' interests through common means. These platoon-families of civic organizations, professional societies, and religious congregations serve as an intermediate entity between the individual and the vast state apparatus.

Today, civil society encompasses a wide variety of groups and associations. For example, the Boy Scouts of America is an exemplary instance of a civic organization that enriches our daily lives. The Scouts encourage education, habits, and virtues that lead to personal success, and teach our youth the importance of contributing to the public good. Other common examples include neighborhood watch committees, school carpools, little league, the Farm Bureau, and the Red Cross.

Civil society's broad reach makes it uniquely qualified to cater to people's needs. However, even in Tocqueville's time, there were individuals and interests who tried to replace responsive private associations with government. Some of these people were well-intentioned, believing that a one-size-fits-all government bureaucracy could actually serve citizens better than local, custom-designed, voluntary associations could; others knew that an expanded government bureaucracy would serve their interests at other citizens' expense. Despite the vibrancy of American civil society, Tocqueville presciently predicted that government would eventually usurp many of the duties that private associations performed so effectively:

> But what political power could ever carry on the vast multitude of lesser undertakings which the American citizens perform every day, with the assistance of the principle of association? It is easy to foresee that the time is drawing near when man will be less and less able to produce, by himself alone, the commonest necessaries of life. The task of the governing power will therefore perpetually increase, and its very efforts will extend it every day. The more it stands in the place of associations, the more will individuals, losing the notion of combining together, require its assistance: these are causes and effects that unceasingly create each other.... The morals and the intelligence of a democratic people would be as much endangered as its business and manufactures if the government ever wholly usurped the place of private companies. Feelings and opinions are recruited, the heart is enlarged, and the human mind is developed only by the reciprocal influence of men upon one another.[9]

Both Tocqueville and the Founders realized that government could not and should not replace civil society, because the static and singular nature of government cannot accommodate the manifold needs of American citizens. When government intervenes in any field served by civil society, it shrinks the size and scope of civic life, taking more of the money that would otherwise be available for private associations. Furthermore, when the government intervenes, it often lassoes private associations with new and cumbersome rules and regulations that discourage new membership and sap further initiative by private citizens. As civic society diminishes, those in need are forced to turn to the bureaucratic institutions that have assumed a dominant position. This creates greater and greater dependence on ineffectual and stultifying government action, and individuals become less free, less virtuous, and less well-served.

The more government centralizes social programs, the more it tends to depersonalize and alienate the individuals it is meant to protect and serve. It reduces the individual, to paraphrase Karl Marx, to an "appendage of the bureaucratic state," which tries to assume control of more and more of our personal responsibilities. This bureaucratization of American life erodes people's dignity and alienates them from one another, as they depend on government to solve problems instead of working together. As the bureaucratic state grows, the citizen becomes smaller, more lonely, and more vulnerable to arbitrary government actions. Transforming from independent citizens into dependent subjects, we lose our ability to organize spontaneously and creatively, instead merely following the rules laid out by a distant, impersonal, and unknowing bureaucracy. Tocqueville described this debilitating process:

> For their happiness such a government willingly labors, but it chooses to be the sole agent and the only arbiter of that happiness; it provides for their security, foresees and supplies their necessities, facilitates their pleasures, manages their principal concerns, directs their industry … what remains, but to spare them all the care of thinking and all the trouble of living? Thus it every day renders the exercise of the free agency of man less useful and less frequent; it circumscribes the will within a narrower range and gradually robs a man of all the uses of himself.[10]

To maximize freedom, power should be vested as close to the individual as possible. This principle of localism, or what is described in Christian social teaching as subsidiarity, acknowledges that the smaller and more decentralized the decision-maker, the better the decision-maker can *personalize* the decision to the individuals affected and protect their dignity and freedom. Centralization alienates the decision-maker from its object and robs the individual of his right and responsibility to self-govern.

Government's activities should be limited to those enumerated in the Constitution and to functions that individuals and local groups cannot do themselves. The Founders enshrined this principle in the Tenth Amendment: "The powers not delegated to the United States by the Constitution, nor prohibited by it to the States, are reserved to the States respectively, or to the people." As the Founders intended, power must reside, wherever possible, in individuals and in the free institutions that they voluntarily create, join, build, and dissolve.

PHILANTHROPY: FREEDOM'S WAY OF SPREADING THE WEALTH AROUND

Americans have proved to be the most selfless people in the world, voluntarily giving more of their time and money to their fellow countrymen and to people across the globe than any civilization in history.

Compared to other democracies, America stands out for its philanthropy and its thriving private institutions of learning, advocacy, and mutual interest. The U.S. non-profit sector is much larger than any other nation in the world, with our closest competitor, the United Kingdom, only reaching 14 percent of the U.S. total. As Arthur Brooks notes, "Even more exceptional is the fact that so much of the support of the [non-profit] sector is purely voluntary." Charitable contributions in the United States amount to $300 billion dollars a year, with three-quarters donated from private individuals. The average family gives over $1,800 annually, and more than half of Americans also volunteer their time.[11]

Burke noted in his time that this generosity extended far beyond our shores, inextricably linking us with the rest of the world—and this remains true today. After the devastating Indonesian tsunami, President Bush pledged military and humanitarian aid to the people and nations affected, including $350 million from U.S. coffers in direct assistance. But the governments of Japan, Germany, and Australia each pledged more, provoking a UN bureaucrat to label the United States "stingy." This illustrates a common misunderstanding of the American system of charity.

Americans are not stingy, we just prefer to engage in charity directly instead of leaving it to the government—a consequence of our civic traditions. After the Indonesian tsunami, individual Americans donated more than $1.5 billion in aid through private organizations, including $400 million to the Red Cross alone. Doctors without Borders was so inundated with American checks that it stopped accepting donations after two weeks.[12]

The story of American industrialist and Scottish immigrant Andrew Carnegie also illustrates our long-standing attachment to private charity and philanthropy. When Carnegie was a boy, a local military veteran, Colonel James Anderson, opened his personal library to working boys of Pittsburgh every Saturday night. Carnegie leapt at the opportunity, later attributing his spectacular entrepreneurial success to his self-education. Decades later, by then one of the world's wealthiest men, Carnegie decided to build 2,500 libraries to provide others with the opportunity for education and self-improvement that he had enjoyed.[13]

Civil society institutions were often designed to inculcate this love of education and knowledge. As Moses Mather, an American preacher and Founding Father, stated, "The strength and spring of every free government is the virtue of the people; virtue grows on knowledge, and knowledge on education."[14]

CIVIL RIGHTS AND CIVIL SOCIETY

Civil society has served as an engine of social change throughout American history, and the civil rights movement is one of its greatest triumphs. After nearly a century of state-sanctioned discrimination and violence, justice-seeking individuals united to right the wrongs of Jim Crow laws. They formed diverse political, religious, and humanitarian associations and built networks to share information, communicate with the public and government officials, and initiate a peaceful campaign to integrate the South. Martin Luther King Jr. described how civil society underpinned his actions in Birmingham:

> I have the honor of serving as president of the Southern Christian Leadership Conference, an organization operating in every southern state, with headquarters in Atlanta, Georgia. We have some eighty-five affiliated organizations across the South, and one of them is the Alabama Christian Movement for Human Rights. Frequently we share staff, educational and financial resources with our affiliates. Several months ago the affiliate here in Birmingham asked us to be on call to engage in a nonviolent direct action program if such were deemed necessary. We readily consented, and when the hour came we lived up to our promise. So I, along with several members of my staff, am here because I was invited here. I am here because I have organizational ties here.[15]

The civil rights movement's marches, sit-ins, freedom rides, and voter registration drives were directed against the power of government. Individuals ranging from northern university students to southern ministers organized themselves into hundreds of associations that kept up continual pressure on political leaders and officials to reconsider the immoral policies of segregation. These groups, as King noted, shared resources and coordinated their message and efforts through free institutions. They worked diligently, against great odds and under great duress, to protect the dignity and freedom of the individual against unjust laws.

OPENING DOORS TO NEW AMERICANS

In contrast to their prominent role in the civil rights movement, civic groups often operate less visibly, though just as effectively. Families and local community groups quietly provide community aid and serve countless needs on a daily basis.

One example can be seen in the resettlement of Jewish refugees in the United States. In 1975, following grass-roots pressure from U.S.-based Jewish organizations and religious-freedom groups, the United States successfully pressured the Soviet Union to allow the emigration of Russian Jews and other persecuted religious minorities. Over 600,000 such refugees ultimately settled in the United States.[16]

Their reception in their new homeland was another triumph of American civil society. A network of local Jewish agencies and families helped pay for the refugees' travel expenses, met them at the airport, hosted and helped resettle them, and assisted them in finding English classes and job counseling. A family matching program was also created to give practical and emotional support to the new arrivals.[17] The director of the Jewish Federation of Los Angeles that coordinated the assimilation and resettlement program, a Jewish refugee herself, noted the program's success: "[O]ppressed Jews from all over the world [came] here to live in freedom. And now we've got such a thriving immigrant community, with people connecting with their Jewish identity and contributing to society."[18]

A similar example is evident in the southeast Asian refugee crisis of 1975. With the fall of south Vietnam, Cambodia, and Laos to the Communists, thousands—and eventually millions—of those nations' citizens fled their new dictatorships. Rising to the occasion, President Gerald Ford organized an emergency military effort to evacuate refugees to the United States. American civil society also answered the call, assisting the refugees' resettlement in countless ways. Churches, synagogues, military families, and civic groups petitioned to sponsor evacuees, while the nonprofit International Rescue Committee coordinated the effort. Within days of their arrival on American shores, refugees were placed with sponsors throughout the nation. Less than a year after his arrival, refugee Dang Nguyen lauded the informal support network that had aided him: "I have a steady job, regular raises, a nice place to live, the children work hard, my wife and I are well, we have grandchildren, and next month there will be a big event in our family: We will all get our citizenship papers!"[19]

Generous and capable, American civil society helped to cultivate new and proud Americans. One of these refugees, Joseph Cao, recently represented New Orleans in the U.S. Congress. Having left Vietnam as a boy, Cao and his family were taken in "by a Lutheran family, the Shrocks family in Goshen, Indiana," with whom they lived for four years.[20] Although Cao's story is not unique, it is emblematic of the vital—and often invisible—role civil society plays in American lives.

WELFARE REFORM: ANOTHER SUCCESS FOR CIVIL SOCIETY

The U.S. government adopted comprehensive welfare reform in 1996, with bipartisan support from a Republican Congress and a Democratic president. As a leader of this effort, I can attest that the long road to this vital reform originated with grassroots civic groups and philanthropists who recognized that the Great Society welfare state was destructive to the efficacy of government, to civil society's free institutions, and to the lives of the people it was designed to help.

The campaign began decades earlier in California, where an independent network of 120 citizens' welfare reform committees and local chambers of commerce organized initiatives to educate voters and politicians on the need for government to return power to civil society and individuals. The groups found success when California governor Ronald Reagan overhauled the state's welfare system, providing a model for reform in states like Michigan and Wisconsin. Soon, a national movement gained steam to encourage all states—the "laboratories of democracies"—to undertake their own reform experiments, and to urge the federal government to follow suit.

Think tanks and other advocacy groups pressured government officials for more than two decades until the dam broke in the 1994 congressional election. Acting on ideas shaped by grassroots reform activists, the new, Republican-led Congress returned power to local authorities and private institutions over major social welfare programs. Although welfare reform is far from complete, citizen activists reclaimed some substantial ground for civil society that had been lost to government expansion.[21]

THREATS TO CIVIL SOCIETY

The biggest threat to civil society today is the growth of Big Government.

Beginning in the Progressive and the New Deal eras, and especially since the time of the Great Society, liberal politicians and social thinkers have viewed the unpredictable and dynamic nature of organic society as a problem that needs to be solved. They believe that, unlike the great men and women who came before them, *they* can resolve major social problems and transform America into a better, fairer, more prosperous country. The instrument used to bring about this ideal society, of course, is government, which is meant to instill virtue, knowledge, prosperity, and dignity in the people and bind them together in pursuit of common national goals and ideals. Yuval Levin summarizes their beliefs:

> From birth to death, citizens should be ensconced in a series of protections and benefits intended to shield them from the harsh edges of the market and allow them to pursue dignified, fulfilling lives: universal child care, universal health care, universal public schooling and higher education, welfare benefits for the poor, generous labor protections for workers, dexterous management of the levers of the economy to ease the cycles of boom and bust, skillful direction of public funds to spur private productivity and efficiency, and, finally, pensions for the elderly. Each component would be overseen by a competent and rational bureaucracy, and the whole would make for a system that is not only beneficent but unifying and dignifying, and that enables the pursuit of common national goals and ideals.[22]

In order to organize society according to this kind of predetermined blueprint, Americans would have to be like-minded and complacent, willing to fall in line with the government plan—or else the government has to resort to coercion. The problem is that Americans are a diverse, entrepreneurial, and independent bunch who often disagree with government blueprints. In fact, as Levin notes, no nation anywhere seems uniform enough for successful central planning:

> Human societies do not work by obeying orderly commands
> from central managers, however well meaning; they work
> through the erratic interplay of individual and, even more, of
> familial and communal decisions answering locally felt desires
> and needs. Designed to offer professional expert management,
> our bureaucratic institutions assume a society defined by its
> material needs and living more or less in stasis, and so they
> are often at a loss to contend with a people in constant motion
> and possessed of a seemingly infinite imagination for cultural
> and commercial innovation. The result is gross inefficiency—
> precisely the opposite of what the administrative state is
> intended to yield.[23]

Far from increasing freedom and prosperity, government welfare programs, especially under the Great Society initiated by President Johnson,
had the perverse effect of entrenching poverty and ignorance. In the
"beneficiary" communities, education, the family, prosperity, the work
ethic, charity, and civil society institutions all disintegrated, crowded out
by the government's expanding role. Instead of making recipients more
independent, welfare programs accomplished the opposite, encouraging
dependency on the government's largesse.

A government-directed society, facing no competition or need for
innovation, is ineffective, wasteful, and worse, it drains the vitality out
of people's lives. When government tries to fulfill our every want and
need, and tries to make easier the difficult things in life—working, loving,
learning, living, and dying—it robs our lives of the meaning we get from
independently carrying out our own duties and responsibilities. As
Charles Murray notes, "Almost anything that government does in social
policy can be characterized as taking some of the trouble out of things."[24]
He continues,

> Families are not vital because the day-to-day tasks of raising
> children and being a good spouse are so much fun, but because
> the family has responsibility for doing important things that
> won't get done unless the family does them. Communities are

not vital because it's so much fun to respond to our neighbors' needs, but because the community has the responsibility for doing important things that won't get done unless the community does them. Once that imperative has been met—family and community really do have the action—then an elaborate web of social norms, expectations, rewards, and punishments evolves over time that supports families and communities in performing their functions. When the government says it will take some of the trouble out of doing the things that families and communities evolved to do, it inevitably takes some of the action away from families and communities, and the web frays, and eventually disintegrates.[25]

As government expands, the social fabric that supports the less fortunate disintegrates. We become more isolated and alienated from one another, and less willing to cooperate with each other, help those in need, or assist our neighbors and communities. This in turn gives government an excuse to assert even more responsibility over our daily lives.

THE RISING COSTS OF THE WELFARE STATE

Despite some successful reforms, the expansive welfare state is assuming more and more of the role that our Founders reserved for churches, community organizations, and private philanthropy. This trend threatens the health and ultimately the survival of our robust and dynamic civil society.[26]

Expansive government rapidly becomes expensive government, and that requires new and higher taxes. The transfer of money from citizens to the bureaucracy then further weakens civil society and leads to even more expansive and even more expensive government.

The effort to finance Big Government through higher taxes is a direct assault on civil society, and the "death tax" is a prime example. This tax, which is in a constant state of flux and was resurrected in 2011 after effectively disappearing in 2010, falls especially hard on small business. That sector contributes immensely to America's social and economic dynamism, often acting as the cornerstone of community organizations and local philanthropy. Entrepreneurs and shopkeepers are community leaders and, when prosperous, are generous with their time and money. Prosperity and generosity are highly correlated, as those with more to give feel obliged to give more.

Take Sukup Manufacturing in rural Iowa. This family-owned business helped build the local playground, swimming pool, and childcare center, and helps maintain the senior citizen center, local church, and Boys and Girls Club. But when its founder dies someday, the federal estate tax will likely force the family to sell the business to pay the hefty tax bill, erasing overnight the Sukup family's philanthropy and job creation.[27] The community relationships fostered by the Sukup-funded institutions will fray, and no amount of government largesse and rule-making can replace those social ties.

An Obama administration proposal to change the rules on charitable deductions would also erode the incentives for charitable giving. Currently, philanthropists receive a deduction of their gift from their taxable income. For a $10,000 gift by someone who earns over $250,000 a year, the giver would save $3,500 in federal taxes. Obama's budget would reduce that write-off by almost 30 percent, or $700, inevitably suppressing charitable giving and weakening civil society.

Elsewhere, lawmakers threaten to further devalue civil society by dictating the inner workings of private associations. In California, the state assembly introduced a bill mandating that charities and non-profits disclose the racial and gender composition of their board members and staff—a bald attempt to force charities and voluntary associations into adopting racial and gender quotas. The proposal further demanded that charities and non-profits demonstrate how their activities "serve minority-interests."[28] The bill was withdrawn after California's biggest foundations agreed to spend tens of millions of dollars on minority-led organizations,[29] but the effort encouraged similar attacks on foundations in states like Florida. However, legislators in the Sunshine State, in sharp contrast to their liberal counterparts in California, responded by passing a law *defending* the independence of foundations and protecting them from these kinds of intrusive regulations.[30]

In their relentless attempt to replace the private sector, government bureaucrats won't hesitate to attack even the most beneficent institutions. In January 2011, a Houston couple, the Herrings, launched "Feed a Friend" to serve hot meals to the homeless. Their program expanded quickly, attracting volunteers who helped to feed up to 120 people every night for more than a year. Nevertheless, the City of Houston shut them down. Their violation? The group could not get the required permit because its meals were not prepared in a kitchen inspected by local bureaucrats and run by officially approved managers.[31] A similar program in Dallas organized by local restaurant-owners, Hunger Busters, met the same fate in 2005 after city bureaucrats complained that the program's policy of feeding the hungry "wherever they are" created litter.[32]

Even the most high-minded government programs can harm civil society, since the taxes and fees needed to fund these programs leave less money with private individuals who might otherwise donate it to civic groups. Government can also distort the market for donations by attaching various conditions to their aid—such "strings" tend to narrow a civic group's mission and undermine its independence from government. Through such means, the government ends up picking winners and losers in civil society, thereby reducing the diversity and dynamism of free institutions. Civic groups are taught to look to the government for approval rather than to their donors and volunteers. This is fundamentally destructive of a free society's most important habits.

Such government intrusions into civil society, according to Ryan Messmore from the Heritage Foundation, turn "the dial of social responsibility one more notch in the direction of the state at the expense of local institutions that serve the poor more personally and efficiently."[33] The static and coercive nature of the state limits choice and proves a poor substitute for civil society. Nevertheless, bureaucrats remain convinced they know best how we should pursue happiness. And of course, it's not their natural tendency to surrender any authority they have seized—their encroachments are only reversed when engaged citizens demand it.

REASSERTING AND REBUILDING CIVIL SOCIETY

Civil society can and will reclaim its rightful place from government, especially in the one realm that represents perhaps the biggest failure of government over-reach: education. For decades, as the government assumed a greater and greater role in education, the resulting bureaucracies became lobbies for their own interests above the interests of children and families. Good schools stagnated while bad schools grew worse, and failing schools were accountable only to the self-serving bureaucrats and unions that contributed to their failure.

However, in recent years, civil society has struck back on behalf of higher quality and local control of education. Faced with abject failure—Detroit, for example, graduates barely 25 percent of its high school students on time despite applying low standards[34]—civil society is saying "no more."

The scope of today's reform efforts is broad and deep: grassroots reformers are working to spread innovation throughout the education system and to return authority over education to the states, localities, and parents; enterprising teachers are establishing independent public schools to cater to the students left behind by the education bureaucracy; parents are demanding that their children have access to well-performing private schools through vouchers or other initiatives; and charter schools like KIPP have thrived, proving more innovative and practical than traditional public schools.[35]

Of course, nearly every reform effort encounters the determined opposition of those vested in the current system. Consider Compton, California. By 2010, the city's perpetually failing schools had been repeatedly taken over by the state without any improvement, as state education bureaucrats proved no more effective than local education bureaucrats. Under pressure from parents' groups and school reform coalitions, California lawmakers passed a "trigger" law allowing charter school operators to take control of a failing school if a majority of the parents ask for it to do so. The first city where this occurred was Compton, where 61 percent of parents signed a petition calling on a charter school operator to run their dysfunctional local elementary school. Marion Orr, a Brown University public policy professor, commented on the historic reform: "We've never seen anything like this before....[It] could create real challenges for public officials who believe they know best how to run school districts."[36]

Predictably, those public officials—teachers' union representatives and school board members—are vociferously opposing the attempt to force accountability on them. The school board has resorted to particularly desperate and underhanded measures to thwart the parents' will. It first announced that all parents who signed the petition had to appear before them with a photo ID to verify their signature—a clear attempt to intimidate parents who may be in violation of immigration laws. When a court rejected this requirement, the board looked through the petition's 275 signatures and ruled every single one invalid.[37] At the time of this writing, the battle between parents and bureaucrats in Compton is still ongoing.

Aside from education, civil society is reasserting itself in other realms, and indeed has begun energetically reclaiming its traditional role from government. The most potent force here, of course, is the tea party movement. Dedicated to countering the growing and unaccountable power of government, the tea party is a diffuse network of tens of thousands of local organizations that is changing the way their fellow citizens and especially our elected leaders conceive of government power.

Consider just one example of tea party activism: in Ohio, tea party groups have united with other liberty-minded citizens to launch the Ohio project. This grassroots effort aims to gather support for a state constitutional amendment to preserve Ohioans' freedom to choose their healthcare and health insurance. The effort has dozens of affiliates, thousands of volunteers, and has gathered more than 300,000 signatures to get this issue on the ballot.

The project's organizers and volunteers are driven to action because ObamaCare, according to the group, is an "unprecedented concept of federal power [that] would redefine the nation as we know it."[38] That is the same redefinition of government's role that Tocqueville predicted would create a culture of increasing dependency.

The tea party is demonstrating that the free institutions of civil society can reassert their rights and restore government to its limited role through strong cooperative efforts. As shown by tea partiers' remarkable grassroots activism, by the noble fight of Compton's parents, and by many other community efforts that occur every day but don't make the newspaper headlines, despite the government's myriad intrusions, the civil society tradition in America lives on.

CHAPTER SEVEN

THE RULE OF LAW

ONE NATION, UNDER GOD, EQUALLY PROTECTED

*S*ince 1952 the family-owned Bailey Brake Service of Mesa, Arizona, has been located on the corner of Main Street and Country Club Drive, one of the busiest intersections in town. Wanting the property for himself, the owner of a hardware store convinced local authorities that he would provide more tax revenues if he owned the spot. So town officials initiated eminent domain proceedings against Bailey's in order to give its private property to the hardware store owner.

But Randy Bailey fought back. With the help of lawyers from the Institute for Justice, Bailey prevailed in court after a two-year legal battle with the Mesa City Council and the town mayor. The Arizona Court of Appeals ruled unanimously in 2002 that the condemnation of Bailey's property did not satisfy the "public use" requirement of the Arizona Constitution.

Bailey told Mike Wallace of 60 Minutes, "If I had a 'for sale' sign out there, it'd been a whole different deal. For them to come in and tell me how much my property was worth and for me to get out because *they're bringing in somebody else, when I own the land, is unfounded to me. It doesn't even sound like the United States."*

Americans have a long tradition of hostility to arbitrary, unlawful, or unconstitutional government actions. We fight these usurpations every day in courts of law and in the court of public opinion.

Americans know that arbitrary government replaces the rule of law with the rule of men. When government violates the rule of law, government officials are acting in their own interests in violation of the people's unalienable rights.

The ancient doctrine of the rule of law is described with clarity and power in James Madison's articles in the Federalist Papers. The rule of law means that government is vested with authority from the people to exercise power in predictable and even-handed ways according to the laws it enacts through constitutionally established means. In describing the House of Representatives in Federalist no. 57, Madison explains why the rule of law is such a powerful defense against tyranny:

> [T]hey can make no law which will not have its full operation on themselves and their friends, as well as on the great mass of the society. This has always been deemed one of the strongest bonds by which human policy can connect the rulers and the people together. It creates between them that communion of interests and sympathy of sentiments, of which few governments have furnished examples; but without which every government degenerates into tyranny. If it be asked, what is to restrain the House of Representatives from making legal discriminations in favor of themselves and a particular class of the society? I answer: the genius of the whole system; the nature of just and constitutional laws; and above all, the vigilant and manly spirit which actuates the people of America—a spirit which nourishes freedom, and in return is nourished by it.
>
> If this spirit shall ever be so far debased as to tolerate a law not obligatory on the legislature, as well as on the people, the people will be prepared to tolerate anything but liberty.

James Madison, meet Randy Bailey. His "vigilant and manly spirit" should be as familiar to you as it is reassuring to us.

THE RULE OF LAW AND THE FOUNDING GENERATION

The Founders knew from bitter experience about the rule of men.

King George III, who came to the throne in 1760 at age twenty-two, was constrained by the English Bill of Rights of 1689 from imposing taxes without the consent of Parliament. But he claimed this restriction did not limit his power to tax residents of Britain's colonies. After Britain's victory over France in the French and Indian War, King George looked for ways to find new tax revenue to repay Britain's enormous war debt. With Parliament unwilling to raise taxes in Britain itself, the young king moved to begin imposing taxes on his subjects in America. But the colonists steadfastly resisted these efforts, believing them unjust because the colonists had no direct representation in Parliament. Outraged by the colonists' defiance, King George and his majority in Parliament then committed myriad abuses against the colonials: holding them without trial, refusing to enact laws for their general welfare, undermining judicial independence in the colonies, and perpetrating other injustices that substituted the king's will for the rule of law.

The otherwise loyal citizens of Britain's North American colonies at first vociferously argued against the king's authority to undertake these measures, and eventually took up arms to settle their fundamental disagreement with him over their constitutional rights as Englishmen.

These circumstances are reflected in the Declaration of Independence. When we read the Declaration today, we're naturally drawn to the famous prologue with its universal description of the natural rights of man. We then tend to skip the large middle section—a chronicle of twenty-seven specific grievances against King George—and go right to the rousing closing lines in which the Founders pledge to each other "our lives, our Fortunes, and our Sacred Honor."

Yet it is those grievances that fired the fury of American patriots and justified the American Revolution. And the fact that the bulk of them—twenty-one out of twenty-seven—concerned violations of the rule of law shows that the Founders believed the rule of law to be indispensible to a just society.

THE RULE OF LAW AND PROPERTY RIGHTS

Property rights stand at the forefront of the securities provided by the rule of law. In America, an individual is entitled to the legal protection of his or her property and the fruits of such property. Unless a person breaks the law, no government bureaucrat or business competitor should have the power to infringe on that individual's property rights.

Although the government today exceeds its constitutional powers in many realms, protecting private property is a legitimate—and indeed vital—government responsibility. Throughout the world, property has historically "belonged" to whomever had the power to take it and defend it. In fact, in the state of nature described by John Locke, protecting property was the singular reason people agreed to institute governments in the first place.

The government must do three things to protect property: recognize private titles, provide a reliable system for registering those titles, and maintain a judiciary that protects those titles and enforces contracts. These protections provide a simple benefit: people can keep what they earn. It means no scheming competitor or conniving government official—like those who conspired against Randy Bailey and his brake shop—can arbitrarily take your land or belongings. And for the dreamers and innovators in our society, it means you are entitled to whatever benefits your risks, creations, and hard work may yield.

From Jamestown to Google, the American commitment to private property rights has provided the framework for American prosperity. Although we tend to take this commitment for granted, billions around the world are subject to the whims of an arbitrary government or a thuggish neighbor.

It was the absence of legally protected private property that sparked the revolutions now sweeping through the Middle East. It all began in Tunisia with a simple street vendor, Mohammed Bouazizi, who operated a fruit cart in an outdoor market. Bouazizi's little business was unlicensed—a common situation throughout the region, where many would-be entrepreneurs can't afford the galaxy of fees and bribes needed to secure work permits. Lacking basic legal protection for their property, vendors like Bouazizi were at the mercy of corrupt policemen, as Marc Fisher described in the *Washington Post*: "Arrogant police officers treated the market as their personal picnic grounds, taking bagfuls of fruit without so much as a nod toward payment. The cops took visible pleasure in subjecting the vendors to one indignity after another—fining them, confiscating their scales, even ordering them to carry their stolen fruit to the cops' cars."[1]

On December 17, 2010, Bouazizi tried to stop a policewoman from stealing his fruit. The woman and some other officers then hit the vendor with a baton, pushed him to the ground, tried to steal his scale, and slapped him in the face. Fisher related Bouazizi's pained response: "'Why are you doing this to me?' he cried.... 'I'm a simple person, and I just want to work.'" After being told at city hall that he could not register a complaint about the incident, Bouazizi immolated himself in an anguished act of protest.[2]

Bouazizi's suicide sparked widespread protests in Tunisia that toppled the country's dictator, Zine el-Abidine Ben Ali, and then spread throughout the region. The next strongman to fall was Hosni Mubarak in Egypt, a country that, much like Tunisia, had failed to develop even rudimentary property law protections. In 2004, 92 percent of Egyptians held real estate without legal title, meaning virtually the entire economy lacked any common mechanism for selling, buying, or borrowing against landed property. According to Peruvian economist Hernando de Soto, author of *The Mystery of Capital,* this lawlessness created a terrifying state of nature in Egypt, with businesses and property owners living in constant fear that government officials or someone else would seize their property.[3]

This problem is hardly confined to the Middle East. From southeast Asia to sub-Saharan Africa, deficient property rights protections have bred corruption and economic stagnation. And even democratic government is no guaranteed cure for these problems. Following the collapse of Latin American dictatorships in the 1980s and the fall of Eastern European Communist regimes shortly thereafter, many Western observers were surprised at how slowly free enterprise spread. As de Soto explains, these states may have embraced capitalism, but they lacked its necessary legal underpinnings:

> The reason [capitalism] doesn't work for the majority is because the system can only work with property rights. Markets and capitalism are about trading property rights. It's about building capital or loans on property rights. What we've forgotten, because we've never examined the poor, we've sort of thought that the poor were a cultural problem, is that the poor don't have property rights. They have things, but not the rights.
>
> And when you don't have the rights, you don't have a piece of paper with which to go to market. You don't have a legal system that undergirds that piece of paper and allows it to circulate in the market.[4]

One hopes that the Tunisian and Egyptian people will finally get the chance to choose their own leaders. But even if they are democratically elected, if those leaders fail to firmly secure private property rights, we should expect to see no end to the corruption, lawlessness, and lack of economic opportunity that provoked the rebellions against their predecessors.

CONTEMPORARY THREATS TO THE RULE OF LAW

Today, some of the biggest threats to our liberties derive from abuses of the rule of law—just as was the case in our Founders' time, as shown in the grievances listed in the Declaration. Specifically, the rule of law faces three principal threats:

- The corrupting influence that Big Government exerts on government officials themselves.
- The requirement in ObamaCare that all Americans purchase health insurance.
- The federal judiciary's claim of judicial supremacy and its subjugation to radical secularism.

This chapter will explain each of these threats and why each marks a dramatic departure from the Founders' understanding of the rule of law.

BIG GOVERNMENT'S CORRUPTION OF
THE RULE OF LAW

The Founding Fathers had a precise term to describe the kind of backroom deal-making and vote-buying we witnessed in Congress during the passage of ObamaCare—"corruption." The Founders used that word not only to describe outright criminal behavior, but also to refer to political acts that corrupt our constitutional system of checks and balances. They frequently accused the British Parliament of corruption, citing practices such as the Crown's use of "placemen"—members of Parliament who also held royal appointments, or were granted lucrative pensions by the Crown, in exchange for supporting the king's agenda.

In *The Creation of the American Republic*, Gordon Wood, a scholar of the American Revolution, describes the roots of the Founders' conception of corruption:

> When the American Whigs described the English nation and government as eaten away by "corruption," they were in fact using a technical term of political science, rooted in the writings of classical antiquity, made famous by Machiavelli, developed by the classical republicans of seventeenth-century England, and carried into the eighteenth century by nearly everyone who laid claim to knowing anything about politics. And for England it was a pervasive corruption, not only dissolving the original political principles by which the constitution was balanced, but, more alarming, sapping the very spirit of the people by which the constitution was ultimately sustained.[5]

Wood then describes the growing sentiment in colonial America that its mother country was corrupt. Despite the reforms of the Glorious

Revolution [of 1688], the Crown had still found a way to "corrupt" the supposedly balanced English government:

> England, the Americans said over and over again, "once the land of liberty—the school of patriots—the nurse of heroes, has become the land of slavery—the school of parricides and the nurse of tyrants." By the 1770's the metaphors describing England's course were all despairing: the nation was fast streaming toward a cataract, hanging on the edge of a precipice; the brightest lamp of liberty in all the world was dimming. Internal decay was the most common image. A poison had entered the nation and was turning the people and the government into "one mass of corruption." On the eve of the Revolution the belief that England was "sunk in corruption" and "tottering on the brink of destruction" had become entrenched in the minds of disaffected Englishmen on both sides of the Atlantic.[6]

More generally, professor John Wallis at the University of Maryland explains that such corruption occurs when "a group of politicians deliberately create rents by limiting entry into valuable economic activities, through grants of monopoly, restrictive corporate charters, tariffs, quotas, regulations, and the like. These rents bind the interests of the recipients to the politicians who create the rents. The purpose is to build a coalition that can dominate the government."[7]

The result, Wallis says, is the creation of "groups within the government whose interest 'is that of men attached to the government; or to speak more properly, to the persons of those who govern; or, to speak more properly still, to the power profit, or protection they acquire by the favour of these persons, but enemies to the constitution.'"[8]

Congress today is mired in this sort of corruption, as its independence is compromised by politicians who no longer serve the people based on their independent judgment, but act instead to create rents, restrict economic activity with regulations, form constituencies who depend on their largess, and of course, "build a coalition that could dominate the government." For example, let's examine a mere partial record of the maneuvers undertaken to pass ObamaCare, some of which had to be abandoned after provoking a public outcry:

- Louisiana senator Mary Landrieu's vote for ObamaCare was secured after her state was granted an additional $300 million as a Medicaid "fix"—a transaction infamously known as the "Louisiana Purchase." Following widespread criticism of the deal, Landrieu defiantly responded, "I am not going to be defensive.... And it's not a $100 million fix. It's a $300 million fix."
- For his vote, Senator Ben Nelson secured an additional $100 million in Medicaid funding for Nebraska, now known as the Cornhusker Kickback.
- Senator Bill Nelson approved ObamaCare after demanding that Florida's senior citizens be spared from the billions in cuts to the Medicare Advantage program that would affect seniors everywhere else. Nelson's bribe is called Gator-Aid.
- In final negotiations to secure key votes in the House, unionized employees watered down higher taxes on their "Cadillac" health plans.

These are textbook examples of what the Founders called corruption—and we need to expose it, denounce it, and fight it just as passionately as the Founders did. Such corruption robs legislators of their freedom to follow their own conscience, listen to the will of the people, and protect the citizens' liberties. Instead, they come to rely on their own power to direct special benefits and payments to favored recipients in exchange for the recipients' political support. Crucially, the prevalence of these sordid transactions in Congress diminishes the rule of law, as politicians increasingly gear their activities toward passing laws that privilege their most powerful and influential supporters.

BIG GOVERNMENT'S CORRUPTION OF THE ENFORCEMENT OF LAWS

The enforcement of broad-based legislation like ObamaCare presents another major form of Big Government corruption of the rule of law. Today, elected lawmakers and judges no longer play the primary role in working out the details of the laws that regulate most aspects of American life. Since the Progressive Era, beginning at the turn of the twentieth century, many of these essential functions have been delegated to bureaucrats who are neither directly accountable to the American people nor insulated from politics.

These bureaucrats should be non-partisan technocrats who faithfully implement laws according to the directives of Congress. But too often, they abuse their discretion to effectively create their own laws. This is accomplished through increasingly intrusive means, including through regulations, interpretive notices, adjudications, bulletins, permits, licenses, waivers, and private letter rulings. In fact, administrative agencies have become so powerful, they are now widely referred to as a fourth branch of government.

For example, the Federal Trade Commission has been "empowered and directed" by Congress "to prevent ... unfair methods of competition in or affecting commerce and unfair or deceptive acts or practices in or affecting commerce" [15 U.S.C. § 45(a)(2)]. But Congress has left it to the FTC to promulgate regulations defining "unfair or deceptive acts or practices," and the commission has produced pages of regulations identifying unfair practices in everything from blog posts (16 C.F.R. 255.5) to imitation leather (16 C.F.R. § 24.2).

In addition to making the rules, the FTC interprets and enforces them. If the FTC decides that a person or business is not following its regulations, it can initiate cease-and-desist proceedings against the person [15 U.S.C. § 45(b)]. The person is then required to appear at a hearing, where one FTC lawyer acts as a prosecutor and presents evidence against the accused to another FTC lawyer, who acts as an administrative law judge and decides whether the evidence is sufficient to establish that the FTC's rules—written by another FTC lawyer—have been violated (16 C.F.R. §§ 3.2, 3.41). If the "judge" finds a violation, he may enter an order requiring the accused to cease and desist from any practices that are determined to be unfair (16 C.F.R. § 3.51). Violating a cease and desist order can result in civil penalties of up to $10,000 per day and additional penalties if the violation is intentional [15 U.S.C. 45(l)-(m)].

The "judge's" decision can then be appealed to the FTC commissioners who decide the appeal by majority vote, like an administrative version of the Supreme Court (16 C.F.R. § 3.54). After completing this often lengthy administrative process, the accused can appeal the FTC's decision to a real federal court, established under Article III of the Constitution, but the court's review of the FTC's decision is highly deferential and quite limited.

The FTC, like many administrative agencies, is thus a miniature government unto itself, with its own legislature, executive, and judiciary. The Constitution, of course, contains no provision for creating such mini-governments, and this is no accident. In Federalist no. 47 James Madison warned that "[t]he accumulation of all powers, legislative, executive, and judiciary, in the same hands, whether of one, a few, or many ... may justly be pronounced the very definition of tyranny." The Constitution's separation of powers was supposed to guard against precisely this kind of concentration of power.

Agency decision-making is often highly politicized. Agency heads are typically Washington insiders with good political connections, and are often positioning themselves to run for local or national political office or to become lobbyists. In order to advance their own political careers and also to protect their agency's budget, senior agency bureaucrats are closely attuned to the needs of the president, Congress, lobbyists, and the rest of the Beltway scene. But they have no constituency among U.S. citizens, no direct accountability to voters, and little contact with the average American.

By giving these agencies such wide latitude to interpret and implement laws, Congress has essentially outsourced a significant part of its legislative authority, leaving the courts to decide whether to take a share of that power for themselves or leave it to the agencies. In doing so, Congress knows it can always reclaim this authority when it wishes. But the main reason Congress does this is, paradoxically, because it makes Congress more powerful.

Here's how it works: the Founders intended lawmaking to be difficult, with proposed bills requiring the approval of three different entities—the House of Representatives, the Senate, and the president—to become law. This structure was designed to produce moderation and compromise—a system in which laws were adopted slowly and only in response to a widespread consensus in their favor.

By outsourcing the task of devising a law's fine details, Congress creates more opportunity to pass new laws. That's because the more detailed a proposed law is, the more people might find something in it they oppose. If enough details offend enough people, the bill doesn't get passed. So legislators craft laws with vague language reflecting broad, popular principles. They punt the difficult part of lawmaking—working out the details in a way that is fair, sensible, and acceptable to a majority—to agencies.

Moreover, this process allows congressmen to avoid accountability. When a law proves unpopular, Congress calls a hearing to berate whichever unfortunate bureaucrat heads the agency that implements it. Congressmen then get to swoop in and save the public from the agency's high-handedness—never mind that Congress gave the job to the agency in the first place.

The administrative state has dramatically expanded the federal government since the administrations of Theodore Roosevelt and Woodrow Wilson. Appropriating many of the powers previously reserved to Congress and the courts, the administrative state essentially makes the laws, interprets them, and enforces them—a significant and growing departure from the rule of law principle that has historically made our nation the freest and fairest in the world.

THE RULE OF LAW AND OBAMACARE

ObamaCare is a radical departure from our tradition of rule of law, which holds that Congress can only exercise those powers clearly enumerated in Article 1, Section 8 of the Constitution.

ObamaCare's so-called "individual mandate," which requires every American to procure "minimum essential [healthcare] coverage" or pay a financial penalty, is an unprecedented expansion of federal power. The government has assumed the authority to deem you a law-breaker if you don't buy a specific product—health insurance—according to its decrees.

When a Democrat-controlled Congress approved ObamaCare, the bill's supporters argued that the individual mandate was constitutionally justified under the Commerce Clause, a provision that gives Congress the power to "regulate Commerce ... among the several States." The Founders designed this clause to prevent American states from imposing tariffs on each other or engaging in other restrictive trade practices that would hamper the economy. But in the last century, Big Government advocates have misused this stipulation to justify federal regulation of energy, trucking, financial services, and assorted other activities that cross state lines.

ObamaCare takes this overly broad interpretation of the Commerce Clause to an absurd extreme.

If the government can coerce individuals—by threat of fines—to buy health insurance, what is stopping it from forcing Americans to buy other products? For example, energy supplies regularly cross state lines. What's to stop the federal government, in the interests of "national energy security," from requiring every homeowner to purchase some percentage of his electricity from the kind of expensive renewable sources whose cultivation is a top priority of the Obama administration and congressional Democrats? Or consider General Motors. Having become deeply involved in GM's operation, the federal government has a vested interest in the company's success. So what is stopping it from requiring all Americans—under threat of penalty—to buy a GM car?

The specter of unrestrained federal power embodied in ObamaCare has provoked a sustained, nationwide backlash. Millions of Americans showed their disapproval during the 2010 elections, expelling the Democrats from their House majority, reducing their Senate majority, and increasing Republican representation in state legislatures by a record 680 seats (with the GOP gaining an additional twenty-five seats due to post-election party switching by former Democrats).

Additionally, dozens of state attorneys general have filed suit against ObamaCare, charging that the individual mandate is unconstitutional. Judges have offered divergent opinions so far, but ObamaCare opponents scored a big victory in January 2011 in *State of Florida v. United States Department of Health and Human Services*, in which Florida Federal District Court judge Roger Vinson ruled that "Congress exceeded the bounds of its authority" by approving ObamaCare's individual mandate.

Vinson held that Congress's interpretation of the Commerce Clause is a "radical departure" from historical precedent. By penalizing Americans who do not buy health insurance, he argued, the government is taking the unprecedented step of regulating "inactivity." His decision contained a stark warning: if the legislature is granted this authority, "it is not hyperbolizing to suggest that Congress could do almost anything it wanted." As a result, Vinson held that the entire ObamaCare law is unconstitutional. This case followed the same reasoning as *Commonwealth of Virginia v. Kathleen Sebelius*, in which Judge Henry Hudson found ObamaCare's individual mandate to be unconstitutional.

Aside from this mammoth expansion of federal power, ObamaCare also violates the rule of law in its granting of vast discretion to administrative agencies. The bill contains 1,968 specific grants of power to the Washington bureaucracy,[9] including numerous expensive requirements on employers (which are especially damaging to small businesses) and on the states. Earlier in our history, as these regulations took effect, their unpopularity would have forced Congress to scrap the bill and start over. But the administrative state offered Congress an easier fix. Instead of changing the bill, Congress simply empowered the secretary of health and human services, who administers ObamaCare, to issue waivers that exempt recipient companies and organizations from some of the bill's onerous requirements. To date, HHS has issued over *a thousand* waivers, including one waiver to the entire state of Maine.

Instead of writing a law that applies to all, Congress has written a law that applies to some but not to others. Waivers are generously distributed to those with political connections and clout or those who can afford expensive lawyers and lobbyists. Powerful supporters of the Democratic

Party like Big Labor are also major recipients of ObamaCare waivers. This is all profoundly unfair to the millions of small businesses who lack the money and resources to influence Washington. As legal scholar Richard Epstein wrote in *Forbes* magazine,

> Waivers are by definition an exercise of administrative discretion that benefits the party who receives its special dispensation. Yet nothing in Obamacare explains who should receive these waivers or why.
>
> The dangers from this uncertainty are enormous. Make no mistake about it, a waiver gives the favored organization a competitive advantage over its rivals. But it is not only one applicant that pulls out all the stops. Its competitors often follow suit while simultaneously trying to block the waiver for the original applicant. Administrative expertise quickly takes a back seat to old-fashioned political muscle and intrigue.[10]

This arbitrary "rule by waiver" is a fundamental violation of the rule of law. In fact, it negates the rule of law and replaces it with the rule of Secretary Sebelius, President Obama, and the Democratic Party.

THE RADICAL USURPATIONS OF
JUDICIAL SUPREMACY

Ever since its 1958 decision in *Cooper v. Aaron*, the Supreme Court has held that the federal judiciary is supreme among the three branches of government in deciding the meaning of the Constitution. As Stanford Law School dean Larry Kramer explains, the decision was an historic power grab:

> In 1958 ... all nine Justices signed an extraordinary opinion in *Cooper v. Aaron* insisting that *Marbury* [*v. Madison*] had "declared the basic principle that the federal judiciary is supreme in the exposition of the law of the Constitution" and that this idea "has ever since been respected by this

Court and the Country as a permanent and indispensable feature of our constitutional system." This was, of course, just bluster and puff. As we have seen, *Marbury* said no such thing, and judicial supremacy was not cheerfully embraced in the years after *Marbury* was decided. The Justices in *Cooper* were not reporting a fact so much as trying to manufacture one....The declaration of judicial interpretive supremacy evoked considerable skepticism at the time. But here is the striking thing: after *Cooper v. Aaron*, the idea of judicial supremacy seemed gradually, at long last, to find wide public acceptance.

Having declared itself superior to the legislative and executive branches, the Supreme Court has largely removed the constitutional checks and balances on its powers. This is a radical departure from the vision of our Founders, none of whom believed in judicial supremacy. To the contrary, in Federalist no. 78 Alexander Hamilton characterized the judiciary as the weakest of the three branches. Likewise, in a letter to William Jarvis in 1820, Thomas Jefferson expressed his *fear* of judicial supremacy:

> [T]o consider the judges the ultimate arbiters of all constitutional questions [is] a very dangerous doctrine indeed, and one which would place us under the despotism of an oligarchy. Our judges ... and their power [are] the more dangerous as they are in office for life, and are not responsible, as the other functionaries are, to the elective control. The Constitution has erected no such single tribunal, knowing that to whatever hands confided, with the corruptions of time and party, its members would become despots. It has more wisely made all the departments co-equal and co-sovereign within themselves....When the legislative or executive functionaries act unconstitutionally, they are responsible to the people in their elective capacity. The exemption of the judges from that is quite dangerous enough. I know of no safe depository of the ultimate powers of the society, but the people themselves.[11]

Jefferson reiterated his concerns in a letter he wrote a year later: "The great object of my fear is the federal judiciary. That body, like gravity, ever acting, with noiseless foot, and unalarming advance, gaining ground step by step, and holding what it gains, is engulfing insidiously the special governments into the jaws of that which feeds them."

Judicial supremacy was also decried by Abraham Lincoln—a man who, we should remember, reentered politics largely as an outraged response to the Supreme Court's pro-slavery decision in the *Dred Scott* case. In his inaugural address, Lincoln declared, "[T]he candid citizen must confess that if the policy of the government upon vital questions affecting the whole people is to be irrevocably fixed by decisions of the Supreme Court, the instant they are made in ordinary litigation between parties in personal actions, the people will have ceased to be their own rulers, having to that extent practically resigned their government into the hands of that eminent tribunal." For Lincoln, judicial supremacy necessarily entailed a surrender of self-government.

Today, a decisive battle is being waged that will determine the future of American self-government. The flash point is whether the U.S. Constitution allows the federal government and state governments to pass laws defining marriage as between one man and one woman. The federal government passed such a law in 1996, the Defense of Marriage Act (DOMA), and many state governments have passed similar laws or constitutional amendments.

The stakes for self-government could not be higher. If the Supreme Court usurps the power to define marriage, then the American people will have truly lost the right to rule themselves. The Constitution gives the judiciary no authority to adjudicate this issue, and it defies belief that the "weakest" branch of government has the power to overturn an institution so vital to the Founders—marriage—that none even entertained the idea of someone challenging it.

More than thirty states have held referenda on gay marriage, and voters in every one of those states have chosen to defend traditional marriage. But to those who would replace the rule of law with the rule of men—or specifically, the rule of a clique of judges—the consent of the governed is less a cherished principle than an obstacle to be overcome.

RADICAL SECULARISM:
THE OFFICIAL RELIGION OF THE UNITED STATES

Radical secularists posit that religion and morality have no role to play in lawmaking. For them, the only legitimate source of legislation is the tenets of radical secularism itself. Ironically, the dogmatic intolerance they display toward any ideas outside their own ideology shows they are, in fact, members of the exact type of religious sect the Constitution deems ineligible of government sponsorship. Worse still, in flagrant violation of the anti-establishment clause, today the judiciary is effectively establishing this radical secularist religion as the official religion of the federal government.

The Founders banned the establishment of an official federal religion out of fear that, as was the case in Europe, such a privileged institution would infringe on the people's liberties. And this has indeed been the result of the government's embrace of radical secularism. Supreme Court justice Potter Stewart warned of this danger in his lone dissent to the Court's 1963 decision in *School District of Abington Township, Pennsylvania v. Schempp*, which held that it was unconstitutional to read the Bible in school or recite the Lord's Prayer:

> It might also be argued that parents who want their children exposed to religious influences can adequately fulfill that wish off school property and outside school time. With all its surface persuasiveness, however, this argument seriously misconceives the basic constitutional justification for permitting the exercises at issue in these cases. For a compulsory state educational system so structures a child's life that, if religious exercises are held to be an impermissible activity in schools, religion is placed at an artificial and state-created disadvantage. Viewed in this light, permission of such exercises for those who want them is necessary if the schools are truly to be neutral in the matter of religion. And a refusal to permit religious exercises thus is seen not as the realization of state neutrality, **but rather as the establishment of a religion of secularism,** or, at the least, as government support of the

beliefs of those who think that religious exercises should be conducted only in private. (Emphasis added)

The judiciary has been the key instrument in enshrining radical secularism as an official, privileged religion. Here's how it does it. In analyzing whether laws violate constitutional rights such as equal protection or free speech, the Supreme Court has long held that courts should consider whether the challenged law furthers a legitimate state interest. For over a century the courts recognized a standard list of these state interests (also called police powers): "the health, safety, morals, and general welfare of the public."

As this list shows, the public's moral judgments were viewed as a legitimate basis for legislation. Relying on this principle, courts have upheld the constitutionality of laws prohibiting conduct widely recognized as immoral, such as public indecency, prostitution, polygamy, child pornography, and animal cruelty. For example, in 1991 the Supreme Court upheld a state law prohibiting public nudity, explaining that the law was justified by "a substantial government interest in protecting order and morality."[12]

However, in a series of cases starting with *Roe v. Wade*, the Supreme Court and lower federal courts have steadily undermined this principle. Surveying the nation's long history of prohibiting abortion based on moral views, the Court acknowledged in *Roe* that "the moral standards one establishes and seeks to observe, are ... likely to influence and to color one's thinking and conclusions about abortion." Nevertheless, it held that states do not have a sufficiently compelling moral interest to justify outlawing abortion.

In recent years, as the gay rights movement has taken its cause to the courts, the Supreme Court has again waffled on whether the Constitution permits the American people to enact laws reflecting their moral judgments. In 1992—the year after the Court upheld state bans on public nudity—the people of Colorado approved a statewide referendum to amend the state's constitution to invalidate local laws and ordinances establishing special protections for homosexuals. In *Romer v. Evans* the Supreme Court struck down the amendment. Studiously avoiding the question of whether the moral judgments of the people of Colorado are a legitimate basis for legislation, the Court simply concluded that the amendment did not "further a proper legislative end."[13]

Less than a decade later, the Court concluded in *Lawrence v. Texas* that a Texas law banning homosexual conduct, while "firmly rooted in Judeo-Christian moral and ethical standards ... further[ed] no legitimate state interest which can justify its intrusion into the personal and private life of the individual."[14]

But Justice Sandra Day O'Connor was more explicit in a concurring opinion, arguing that "[m]oral disapproval of a group cannot be a legitimate governmental interest," and equating "moral disapproval" of a group with a "bare desire to harm the group."[15] This was a radical assertion with enormous consequences for American jurisprudence. As Justice Scalia pointed out in dissent, "This effectively decrees the end of all morals legislation," including "criminal laws against fornication, bigamy, adultery, adult incest, bestiality, and obscenity."[16]

Lower court opinions in the wake of *Lawrence* reveal continuing confusion surrounding the basic question of whether laws can be based on moral considerations. While some courts have concluded that, after *Lawrence*, "public morality likely remains a constitutionally rational basis for legislation,"[17] others have found the opposite and struck down, for example, a federal law banning the distribution of obscene materials and a Texas law prohibiting the sale of sex toys.[18]

These conflicting decisions provide some telling insights about radical secularism. First, something has gone wrong when courts question whether widespread public judgments rooted in Judeo-Christian morality and centuries of American tradition are a legitimate basis for making law. The entire corpus of thought left by our founding generation, including both public and private correspondence, indicates they would have been appalled by the proposition that public morals were not a legitimate state interest.

Second, the logic of radical secularism not only displaces traditional moral judgments, it affirmatively condemns them. As Justice Scalia pointed out in his dissents in *Romer* and *Lawrence*, once morality is no longer a legitimate state interest, relying on moral considerations in law-making becomes a form of bigotry akin to racism.

Finally, radical secularist thinking is ultimately sectarian and partisan. It turns the coercive power of government against the Judeo-Christian tradition that animated America's founding, and indeed, the advent of Western civilization. Traditional moral reasoning is displaced and stigmatized in order to make room for unelected judges' arbitrary moral views. As a Texas judge recently observed in dissenting from one such affirmation of radical secularism, "The Court ignores that by creating morality-based, non-textual rights it does nothing more than substitute its own moral compass for that of the People."[19]

The balancing of individual rights and the public's interest in morality has always been, and will always be, a difficult question. These issues have traditionally been subject to public debate and decided by the people's elected legislators. But with radical secularism becoming established as the judiciary's guiding ideology, that debate is being taken from the people and lorded over by enrobed activists whose moral compass is drastically at odds with that of the vast majority of their countrymen.

THE ATTACK ON DOMA

The recent decision by President Obama and Attorney General Eric Holder not to defend the constitutionality of the Defense of Marriage Act (DOMA) in federal court is yet another example of the abandonment of the rule of law.

In February 2011, Holder informed the congressional leadership that Obama had decided to cease defending DOMA in the courts because the president believes the law is unconstitutional. According to Holder's letter,

> the legislative record underlying DOMA's passage contains discussion and debate that undermines any defense [of the law]....The record contains numerous expressions reflecting moral disapproval of gays and lesbians and their intimate and

family relationships—**precisely the kind of stereotype-based thinking and animus the Equal Protection Clause is designed to guard against.**"[20] (Emphasis added)

The letter expresses the following logic: if lawmakers engage in "stereotype-based thinking" when they vote for a law—as Holder and Obama claim was the case with DOMA supporters—then that law is unconstitutional.

This novel understanding of constitutional law becomes even more ludicrous when one realizes that the ostensibly bigoted thinking they found objectionable was *Judeo-Christian morality*. This was further clarified in a footnote to the letter that described what constitutes supposedly unconstitutional thinking:

> *See, e.g.,* H.R. Rep. at 15–16 (judgment [opposing same-sex marriage] entails both moral disapproval of homosexuality and a moral conviction that heterosexuality better comports with traditional (especially Judeo-Christian) morality"); *id.* at 16 (same-sex marriage "legitimates a public union, a legal status that most people ... feel ought to be illegitimate" and "put[s] a stamp of approval ... on a union that many people ... think is immoral"); *id.* at 15 ("Civil laws that permit only heterosexual marriage reflect and honor a collective moral judgment about human sexuality"); *id.* (reasons behind heterosexual marriage—procreation and child-rearing—are "in accord with nature and hence have a moral component").[21]

Here, President Obama and Attorney General Holder essentially argue that Judeo-Christian morality cannot serve as a legitimate source for American lawmaking in general and for defining marriage in particular, since Judeo-Christian morality is, for them, "precisely the kind of stereotype-based thinking and animus the Equal Protection Clause is designed to guard against."

This may seem like a strange position for Obama to take, considering that in his book *The Audacity of Hope* he alludes to his religion as the reason for his own opposition to same-sex marriage.[22] Then again, Obama has stated that his position on this issue is "evolving." That apparently means he now believes that supporters of traditional marriage are mere bigots, that the Constitution demands the legalization of same-sex marriage, and that he believes this so strongly that he can violate his duty to uphold laws passed by Congress. But because most Americans still support traditional marriage, he lacks the audacity to simply say what everyone already knows—that he supports gay marriage and believes the courts should impose it.

With their letter, Obama and Holder have registered their support for radical secularism as the established church of the United States. Believing themselves to be part of an enlightened political class, they use state-sanctioned radical secularism as a means to diminish the influence of Judeo-Christian morality, which they regard as a collection of bigoted superstitions. As a result, believing Christians and Jews are stripped of their rights to freely exercise their faith and to participate equally in the political process.

Radical secularists resent religion for many historical, philosophical, and psychological reasons. But in light of their quest to impose their will upon the judiciary, the federal government, and ultimately the American people, they primarily begrudge religion for one reason: because faith reminds us of the need for humility, and of the limits and dangers of men who wield power.

* * *

In 1998, the Iowa legislature passed a law defining marriage as between one man and one woman. In 2009, all seven judges of the Iowa Supreme Court found the law unconstitutional.

Believing otherwise, Iowans banded together to reclaim the authority seized by their rogue judges. Led by groups like Iowa for Freedom, an organization formed by former gubernatorial candidate Bob van der

Plaats, Iowans launched a campaign to remove the three judges who were on the ballot in a retention election in November 2010. On Election Day, all three judges were defeated. Like the Founders, Iowans understood that the best safeguard against threats to the rule of law is an informed, active citizenry.

Americans everywhere should follow the example of the people of Iowa. We cannot be mere spectators as radical secularists and judicial supremacists undermine our system of government and the Judeo-Christian morality that inspired its architects.

If these groups continue chipping away at the rule of law, the biggest victims will be the weakest elements of society. Without the rule of law, the strong can still defend their interests through bribes and personal connections; it is the average person and the weak and the poor who are left with no recourse and come most firmly under the boot of arbitrary rulers.

CHAPTER EIGHT

SAFETY AND PEACE

AMERICA, THE INDISPENSIBLE NATION

*I*t is June 4, 1942, and America is losing a war. Off the east coast, enemy U-boats hunt down and sink American-flagged ships with impunity. In the Pacific, the Japanese military, driven by a samurai code of relentless attack, has driven us back on every front. On this morning, a huge Japanese invasion fleet is bearing down on a tiny, American-held atoll called Midway. The Japanese are confident in their ability to fully destroy the minuscule American fleet they believe awaits them.

Unbeknownst to the aggressors, however, three of our carriers, all that remains of our entire carrier force in the Pacific, are waiting to attack. On the USS Hornet, *the Torpedo 8 bomber squadron stands ready to launch. Only hours before, the planes' crews were filmed smiling, grinning, and posing next to their aircraft, eager for a chance to prove themselves in combat. After a scout plane reports that the enemy carrier*

*fleet has been located, Torpedo 8, along with other bomber squadrons
and some fighter jets, takes off to its rendezvous with destiny.*

*The bravado of the squadron's crews had masked the grim reality of
their situation—they are flying antiquated "Devastator" single-engine
bombers that are under-armed, bulky, and slow. In this battle, their pilots
will have to line up miles out from their target and then fly straight into
a storm of flak at just 120 mph, closing to a suicidally close torpedo drop
range of half a mile out, while the lone gunner aboard fights to ward off
diving attacks from fighters flying three times as fast and armed with 20
mm cannons.*

*After launch, with their fighter escorts and the other bomber squadrons
having become lost in the clouds, the pilots of Torpedo 8 spot their target—including carriers that had launched the deadly attack on Pearl Harbor six months ago. But there is no support and no cover. The wall of flak
from all the ships is aimed straight at them, while from every direction the
legendary Japanese Zero fighter aircraft come diving in for easy kills.*

*Two years before, most Torpedo 8 members were college students,
perhaps members of their campus Naval Reserve flight training programs.
They probably did not anticipate that the war clouds over Europe and
Asia would affect them personally, but now they are here, squaring off
against a skilled, experienced, and high-tech Japanese air force. They are
essentially amateurs, but they have accepted their mission like warriors—
and that's how they die. Every one of the squadron's fifteen planes at
Midway is shot down, and only one of the thirty crew members survives.*

*The Japanese exult in their easy victory. Zero pilots return to their
ships, eager to have yet more American flags painted on the side of their
planes to celebrate their kills. And yet, amidst all the celebration and
laughter, it is reported that one Japanese commander stands silent,
stricken. Turning to his staff, he proclaims, "My God, the Americans
have Bushido."*

*Even in their defeat, the Americans' bravery and warrior ethos caught
the attention of the Japanese leader. And his statement proves to be an
ominous portent for his own fleet—for at that instant, the lost American
squadrons find the Japanese fleet, and not a single enemy fighter is in the
sky to protect them. They dive in screaming, bent on vengeance. What*

follows, what historian Walter Lord calls "the incredible seven minutes," is payback for Pearl Harbor, and for the unrelenting defeats of the previous six months.

In seven minutes the pride of the Japanese fleet, three of their four best carriers, are transformed into flaming hulks, with their fourth suffering the same fate later in the battle.

It is a blow from which the Japanese never recover. The day after the sacrifice of Torpedo 8 and the terrible vengeance of their comrades, Japan's leaders should have realized what they were up against and sought terms of surrender. Though it would take three more years, the end result was now inevitable—the aroused American people had begun to strike back. And they would not stop until the terms of surrender were signed in Tokyo Bay, while overhead a thousand of our newest warplanes—B-29s, Corsairs, and Helldivers—circled as a symbol of our strength and perseverance.

Without safety, freedom itself is threatened.

If the people's safety cannot be assured, the unalienable rights to life, liberty, and the pursuit of happiness are meaningless, which is why the first responsibility of government is to defend the nation. In the preamble to the Constitution, providing "for the common defense" is identified as a primary reason for forming the new government.

Our Founding Fathers knew it would require extraordinary courage and material provision to defend their new nation in a dangerous world. In fact, the American experiment could have perished in its infancy in the frigid winter of 1777–78 had it not been for the bravery, leadership, and vision of a few men at Valley Forge who kept the dream of independence alive.

That nation almost collapsed nearly ninety years later during the excruciating four-year Civil War. And in the most heated moments of the Cold War, we were one miscalculation away from a nuclear conflict that could have destroyed the country as we know it.

But we have persevered.

Even in our darkest hours, America's leaders and the American people have believed that our way of life is worth defending—no matter how big the sacrifice. From Valley Forge and Yorktown, to Omaha beach and the black volcanic sands of Iwo Jima, and at this very moment the distant front lines of Afghanistan, the price has been steep and painful, but necessary in a fallen world where tyranny endures, waiting for those who falter and lose faith in themselves and in their destiny. Again and again in American history, even during the most trying of times, ordinary Americans have risen up to defend a simple idea: that God has endowed every man and woman with the capacity to be free.

No other nation has done that. No other nation has been so inextricably tied with the fate of freedom throughout the world. America is indeed the last best hope for mankind.

The world is no less dangerous today than it was in our Founders' time. Facing a variety of contemporary threats, America must reverse its current trajectory of appeasement, self-abasement, and submissiveness. As our Founders understood, the best way to stay safe is by proudly professing our values and defending them with unwavering strength and conviction.

PEACE THROUGH STRENGTH

The courage to be free is only sustained by the moral capacity to distinguish between good and evil. If evil cannot be called by name, we will not be able to deter—or even recognize—threats to our nation. Likewise, if we cannot proclaim the righteousness of our traditional values, then we won't be able to mobilize the fighting spirit necessary to defend America.

Throughout most of American history, our leaders have not been hobbled by the kind of moral ambiguity that characterizes our present administration. In 1858, during one of the famous Lincoln-Douglas debates, Abraham Lincoln identified the nature of the constant moral choice America faces: "It is the eternal struggle between these two principles—right and wrong—throughout the world. They are the two principles that have stood face to face from the beginning of time; and will ever continue to struggle. The one is the common right of humanity, and the other the divine right of kings."

Likewise, in an impassioned fireside chat in May 1941, as Europe was being overrun by Nazi Germany, Roosevelt offered a profound moral defense of our civilization: "Today the whole world is divided between human slavery and human freedom—between pagan brutality and the Christian ideal. We choose human freedom—which is the Christian ideal." And then, with his remarkable foresight of the deadly struggle to come, he warned us: "No one of us can waver for a moment in his courage or his faith."[1]

American presidents set the moral tone for our struggles. But their calls would be meaningless if not for millions of ordinary Americans who willingly rise to the challenge to defend their rights, providing an example to millions across the world who take inspiration from our way of life. President Ronald Reagan paid tribute to this American courage in his first inaugural address:

> Above all, we must realize that no arsenal, or no weapon in the arsenals of the world, is so formidable as the will and moral courage of free men and women. It is a weapon our adversaries in today's world do not have. It is a weapon that we as Americans do have. Let that be understood by those who practice terrorism and prey upon their neighbors.[2]

Two years later, in his famed Evil Empire speech, President Reagan offered an extended meditation on the need to make moral judgments and embrace our history, even if we have not always lived up to our founding ideals:

> Now, obviously, much of this new political and social consensus I've talked about is based on a positive view of American history, one that takes pride in our country's accomplishments and record. But we must never forget that no government schemes are going to perfect man. We know that living in this world means dealing with what philosophers would call the phenomenology of evil or, as theologians would put it, the doctrine of sin.
>
> There is sin and evil in the world, and we're enjoined by Scripture and the Lord Jesus to oppose it with all our might.

Our nation, too, has a legacy of evil with which it must deal. The glory of this land has been its capacity for transcending the moral evils of our past. For example, the long struggle of minority citizens for equal rights, once a source of disunity and civil war, is now a point of pride for all Americans. We must never go back. There is no room for racism, anti-Semitism, or other forms of ethnic and racial hatred in this country.

I know that you've been horrified, as have I, by the resurgence of some hate groups preaching bigotry and prejudice. Use the mighty voice of your pulpits and the powerful standing of your churches to denounce and isolate these hate groups in our midst. The commandment given us is clear and simple: "Thou shalt love thy neighbor as thyself."

But whatever sad episodes exist in our past, any objective observer must hold a positive view of American history, a history that has been the story of hopes fulfilled and dreams made into reality.

Especially in this century, America has kept alight the torch of freedom, but not just for ourselves but for millions of others around the world.

As American presidents have traditionally found, our nation's peace and safety is best maintained through a robust military capacity, tireless vigilance, and a clear strategy for identifying and countering potential threats—a policy widely known as "peace through strength." Adherents of such a policy do not seek out confrontation. To the contrary, America leads the world in spending on the military and on national security precisely to ensure that our wars are as rare and as swift as possible.

A strong military dissuades enemies and potential enemies from challenging us, while encouraging our friends and allies to stand up to aggressors rather than appease them. When we convey weakness and confusion, we become most vulnerable to attack—whether it is the Japanese raid on Pearl Harbor in 1941, Iranian revolutionaries seizing American hostages in 1979, or radical Islamists attacking the United States on September 11, 2001.

REAGAN AND CARTER:
LESSONS IN STRENGTH AND WEAKNESS

America emerged from its victory in World War II as a superpower. We had liberated nations around the world from the evils of Nazism and Japanese totalitarianism, and millions looked to us to guarantee peace, security, and freedom in the post-war world. We did not seek that role. We entered World War II as a response to an unprovoked military attack, and most Americans assumed once the enemy had been defeated we would simply return home. But by 1945 nearly all could see that after so many years of suffering and tens of millions dead around the world, it was time for America to stand forth and save the world from another such conflict. Accepting the challenge, we assumed leadership of the free world's struggle against Communism.

Most U.S. presidents fought the Cold War with steeled purpose and moral clarity. From Truman's Berlin Airlift to Reagan's military buildup, American leaders saw the conflict for what it was: a struggle between good and evil, and between freedom and tyranny. Aside from a few disgruntled academics and media figures, the overwhelming majority of Americans also viewed the Cold War through this prism.

When America stood strong against the Communists, we kept them on the defensive. In every available venue, from dinner-table conversations to presidential UN addresses, we denounced their claims to legitimacy and their refusal to allow their own people to speak and worship freely, pursue private enterprise, or even leave their own country. We constantly pointed to the Berlin Wall as the ultimate symbol of Communism's failure, and we championed imprisoned dissidents who took comfort in knowing their suffering and sacrifice was not going unnoticed. In Hollywood movies and throughout popular culture, we ridiculed the hypocrisy, self-evident abuses, and absurd contradictions of Communist regimes—in just one example, after Nikita Khrushchev was overthrown as Soviet leader, this anti-Western stalwart could only publish his memoirs by having them smuggled to the West.[3]

This was the kind of unity, strength, and clarity of purpose we summoned for more than forty years to win the Cold War. Yet not every president subscribed to the consensus. Some presidents, especially in the

1970s, were less certain that military strength and constant vigilance were the best ways to defeat Communism. At this point, let's briefly look at that decade in general and the Carter presidency in particular as a cautionary tale for future leaders.

JIMMY CARTER'S DOCTRINE OF WEAKNESS

In the early- to mid-1970s, Washington began scaling down our military commitments, cutting national security spending, and disengaging from our allies in south Vietnam. This accompanied the policy of "détente" adopted by the Nixon and Ford administrations, a posture that focused on managing relations with the Soviets through direct diplomacy. Some welcomed détente as a less confrontational approach that lowered international tensions between the two nuclear-armed superpowers. However, the policy required U.S. leaders to mute their rhetoric about the criminal nature of Communism and, to a large extent, to stop questioning the Soviet regime's legitimacy or that of its Eastern European client states.

Upon taking office, President Jimmy Carter introduced what might be regarded as an extreme form of détente. Denouncing America's "inordinate fear of communism," he felt no need to speak about the fundamental threat that Soviet totalitarianism posed to America, to the West, and to the entire world. In his view, the world was not as dangerous a place as most Americans had perceived, and at least some of the danger stemmed from Americans' supposed anti-Communist paranoia.

Carter eschewed America's singular role as the world's bulwark against Communism, adopting policies that accepted declining American power in the interests of "peace." He signed the second Strategic Arms Limitation Treaty ("SALT II") with the Soviet Union in 1979, ignoring well-founded concerns that the treaty would erode U.S. strategic advantages. Carter even signed the agreement despite the Soviets' continued deployment of SS-20 intermediate-range nuclear weapons, which were not covered by the treaty and for which NATO had no comparable class of nuclear weapons deployed in Western Europe. In line with America's new, more modest role in world affairs, Carter also looked on passively as Moscow-backed Communist movements seized power throughout Latin America and the Horn of Africa, openly employing surrogate mercenaries from Cuba and other states to do their bidding.

Perhaps Carter's greatest blunder was his incoherent policy toward the Shah of Iran. Alternating wildly between praise and condemnation of the monarch, Carter was paralyzed when the Shah was overthrown and ultimately replaced by an Islamist, pro-terrorist, anti-American regime. On November 4, 1979, less than a year after the Shah's ouster, a group of radical Iranian students and Islamist militants stormed the U.S. Embassy in Tehran and took fifty-two Americans hostage. Aside from a failed rescue attempt, the Carter administration was incapacitated during the crisis, which lasted 444 days until the hostages were released on President Reagan's inauguration day. During this saga, TV news broadcasts kept a constant count of how many days our fellow citizens suffered in captivity, while the Iranian regime heaped scorn on the United States and repeatedly threatened to annihilate us.

Looking at the poor results of Carter's foreign policy, we see that the president failed to understand the natural consequences of scaling back American power—it creates a vacuum that is typically filled by the most aggressive actors. Carter's policies reflected the weariness that some Americans, especially government leaders, felt toward our unique role in defending freedom around the world. They wanted to see America become a nation more like any other, without so many of the special obligations and responsibilities that befall the world's leader.

Leading the defense of the free world entails costs, in terms of money and lives, as well as the human energy required to constantly stand up to evil. It's easy to understand the urge to cast aside these responsibilities and live like everyone else. But as Carter learned, doing so carries its own price—both for America and for freedom throughout the world.

During Carter's presidency, the CIA tapped a group of experts on the Soviet Union—labeled "Team B"—to compare the capabilities of the United States and the Soviet Union. Unsurprisingly, they found that the United States was falling behind the USSR in terms of military strength and global influence. But Americans didn't need a CIA study to tell them

that. The indications were everywhere, especially in the Soviets' decision—one showing utter contempt for Western opinion—to invade
Afghanistan in 1979.

Americans, however, did not stand idly by as our security, prestige,
and the cause of liberty eroded. A passionate, conservative activist movement soon gave voice to the millions of Americans who were concerned
about our waning influence in the world. Citizen activists joined military
and congressional leaders to sound the alarm that Soviet intentions were
not as innocuous as Carter and his officials were making them out to be.
One notable group, the Committee on the Present Danger, brought
together high-profile Democrats and Republicans who supported a
stronger commitment to fighting Communism. They would find a spokesman in America's next president.

RONALD REAGAN: THE ANTI-CARTER

Ronald Reagan denounced Jimmy Carter's naïve and dangerous worldview in his July 1980 acceptance speech for the Republican nomination:

> Adversaries large and small test our will and seek to confound
> our resolve, but we are given weakness when we need strength,
> vacillation when the times demand firmness.
>
> The Carter Administration lives in a world of make-
> believe—every day, drawing up a response to that day's prob-
> lems—troubles, regardless of what happened yesterday and
> what'll happen tomorrow.
>
> But you and I live in a real world, where disasters are
> overtaking our nation without any real response from Wash-
> ington. This is make-believe, self-deceit and, above all, trans-
> parent hypocrisy.[4]

Candidate Reagan then issued a resounding call for a policy of peace
through strength:

> We're not a warlike people. Quite the opposite. We always
> seek to live in peace. We resort to force infrequently and with

great reluctance, and only after we've determined that it's absolutely necessary. We are awed—and rightly so—by the forces of destruction at loose in the world in this nuclear era. But neither can we be naïve or foolish. Four times in my lifetime America has gone to war, bleeding the lives of its young men into the sands of island beachheads, the fields of Europe, and the jungles and rice paddies of Asia. We know only too well that war comes not when the forces of freedom are strong; it is when they are weak that tyrants are tempted.[5]

After taking office in 1981, Reagan asserted the moral will to defend our way of life and devised a comprehensive approach to reverse the string of American setbacks. First, his administration ramped up a defense buildup that the Carter administration had belatedly initiated after the Soviet invasion of Afghanistan, increasing spending on both conventional and nuclear weapons and forging closer ties with our traditional NATO allies. Defense spending as a percentage of GDP increased from 4.7 percent in 1979 to 6.2 percent in 1986. In dollar terms, this was a rise from $116.3 billion in 1979 to $273.4 billion in 1986.[6]

Reagan's defense buildup was accompanied by a crucial moral offensive. The president was unafraid to call evil by its name or to point out the moral failures of Soviet Communism. In March 1983, in a speech to Protestant ministers, he cautioned anyone who was tempted to draw moral equivalency between freedom and Communism:

So, I urge you to speak out against those who would place the United States in a position of military and moral inferiority. You know, I've always believed that old Screwtape reserved his best efforts for those of you in the church. So, in your discussions of the nuclear freeze proposals, I urge you to beware the temptation of pride—the temptation of blithely declaring yourselves above it all and label both sides equally at fault, to ignore the facts of history and the aggressive impulses of an evil empire, to simply call the arms race a giant

misunderstanding and thereby remove yourself from the struggle between right and wrong and good and evil.

I ask you to resist the attempts of those who would have
you withhold your support for our efforts, this administration's efforts, to keep America strong and free, while we nego-
tiate real and verifiable reductions in the world's nuclear
arsenals and one day, with God's help, their total elimination.

While America's military strength is important, let me add
here that I've always maintained that the struggle now going
on for the world will never be decided by bombs or rockets,
by armies or military might. The real crisis we face today is a
spiritual one; at root, it is a test of moral will and faith.[7]

Consistent with his military and moral strategies, Reagan announced just
two weeks later a dramatic initiative that would replace the theory that
had governed U.S.-Soviet relations since the 1950s.

According to "Mutual Assured Destruction," or MAD, a nuclear
attack by one of the superpowers on the other would provoke nuclear
retaliation, assuring the widespread destruction of both countries. This
"balance of terror," it was held, kept both sides safe from nuclear war—
neither side would start a war because neither side could win.

While MAD may have provided effective deterrence, Reagan believed
the doctrine was morally flawed. Repulsed by the thought that American
citizens were living without a defense against nuclear missiles, he believed
it was a moral imperative for him to find a way to defend America against
incoming nuclear missiles.

In March 1983, Reagan announced plans for his Strategic Defense
Initiative (SDI), a ground, air, and space-based weapons program designed
to shoot incoming ballistic missiles out of the air. Derisively referring to
SDI as "Star Wars," critics at home derided the plan as implausible. But
Soviet leaders viewed SDI as a strategic threat that they could not match
or counteract. As a result, they undertook an intensive propaganda cam-
paign, including copious personal insults against Reagan and claims that
SDI would enable him to launch a nuclear attack against the Soviet

Union.[8] Their aim was to gin up international pressure for the president to abandon SDI.

Ignoring liberals' jeremiads that Reagan's firm policies would result in nuclear war, American citizens knew, by the eve of his landslide re-election in 1984, that the president's comprehensive strategy was working. America was far stronger than it had been in 1980 and had gained substantial leverage in its negotiations with the Soviets. In an October 20, 1984 address to the nation, Reagan touted the effectiveness of his "peace through strength" strategy:

> Well, in the past 3½ years, our administration has demonstrated the true relationship between strength and confidence and democracy and peace. We've restored our economy and begun to restore our military strength. This is the true foundation for a future that is more peaceful and free.
>
> We've made America and our alliances stronger and the world safer. We've discouraged Soviet expansion by helping countries help themselves, and new democracies have emerged in El Salvador, Honduras, Grenada, Panama, and Argentina. We have maintained peace and begun a new dialog with the Soviets. We're ready to go back to the table to discuss arms control and other problems with the Soviet leaders.
>
> Today we can talk and negotiate in confidence because we can negotiate from strength. Only my opponent thinks America can build a more peaceful future on the weakness of a failed past.

America's strengthened position was evident in Reagan's summits with Soviet leader Mikhail Gorbachev, beginning with the Reykjavik summit of October 1986, where Gorbachev offered unprecedented concessions. However, concerned by the advantage America would reap from SDI, Gorbachev pressed for restrictions on the program. When Reagan refused, their preliminary agreement to eliminate all U.S. and Soviet offensive ballistic missiles collapsed.

Reagan's own account of that moment is poignant and indeed a profile in courage. Gorbachev offered nearly complete disarmament of ground-based missiles, a political coup for Reagan in the face of progressive critics, but the caveat was that America must remain defenseless against nuclear attack. The temptation to accept the deal was great, but Reagan had the courage to refuse, knowing that the concession would be just that—a concession, a temporary win with the potential of disaster at some future date.

But the Soviets soon softened their position on SDI, allowing both sides a year later to sign the Intermediate Nuclear Forces agreement, which eliminated intermediate range ballistic missiles in Europe. Facing economic decline and an eroding international position, with their very legitimacy facing constant American challenges, the Soviets and their East European satellite governments found it increasingly difficult to control their own restive people. Two years later the Berlin Wall fell, and two years after that the Soviet Union dissolved.

The disappearance of the Soviet Union was the end result of a comprehensive and morality-based strategy to promote freedom around the world. Reagan was assisted in this effort by two other world leaders who were committed to the cause of individual dignity and freedom: Pope John Paul II and British prime minister Margaret Thatcher. Their "triple alliance" combined the strength of America, a renewed vigor from England, and the profound moral convictions of a pope who had survived the tyranny of both Nazism and Communism. These three historic figures confronted Communism without fear or hesitation, harboring no doubts about the righteousness of their cause. They saw no need to flatter Communist leaders or give credence to their grievances against the West. As a result of their unflinching stand for freedom, tens of millions of people have been liberated from their captive governments and have assumed their rightful place in the free world.

RADICAL ISLAMISTS: OUR UNNAMED ENEMIES

The lessons of the Cold War are clear: America is strong and successful when it speaks the truth about our enemies instead of indulging them.

America is the world's foremost advocate of freedom, and it needs to assume the responsibilities that role entails. When we shirk those responsibilities and act like any other nation, the world becomes less free and more dangerous.

The Obama administration, however, has not learned this lesson. Although in the last decade nearly every major terrorist attack or attempted terrorist attack against Americans was carried out by radical Islamists, our current leaders and many of our political elites cannot tell the truth about our enemies or even properly name them—radical Islamist terrorists are referred to by the ridiculous euphemism "violent extremists." Naturally, if you are so paralyzed by political correctness that you can't even name your enemies, it becomes impossible to devise a comprehensive strategy to defeat them.

This moral obtuseness was shockingly displayed in the government's response to the Fort Hood massacre. After radical Islamist Nidal Malik Hasan murdered thirteen people in a terrorist attack on Fort Hood, Obama's Department of Defense investigated the killings and published a report that failed even once to mention radical Islamism as a cause of Hasan's rampage—in fact, the report did not even state Hasan's name. Apparently, our government found it irrelevant that Hasan was a fairly open Islamist who had corresponded with al-Qaeda cleric Anwar al-Awlaki and had shouted "Allahu Akbar" during his killing spree. A Senate investigative committee later denounced the Department of Defense for actively covering up Hasan's obvious Islamist tendencies, and for using vague euphemisms instead of calling our enemies by their rightful name. Ultimately, the committee found that simply recognizing Islamism as a threat and calling it such could have prevented the attack.[9]

We also saw a lack of moral clarity in the heated objections to the March 2011 congressional hearings on Islamist radicalization. In the days leading up to the hearing, its sponsor, Congressman Peter King (R-NY), was widely lambasted in the media as a bigot and a modern day Joe McCarthy—simply for his willingness to discuss and investigate radical Islam. Accusing King of "singling out" Muslims, some insisted his hearings should cover other kinds of extremists, such as neo-Nazis.

King replied during the hearing that he merely sought to investigate the biggest threat to our safety. He argued, "There is no equivalency of the threat between al Qaeda and neo-Nazis, environmental extremists, or other isolated madmen."[10]

Ignoring this undeniable truth, the Left fights tooth-and-nail against any attempt to have an open, honest discussion about the threat of Islamist terrorism. Democratic congressman Bennie Thompson even speculated that King's hearings could *increase* the likelihood of a terrorist attack, exclaiming, "I cannot help but wonder how propaganda about this hearing ... will be used to inspire a new generation of suicide bombers."[11]

Cowed silence may be the politically correct response to the outrages of radical Islamists, but it's hardly a sound basis for developing a strategy to defend ourselves against them.

NO STRENGTH AND NO STRATEGY

The Obama administration could have adopted the Reagan model of peace through strength in order to counter the growing threat of radical Islamism. The president could have spent his first two years in office crafting a comprehensive, innovative plan to isolate, discredit, and defeat those who promote the radical Islamist ideology.

Unfortunately, he opted for an incoherent course whose primary objective seems to be currying favor with foreign governments, particularly hostile ones, by scaling back America's role in the world. With his frequent apologies to foreign audiences for what he perceives to be America's past sins, his demonstrative bowing to foreign leaders, and his indulgence of our enemies' grievances, Obama has willfully sought to undo America's dominance in world affairs.

We saw this inclination early in his presidency. In June 2009, police forces of Iran's clerical dictatorship savagely suppressed a huge opposition movement that had formed to protest the sham reelection of the regime's "president," Mahmoud Ahmadinejad. When the protests first began on June 13, Obama's press secretary, Robert Gibbs, issued a near-farcical statement that serves as a timeless example of moral equivocation and the abdication of American leadership. Instead of clearly condemning the mullahs' theft of the election, Gibbs declared, "Like the rest of the world, we were impressed by the vigorous debate and enthusiasm that this election generated, particularly among young Iranians. We continue to monitor the entire situation closely, including reports of irregularities."[12]

Six days later, after the protests had spiraled into a mass movement and the regime's police forces had begun brutally cracking down, Obama responded by expressing his "concern" at the violence. This meek condemnation was weakened further when Obama derided the protestors by claiming the difference between Ahmadinejad's policies and those of the opposition candidate who actually won the elections, Mir-Hossein Mousavi, "may not be as great as advertised."[13] Obama further explained he did not want to be seen as "meddling" in the elections—a feeble justification for breaking American tradition and refusing to support peaceful protestors as they were beaten and shot in the streets by police-state thugs.

Obama's muted reaction to the Iranian protests stemmed from his naïve goal of "engaging" Iran's mad mullahs in a "dialogue"; an administration official admitted as much to the *New Yorker*, saying, "The core of it was we were still trying to engage the Iranian government and we did not want to do anything that made us side with the protesters."[14] And the administration surely did a good job of that—no one could have mistaken the president for siding with the oppressed Iranian protestors against their despotic rulers.

Obama took a similar approach in his dealings with Russia—and achieved a similar outcome. Believing that tensions with Russia stemmed from our previous administration's supposed intransigence, Obama officials took office pledging to "reset" U.S.-Russia relations. To demonstrate to the world America's new approach, Secretary of State Hillary

Clinton travelled to Geneva and presented the Russian foreign minister with a hokey reset button that was misspelled in the Russian language.

The chief accomplishment Obama touts for his Russia policy is the "New START" treaty on nuclear arms controls. However, as Charles Krauthammer noted, the treaty significantly damages America's national security by impeding our development of missile defense systems, despite Obama's claims to the contrary.[15] Russia has pocketed this concession and demanded more, just as it did with Obama's decision to dramatically scale back our missile defense plans for Eastern Europe—a move that keeps our Czech and Polish allies vulnerable to Russian bullying. In the post-Cold War world, why the president suddenly views Russia's nuclear arsenal as a vital threat is anyone's guess. Meanwhile, Iran continues its furious quest to acquire nuclear weapons, having proven impervious to Obama's repeated pleas for "dialogue."

Finally, there is no better example of Obama's willful determination to downsize America's global influence than his actions in Libya. Having undertaken a humanitarian mission to prevent the massacre of Libyan rebels by their dictator, Muammar Kaddafi, the president stipulated from the beginning that after conducting some initial airstrikes, the United States would play a "supporting" role in the operation. And Obama has kept his word, turning most responsibility for the campaign over to NATO, particularly Britain and France.

This represents a fundamental reorientation of power relations both within NATO and in the world at large. America has always exercised firm leadership of NATO, but that era is apparently over—at America's own behest. Elevating the tool of multilateralism into an end in itself, the Obama administration categorically rejects the very idea of American dominance. The administration's urge to shirk responsibility and account-ability for the Libyan operation is clear; in fact, one U.S. official was quite explicit about it in his comments on Libya to the *New York Times*: "'We didn't want to get sucked into an operation with uncertainty at the end,' the senior administration official said. 'In some ways, how it turns out is not on our shoulders.'"[16]

The predictable result of the abdication of American leadership has been confusion, tension with our allies, and thus far, failure in the Libyan campaign. NATO members—as well as Obama's own officials—have not even been able to agree on what would constitute victory. The *New York Times* reported on the alliance's disarray:

> The United States has all but called for Colonel Qaddafi's overthrow from within—with American commanders on Thursday openly calling on the Libyan military to stop following orders—even as administration officials insist that is not the explicit objective of the bombing, and that their immediate goal is more narrowly defined.
>
> France has gone further, recognizing the Libyan rebels as the country's legitimate representatives, but other allies, even those opposed to Colonel Qaddafi's erratic and authoritarian rule, have balked. That has complicated the planning and execution of the military campaign and left its objective ill defined for now.[17]

The French foreign minister claimed the Libyan campaign would last days or weeks but not months.[18] However, lacking a well-defined strategy or even clear objectives, the operation, at the time of this writing, is well into its second month—with no end in sight. It is astonishing to think that after protecting Western Europe from Communism for forty years, and acting as the linchpin of most of the continent's security for another ten years, NATO's credibility is being severely damaged by an African dictator who no longer fully controls his own country.

★ ★ ★

As previously stated, we pay a price for America's leadership in the world—but there is also a price to pay for withdrawing from it. The entire world is watching as a void develops that American power used to fill. Our enemies are adept at exploiting weakness, and they are already maneuvering to take advantage of America's new reluctance to "meddle" in world affairs.

America is confronted by growing threats from radical Islamism. As we remain engaged in Iraq and Afghanistan, as conditions in Yemen, Bahrain, and Pakistan become more precarious by the day, and as Iran races to develop nuclear weapons, one might be tempted to conclude President Obama lacks any comprehensive strategy for addressing radical Islamism and other threats facing the United States. However, it has recently come to light that the president does, in fact, take a principled approach to leadership.

In the *New Yorker*, an Obama advisor characterized the principle behind the president's actions in Libya as "leading from behind." The magazine explained, based on interviews with a wide range of current and former Obama administration officials, that this is "a different definition of leadership than America is known for, and it comes from two unspoken beliefs: that the relative power of the U.S. is declining, as rivals like China rise, and that the U.S. is reviled in many parts of the world."[19]

This "definition of leadership"—the closest thing we have to an Obama Doctrine—not only violates American Exceptionalism, it is the precise antithesis of American Exceptionalism. This notion—that America should acknowledge its "decline" and abdicate its global leadership at the behest of those who supposedly "revile" us—is a self-fulfilling prescription for our future as a weaker, less respected, and ultimately less safe country.

The world today would be a far different place if not for America's constant, confident push for freedom over the last century. In evaluating the usefulness of American leadership, President Obama should ask the opinion of a survivor of East European Communism, or a survivor of Imperial Japan's depredations throughout Asia, or a survivor of Nazi Germany's horrific atrocities. He should ask Taiwanese or Korean citizens who depend on America to protect their nations from revanchist Communists, or Indonesian or Japanese citizens who benefited from American aid in recovering from a tsunami. Ask them if America is a force for good—and whether the world would be better off if the United States were a nation like any other.

PART III

AMERICA RISING

*The great privilege of the Americans is not only
to be more enlightened than others, but also to have
the ability to make mistakes that can be corrected.*

—Alexis de Tocqueville

CHAPTER NINE

RESTORING AMERICAN EXCEPTIONALISM

The American economy today is in dire straits. The real unemployment rate—which includes those who have stopped looking for work—is around 15 percent. Food, gasoline, and healthcare prices are rising fast. Americans are working longer hours, yet have less disposable income. We remain reliant on unstable, sometimes hostile foreign countries for much of our energy. For the first time since World War II, we face real economic competitors, in China and India. And most threatening to our future, the federal government budget deficit is over $1 trillion a year, pushing our national debt to an astonishing $14 trillion.

Unsurprisingly, Americans feel anxious about our future. A March 2011 Rasmussen poll showed that by a margin of 48 to 34, Americans believe our country's best days are behind us, and just 22 percent of Americans believe the country is headed in the right direction. This pessimism was evident at a town hall event with President Obama in

September 2010, when a woman who voted for Obama told him, "My husband and I ... thought we were well beyond the hot dogs and beans era of our lives, but ... that might be where we're headed again, and, quite frankly, Mr. President, I need you to answer this honestly. Is this my new reality?"[1]

Video of the confrontation went viral on the Internet, because it captured Americans' current fear and frustration. America's traditional can-do optimism, in which every generation is expected to have a better life than the last, has been replaced by a growing concern that our current problems are not, in fact, a temporary bump in the road, but instead, a preview of the tough decades ahead.

THE ECONOMIC COLLAPSE OF THE BIG-GOVERNMENT WELFARE STATE

The deteriorating economy is, in many ways, a symptom of the collapse of the big-government welfare state. Our current governing model is simply proving too slow, too expensive, and too destructive of the core habits of success that have made America exceptional for the past 400 years.

The election of a young, charismatic, liberal president to tackle our economic crisis was seen by our elites as heralding the rebirth of big-government liberalism in America, and as the death-knell of small-government conservatism. "We are all socialists now" blared one typical headline from *Newsweek*. "Whether we like it or not," wrote the authors, "the numbers clearly suggest that we are headed in a more European direction."[2]

Instead, Obama's spasm of big-government intervention—including the extravagant and counter-productive stimulus, the unpopular passage of ObamaCare, and the acceleration of the government debt crisis—vividly demonstrated to the country not a renaissance of Big Government, but its limitations. America is now reassessing what government can and cannot do against the Left's false assurances that government is always the solution.

To understand just how fundamentally the big-government welfare state has failed, it is worthwhile to review how it emerged and why.

During the Progressive era of 1890 to 1916, in reaction to the rapid industrialization of the Gilded Age, the belief spread that America needed the federal government to substantially regulate the private economy. The government approved anti-trust laws and formed agencies such as the Food and Drug Administration to protect consumers from corporate dishonesty and abuse. The Progressives also tried to professionalize the government workforce, both to combat corruption and to introduce scientific planning and new efficiencies to government.

Initially, the welfare state was deemed necessary in order to adapt to new economic realities. Capitalism in the industrial age could produce enormous wealth, Progressives argued, but it also left people at risk of poverty and exploitation. The promise of the big-government welfare state was that government would curb the worst excesses of capitalism through strict regulation of the private sector while providing a system of social insurance to meet everyone's basic needs.

This welfare state, they promised, would be run impartially and scientifically by a professional and competent bureaucracy. Furthermore, the common contribution to the social safety net would provide a sense of community and shared moral purpose among the American people to care for the health and well-being of their neighbors.

During the Great Depression of the 1930s, the government assumed responsibility for providing a basic level of economic security for the American people. The Social Security Administration was created to solve the problem of senior poverty, and unemployment insurance was introduced as part of the new safety net. The Great Society programs of the 1960s saw the government further expand its role in reducing poverty with the advent of Medicare, Medicaid, food stamps, and many other programs. As the number of these welfare and social insurance programs grew, the government needed an ever expanding bureaucracy to administer them, and more and more regulations to guide them. The whole system grew into the big-government welfare state we have today.

This model is both inadequate and inappropriate for the modern world and has generated unforeseen and devastating consequences. Its collapse is driven by simple economic reality. Massive, publicly funded social insurance and benefit systems have proved unsustainable, driven toward bankruptcy by the demographic realities of lower birth rates and aging populations, and by the damage to economic growth caused by the high taxes that fund these entitlements.

The American entitlement system is, essentially, a federally mandated wealth transfer system from one group of people to another. Social Security, for instance, was designed in an age where there were forty-two workers for every retiree and poverty amongst senior citizens was rampant. Today, however, there are three workers for every retiree, with that ratio projected to fall to 2–1 in the coming decades. Furthermore, young people entering the workforce today are more likely to be poor than seniors are. Coupled with Americans' increasing lifespans, a wealth transfer system from, in this case, the young to the old will not serve the economic needs or meet the economic realities facing future generations.

For the first time since its creation, Social Security is now operating in the red. The Congressional Budget Office says it will continue to operate at a loss until its structure is reformed.[3] Medicare is in even worse shape due to demographic realities as well as exploding health costs that are destroying its solvency. The trustees of Social Security and Medicare estimate that the two programs have $46 trillion combined in unfunded liabilities—that's $15,333 per person. Medicaid, which covers the healthcare of the poor, costs an additional half trillion dollars a year. Those costs under the current structure are only going to increase because there are no market-driven pressures to lower costs or to improve benefits.

Entitlement spending eats up a majority—and growing—share of the federal budget. Unless we adopt a different model, our national debt will be nearly twice the size of the economy by 2030. It will become three times the size of the economy by 2050. This is a debt that will be carried by our children, their children, and their children again. The interest payments on the federal debt will rapidly grow beyond the cost of national security and will crush the next generation with a tax burden just to pay interest on the debt they inherited.

The creaking bureaucratic administrative state that operates our regulatory agencies and social insurance programs is also running into the harsh realities of the twenty-first century. The administrative state was fashioned in a time of industrialization, mass production, and top-down hierarchal management. The sprawling federal and state bureaucracies were designed along those same lines, both in their command structure and in the way they view how they serve the American people. Government is not Burger King; you can't have it your way. In fact, it is determined for you to have it the government's way, that is, the bureaucratic way.

Today's economy, however, is marked by customization and personalization. It is increasingly globalized, individualized, and dependent on high-tech information systems. Aside from certain aspects of our military, the bureaucratic structure of government has not adjusted to the new world. That's because, unlike private companies, the government doesn't have to stay competitive. Instead of encouraging economic growth, the big-government welfare state suppresses it by redistributing tax income in a way that discourages work, savings, and investment. The result is an atrophied, exhausted administrative state that is completely unsuited to the demands of the twenty-first century economy. Compare your typical experience shopping at Amazon.com with what you go through at the DMV to understand the difference.

THE MORAL COLLAPSE OF THE BIG-GOVERNMENT WELFARE STATE

In addition to these harsh economic realities, there is a deeper flaw within the premise of the big-government welfare state that has led to its demise: ultimately, it is incompatible with human nature because it does not view American citizens as individuals with inherent dignity and rights.

We have discussed throughout this book how America's extraordinary success can ultimately be attributed to habits of liberty stemming from our founding principles. The Progressives began by "progressing" away from these principles and accepting a European socialist critique of America. According to this view, American wealth inequality proved that the aspects of civil society that the Founders championed—family, religion, charities, and civic groups—were inadequate. They believed that to guarantee the people's well-being, America should transform into a collective state led by an intellectual elite—namely, them. So they developed government programs to meet the people's material needs, in effect creating government substitutes for charities, churches, and other philanthropic civic groups.

The Progressives morally justified the big-government liberal welfare state as a way for the American people to fulfill a shared responsibility for our neighbors' well-being. Their vision was collectivism, the system rejected in the early settlements of Plymouth and Jamestown as a failure. But by having government take the lead role in addressing social problems, the big-government welfare state eroded Americans' historic responsibility to participate in civil society. Whereas the traditional American attitude was to ask "What can I do to help?" the collectivist mindset is, "Why isn't government doing something to help—and who can we tax more to pay for it?"

Furthermore, as the welfare state grew to encompass not only the poor but even much of the middle class, its beneficiaries were relieved of not only responsibility for their neighbors, but for themselves. The result is that too many Americans now approach their government as desperate dependents instead of as autonomous, dignified, and self-sufficient citizens.

Now that so many Americans are dependent on government, we find the big-government welfare state is incapable of meeting the needs of the people. That is because human beings need more than simply material sustenance—they require spiritual and moral fulfillment, and the self-respect that comes from working hard to provide for one's own needs.

Because the welfare state defines the American people solely by their material needs, its administrators are incapable of understanding or predicting the way people will react to their programs. The American people, simply put, have never taken kindly to being bossed around by bureaucrats. Bill Mauldin's grubby, grumbling World War II heroes "Willie & Joe" exemplified our "Greatest Generation" of men who would answer to government authority only until the given task was finished, and even while doing so, behaved in an anti-authoritarian manner that was quintessentially American.

Thus, the scientific efficiency that was supposed to infuse the Progressives' administrative state never materialized; as the big-government welfare state has grown, so too has its incompetence and wastefulness.

As this failure became increasingly clear over time, the Left has invested even more power in the government to try and force people to behave the way they want them to in order to achieve their ideal, efficient society. Friedrich Hayek, George Orwell, Milton Friedman, and many others warned about this willingness among the Left to resort to coercion. As Hayek noted, "The more the state plans, the more difficult planning becomes for the individual."

In short, the central failing of the big-government welfare state is that its designers and current champions do not think of people as individuals with inherent dignity who are capable both of self-government and compassion for their fellow man; they think of citizens as groups of people to be organized, placated, and for some radicals on the Left, to be molded into "new Americans." The famous and influential Progressive activist John Dewey, for one, saw public education as a vehicle to remodel citizens to fit Progressive concepts of the role of the citizen in relationship to the collective state. This violates a core tenet of American Exceptionalism: respect for the inherent dignity of the individual.

The main selling points of the big-government welfare state during the Progressive era—its efficiency, its moral purpose in unifying society, and its economic benefits—are in fact its greatest liabilities. It has become an unresponsive, broken, and destructive apparatus that has brought about huge debts, inefficient and intrusive government bureaucracies, a weakening economy, and a cultural and moral rot that has trapped generations of citizens in poverty and dependence.

WHY AMERICAN EXCEPTIONALISM MATTERS

As the big-government welfare state collapses, the Left has employed every tool at its disposal, no matter how corrupt, to preserve and expand its power base. It may cripple the country, but in the tradition of the urban political machine bosses of old, left-wing leaders figure, "At least we'll own the wreckage."

That is why the Left passed ObamaCare despite the clear opposition of the American people. It's also why it so bitterly resists attempts to make payment of union dues voluntary, not mandatory, and why it is fighting so hard to abolish secret ballot elections for forming unions. The

Left knows that its power rests not on popular support, but on its ability to use Big Government to reward its allies and punish its enemies.

Unfortunately, with some significant exceptions such as Congressman Paul Ryan, the Right has largely failed to offer a comprehensive, alternative vision to the Left's failed model. Too many Republicans only offer cuts to the current welfare state—in other words, "less of the same"—to address our current challenges.

This is inadequate. First, the American people will not tolerate leaving the poor helpless. It is important to note that the big-government welfare state, while fatally flawed, still has an innate attraction for many people because it appeals to a common desire for all Americans to have equality and opportunity.

And second, if we were to keep the current system, the comprehensive cuts needed to stabilize it would be politically impossible to impose. As discussed, a significant portion of the American people, including the middle class, now depend on some sort of government program, such as Medicare and Social Security. The beneficiaries of these programs will not be willing to sacrifice that support without an acceptable replacement. That's why, in the long run, being the "pain party" is a losing proposition for Republicans.

Lincoln once declared, "The dogmas of the quiet past are inadequate for the stormy present. The occasion is piled high with difficulties and we must rise to the occasion....We must disenthrall ourselves and then we shall save our country." Lincoln's counsel holds true today. I believe it is time for the Republican Party to disenthrall itself from the dogmas of being an opposition party, rediscover the fundamental principles of our republic, and based on those principles, work out a comprehensive program for renewing our economy and government. If we remember who we are, we will know what to do. That is why American Exceptionalism matters.

TEN STEPS TO RESTORING AMERICAN EXCEPTIONALISM

Replacing the Left will require not only a fundamental change in policies, but a change in habits. Instead of waiting for government to reform itself, we should immediately start living our lives every day in ways that promote freedom, personal responsibility, and self-government. Fortunately, through their habits of liberty, the Founders provided us with a clear and proven model for the kind of virtuous life that sustains a healthy republic.

The challenge is to apply our Founders' example to twenty-first-century conditions. This is not difficult, but it will require some hard work and a personal commitment to action. Here are ten things you can do to help America's future be as exceptional as its past.

1. LEARN ABOUT AMERICAN HISTORY, EXCEPTIONAL AMERICANS, AND AMERICA'S FOUNDING PRINCIPLES

If we are going to win the argument, we have to be prepared for the argument. One of the left-wing elite's great advantages is that they include many of the most studied and most articulate people in our society. In their positions in the news media, schools and universities, bureaucracies, and judgeships, they can make powerful arguments for their views. They may be wrong, but they sound good.

Americans should learn about the issues and analyze how they relate to the principles and history of American Exceptionalism. In the tradition of Abraham Lincoln, we have to study and master our arguments so we can make our case convincingly against well-prepared opponents.

I am encouraged by the tea party movement's commitment to study groups and by the number of people who now carry a copy of the Constitution and the Declaration of Independence.

Remember, learning always comes first.

2. SPEAK OUT

Once you feel confident in your knowledge, start speaking out in favor of American Exceptionalism.

We live in an age of amazing and diverse media. You can establish your own website. You can tweet. You can communicate on Facebook and by email. You can go on talk radio. You can invent your own online talk radio show. You can write letters to the editors. You can organize events (for example, a public celebration of George Washington's birthday) and see if you can get the media to cover them.

If you are willing to be noisy, you're in luck—because you live in the easiest time in history to be noisy.

3. QUESTION GOVERNMENTAL AUTHORITY AT EVERY TURN

Go to your local school board, city council, or county commission and ask questions. Go to town hall meetings for your state legislators or members of Congress. If they don't hold town hall meetings, go to their office. Go with friends to the state capitol and even to Washington.

Once you're there, argue for the right policies. If those policies don't yet exist, invent them. We are entering an age of citizen-centered politics and citizen-centered government. We need so many new solutions and our problems and challenges are so diverse and so difficult that every citizen should feel empowered to challenge the old order and to help develop new solutions.

4. TEACH THE CHILDREN AROUND YOU

There are many opportunities to teach the next generation about America—its principles, its history, and its heroes. Speak about this topic with your children, grandchildren, nephews, and nieces. You also may have the chance to speak to neighborhood children through organizations like the Boy Scouts and Girl Scouts, Big Brothers Big Sisters, your local church group, etc.

While I strongly believe our schools should teach American history more accurately and more thoroughly, I also think there are many things we can do to fill in the gaps and to build on the work of schools.

The next time you travel with your children, look for historic sites you can visit. Even a brief introduction to a battlefield or a museum or a living exhibit can trigger a lifetime of interest in young people.

If you come to Washington, pick up a copy of *Rediscovering God in America*, a book and movie I created with my wife Callista, and find out how you can spend a day or two in our national capital visiting the monuments and learning about America's founding and America's history.

Look for powerful and entertaining movies to show your children that learning can be interesting and fun—movies like *Glory*, *Amazing Grace*, *Sunrise at Campobello*, and *Chariots of Fire*.

Visit the presidential libraries for half a day. Visit Mount Vernon and its amazing new education center with its great exhibit on George and Martha Washington. And visit living exhibits like Williamsburg, where re-enactors bring the past to life.

5. INSIST ON SCHOOLS THAT TEACH RESPONSIBILITY AND THE FUNDAMENTALS OF AMERICAN CITIZENSHIP

While you are serving as a teacher-mentor, you should also insist, as a citizen, on bringing America back into our schools.

You can start by asking your state legislature to mandate that every year from K through 12 and in every tax-paid freshman year in college, there must be lessons on the Declaration of Independence. By reminding young Americans every year that there are self-evident truths and that we are endowed with unalienable rights by our Creator, we will convey the spiritual and liberating nature of America.

Requiring the Pledge of Allegiance in homeroom every day is a reminder that we are indeed a republic that is united under God.

A moment of silent prayer to open each day would also help. Young people need to be reminded continually that they are part of something much bigger than mere earthly existence. At school, they should be allowed time to reflect upon the spiritual component to their lives.

Textbooks should be reviewed to ensure their factual accuracy. Through bias and censorship, the secular Left has grossly distorted and rewritten history. It is time to insist that our children learn the truth, especially as it relates to the founding and history of America.

To effect this change, you'll need to make your case to your school board, your state legislature, and your governor. In some cases it may mean replacing elected judges who are improperly imposing their radical secularism on American schools.

Insist that your child's school focus on homework, deadlines, and developing a robust work ethic for students. Young Americans are going to be competing in the world market with young Asians who start studying earlier, study longer, and study more intensely. We will not remain the world's economic leader without re-establishing a serious work and achievement ethic in students.

6. DEFEAT AND REPLACE BAD JUDGES

The lawyer class loves judicial supremacy. It makes them the keepers of the secret knowledge of America's future.

In the 1960s, the Supreme Court outlawed voluntary school prayer and instituted tort rules that encourage lawsuits, weakening and in some ways sickening our society. But praying less and suing more has turned out to be a bad experiment with bad results.

Lord Acton warned that "power tends to corrupt and absolute power corrupts absolutely." Note that he dropped the word "tends" in the second half of that sentence. He asserted that absolute power *always* corrupts.

We now have judges who believe they have absolute power. When a majority of California voters reassert that marriage is between a man and a woman in their state, and one federal judge decides his opinion is more important than theirs, there is something wrong. When the Supreme Court empowers politicians to seize citizens' private property and give it to real estate developers, there is something wrong. When justices start citing Zimbabwe and other foreign countries instead of the United States Constitution, there is something wrong.

Judicial supremacists tell us we have no choice except to endure judicial tyranny. Former Speaker of the House Nancy Pelosi once asserted that when the Supreme Court issues a ruling, it "is almost as if God has spoken."[4] Yet as I have noted elsewhere, the Founders designed the judiciary as the weakest branch of the federal government. Additionally, recall that President Jefferson eliminated eighteen of thirty-five federal judges in the Judiciary Act of 1802—and you have to assume Jefferson and his secretary of state, James Madison, had some knowledge of the Constitution.

Our generation must restore the proper balance between the judicial, legislative, and executive branches. A first step is to defeat elected judges who flout the Constitution. Developing a new, Jeffersonian approach to lifetime judicial appointees when they prove to be radically destructive would be another step.

It may well be necessary to abolish the Ninth Circuit Court of Appeals—the most radical and most consistently overturned appeals court. This would be a much more modest step than the Jeffersonian reform of 1802.

And a final step would be to make all new judges meet a higher standard of knowledge of American history and of the principles of American Exceptionalism.

7. REESTABLISH THE WORK ETHIC

In the long-term, our economy cannot be stabilized without first reversing the erosion of the work ethic that has occurred over the last two generations.

For four hundred years, since Captain John Smith decreed that those who don't work won't eat, Americans have worked hard, dreamed big, achieved amazing breakthroughs, and created enormous prosperity.

Whether you want to be a ballerina or a surgeon, a success in business or a success in sports, a good parent or a good citizen, it always takes hard work to achieve your goals.

The most important contribution you can make is to encourage the work ethic in your children by setting an example. Show them that everyone can dream big, but that it takes learning and hard work to make their dreams come true. Every time you instill in young people the understanding that effort leads to reward, you have strengthened America.

8. CELEBRATE AMERICAN HOLIDAYS

Holidays should be more than just a day off work—we should celebrate them as the historic institutions they are. Explain to young people why Memorial Day and Veterans Day exist and the sacrifices those days honor. Spend time on the Fourth of July discussing why we are patriotic and why our Star Spangled Banner celebrates an American victory on our own soil. At Thanksgiving, spend a few minutes remembering the Pilgrims as well as President Lincoln's first Thanksgiving proclamation. Talk about all the things we Americans have to be thankful for.

These simple steps move us toward a patriotic, historically informed citizenry at remarkably little cost.

9. VOLUNTEER IN YOUR COMMUNITY

Restoring a healthy, free, and self-governing society will require an engaged and energetic citizenry.

Tocqueville wrote about the enormous energy and enthusiasm of Americans voluntarily banding together to solve problems and create opportunities. But for two generations we have paid higher and higher taxes to hire more and more bureaucrats to replace citizens with "experts."

That experiment has failed.

If we are to implement the Tenth Amendment and return power to the people, citizens will have to volunteer to fill the gaps that emerge when the bureaucrats are disempowered.

Volunteering your time and encouraging others to volunteer is a major step toward a better, more engaged, and freer America.

10. RUN FOR OFFICE

Your country needs you.

There are more than 513,000 elected offices in America. If you know a better way to run your school board, town, city, or state, take the initiative to do so. Put your convictions to the test by running for office. Convince your fellow citizens that your ideas are practical solutions to specific problems. Drum up support for your program, get elected, and follow through with your plans.

RESTORING AMERICAN EXCEPTIONALISM AND AMERICAN PROSPERITY BY RESTORING THE WORK ETHIC

Out of all our problems, the one that's hurting the most Americans today is unemployment.

It is impossible to balance the budget at 8 or 9 percent unemployment. If there is a significant recession in the next few years, joblessness could hit 12 or 13 percent.

A recent report finding that 42 percent of African American teenagers are unemployed is a warning sign of a looming social crisis. Additionally, some of our greatest cities are becoming ghost towns as economic decay and unemployment destroy the very fabric of the community.

The pain of unemployment is being compounded by inflation, stoked by the Bernanke policy of printing money and the government's mania for economic stimulus. Cheap dollars become expensive oil, gold, silver, and other commodities. Expensive oil translates into expensive food since energy is vital to food production, processing, and distribution. All this threatens to bring back the stagflation of the 1970s, when President Jimmy Carter's destructive policies led to both economic decline and inflation.

There are specific policies that can reverse these damaging trends, as outlined below. But a single value must guide all these policies: the restoration of the work ethic.

A government dedicated to encouraging and rewarding work will empower individuals to determine their own future and their family's future, to pursue success at the risk of failure, and to provide for their own well-being without being stymied by bureaucratic regulation.

In a society whose economic engine was built to run on self-reliance, the dependence fostered by the big-government welfare state has wreaked havoc on our economy and is increasingly undermining the foundation of American liberty itself.

Consider some key areas of public policy in which new policies that emphasize the work ethic would help to reverse our current decline and encourage personal responsibility.

A SIMPLE, LOW TAX SYSTEM

Nothing will restore the work ethic more than policies that reward the creation of wealth instead of just spreading it around. We should begin by approving the 12.5 percent business tax rate that Ireland adopted almost twenty-five years ago, and which raised the Irish standard of living from the second lowest in Europe to the second highest. Our reform program should aslo include: eliminating the capital gains tax, which involves double taxation of capital income on top of corporate and individual income taxes; immediate expensing for investment in tools and equipment, accelerating the productivity and wages of America's workers; and abolishing the death tax, which taxes for a fourth time the lifetime savings of American families. Tax reform for individuals should provide for an optional 15 percent flat tax, with generous personal exemptions of $12,000 per family member.

These reforms will make the United States the world's most attractive country in which to create and grow companies, increasing the reward for hard-working and innovative entrepreneurs.

AN ALL-OF-THE-ABOVE AMERICAN ENERGY PLAN TO LOWER ENERGY PRICES

Since coming to power, the Obama administration has waged a war on American energy that has led to rising gas prices, lost American jobs, strained family budgets, and a greater dependence on foreign oil. For example, due to President Obama's recent moratorium on drilling in the Gulf of Mexico, and his administration's subsequent reluctance to issue new drilling permits, the Energy Information Administration projects that oil production in the United States will decline by an astounding 220,000 barrels per day in 2011, which translates to us sending an additional $10 billion this year to foreign countries instead of investing in American jobs and American energy.

Alongside their heavy restrictions on our own fossil fuel production, President Obama and his officials have consistently distorted the facts about America's true wealth of energy resources. Instead of an all-out effort to increase domestic oil and gas drilling, the Obama administration has naively expressed hope that the often hostile, often unstable countries of OPEC will "continue to support our economic recovery."[5]

Conservative estimates of American resources suggest we have more than a 100-year supply of natural gas and at least three times as much oil as Saudi Arabia locked away in shale in the American West. Offshore we have tens of billions of additional barrels of oil and hundreds of trillions of additional cubic feet of natural gas. We have an enormous capacity to produce more nuclear power, and recent innovations in renewable technologies show great promise for the future. But in order to realize this energy potential, we have to get serious about actually producing American energy, which starts with allowing producers to do what they do best: creating affordable and reliable energy.

What does this have to do with the work ethic? Quite simply, President Obama's energy policies mean that thousands of Americans will lose their jobs due to a worsening economic situation caused by higher energy prices. If we would aggressively develop American fossil fuels, we would create abundant and affordable domestic energy supplies, leading to hundreds of thousands of new jobs. Look no further than the Dakotas to see what producing American energy can do: North Dakota has a booming economy with an unemployment rate of 3.6 percent. In addition to low taxes, the key driver of North Dakota's economic boom is oil and gas production in the Bakken formation. Much of this drilling is taking place on private lands, but the message is clear: encouraging energy production, including more domestic drilling, will create jobs and grow the economy.

With their ideologically driven, counter-productive crusade against fossil fuels, President Obama and liberal Democrats in Congress are failing the American people, compromising our economic strength, undermining our energy independence, and preventing many Americans from earning a living.

WELFARE REFORM 2.0

As explained earlier in this book, in the 1990s, when I was Speaker of the House, we replaced the failing Aid to Families with Dependent Children (AFDC) welfare program by repealing policies that fostered dependence and installing new ones that promoted work and self-reliance.

The old AFDC discouraged work in many ways, especially by failing to limit the amount of time someone could receive assistance and failing to limit the increase in payments a person could obtain by having more children. In contrast, the cornerstone of our new policies was a requirement that beneficiaries either work or go to school, a rule that also increased the incentive for parents to stay together, since at least one parent had to work to qualify for benefits. This helped break the cycle of dependence that trapped people in poverty, undermined the family, and encouraged listlessness.

The welfare reform of the 1990s was the single most successful social policy reform of the latter half of the twentieth century. In light of this undeniable model of success, it is time to apply the same principles— namely, a commitment to work—to other federal welfare programs, including Food Stamps, Medicaid, SCHIP, housing assistance programs, and all other federal means tested programs providing assistance to low-income families. The repeal and replacement strategy that worked for welfare will work in each of these areas, because it reinforces the habits of liberty that empower the individual, strengthen freedom, and support American Exceptionalism.

OFFERING PERSONAL RETIREMENT ACCOUNTS AS AN ALTERNATIVE TO SOCIAL SECURITY

For decades now, the federal government's official reports have shown that Social Security will not be able to pay all promised benefits to the Baby Boom generation—which began retiring this year—without severe, unsustainable tax increases. In fact, possibly as early as 2029, the Social Security trust funds will run out of money to pay promised benefits. Paying all promised benefits to today's young workers would eventually require raising the total payroll tax rate to as much as 44 percent—three times current levels—and ultimately more.

Our current Social Security system operates as a pure tax-and-redistribution system, with no real savings and investment mechanism and no ability to earn investment returns. Consequently, over the long run the system can only pay low, inadequate returns and benefits. Indeed, since the growing Social Security deficit will, under the current structure, ultimately require raising taxes or cutting benefits, the real effective return on Social Security contributions will be zero and eventually negative. A negative return is like putting your money in the bank, but instead of earning interest on it, you pay the bank for holding your deposit.

Instead of propping up this increasingly insolvent system, today's young workers should have the option of replacing the status quo with a new system suited to twenty-first century realities. This system would pay far better benefits while empowering contributors with more responsibility over their own finances, providing a sounder economic foundation for them and their families.

This system has already been proven in the real world. It involves creating personal retirement accounts that would let workers choose between paying into the current Social Security program or saving and investing what they and their employers would otherwise pay into Social Security in personal savings, investment, and insurance accounts. Moreover, if a worker opts for a retirement account, he will still be guaranteed to receive the benefits promised by Social Security if his retirement account ultimately offers a lower return than the existing program.

Chile began allowing workers to choose retirement accounts thirty years ago, an idea they got from young economists who had studied in America under Milton Friedman. Chilean workers overwhelmingly invested in the personal accounts, and today they are reaching retirement earning twice the benefits of the old Social Security system or more, after a lifetime of having paid only half the taxes required by the old system.

We have seen similar results here in America. In 1981, local government workers in Galveston, Texas, opted into their own savings and investment system in place of Social Security. Thirty years later, these workers are enjoying the same results as workers in Chile. Likewise, similar positive results continue to emerge under the Thrift Savings Plan (TSP) for federal employees.

Sound financial principles are essential to a strong work ethic. A system where working people and seniors do not personally control their own retirement money is not operating on sound finance. It makes no more sense to trust the government with our retirement account than it would to trust the government with our personal checking account.

With personal accounts, working people and seniors would enjoy the self-reliance and financial independence that encourage the work ethic. A society based on the dignity of the individual must have a corresponding system of retirement that maximizes independence by empowering citizens to fully provide for their own needs over their entire lifetime.

REAL CHANGE CAN HAPPEN FAST

It would be easy to believe it would take years if not decades to implement the large-scale replacement policies that America needs. But consider the following example.

In 1958, the Green Bay Packers had their worst season ever, winning only one game. But just three years later, they were NFL champions. Amazingly, from the worst team in Green Bay history, fifteen players became all-pro and seven became members of the NFL hall of fame.

What happened that produced such a dramatic turnaround?

Vince Lombardi happened. After becoming head coach in 1959, he created rigorous training regimes, demanded discipline from his players, and developed famous offensive plays like the Lombardi Sweep. He imposed on the struggling team the right values and right policies to win.

In his first year he took the worst team in football and led them to a 7–5 winning season. The next year they advanced to the NFL championship game, losing to the Eagles. After that game, Lombardi told his players this would be the last time they lost a championship game under his leadership—and he was right. The next season, 1961, the Packers won the NFL championship, the first of five the team would win during the 1960s. Under Lombardi's leadership, they never had a losing season.

So why is a story about the Green Bay Packers relevant to America's future? Because it illustrates a simple truth: rapid turnarounds are possible when good leaders implement good policies. This lesson applies as much to countries as it does to football teams. In fact, there are many examples in recent American history.

The first executive order Ronald Reagan signed upon taking office ended price controls on gasoline. It was signed into law on January 28, 1981, when gasoline, adjusted to 2011 dollars, was $3.30 per gallon. Just fifteen months later, gas had dropped over fifty cents a gallon to $2.77. By July 1984 the price was just $2.50 a gallon, and by December 1986 it had dropped almost 50 percent to $1.55 a gallon.

Reagan's bold leadership and effective policies produced a dramatic turnaround in the overall economy, leading to what supply side guru Art Laffer and *Wall Street Journal* chief financial writer Steve Moore call "the twenty-five year boom—the greatest period of wealth creation in the history of the planet."[6]

Reagan's signature economic policy—the Kemp-Roth tax cut—was signed in 1981. Once it was phased in completely in 1983, economic growth, which had been flat for more than a year, exploded almost immediately. GDP growth averaged a whopping 7.75 percent a quarter in 1983, with unemployment dropping from 10.4 to 8.3 percent, and then down to 7.3 percent by the end of 1984.

Reagan also imposed strong anti-inflationary measures. In January 1981, inflation was a staggering 11.2 percent. By the end of 1983, it was down to 3.8 percent.

As shown by both Reagan and Lombardi, the right policies can bring about fast, dramatic change, eliminating even deeply entrenched habits of failure and replacing them with habits that lead to success.

History demonstrates—and much of this book has discussed—just what habits of success have been unique to America and responsible for our remarkable prosperity, safety, and personal freedom. Just as any successful football team depends upon disciplined habits of practice, drills, and training, a flourishing nation depends upon a people that actively embrace the habits of liberty that keep us safe, strong, and free. A government can either establish a framework for public policy that reinforces these habits, or enforce policies that undermine and diminish them.

Indeed, American history is filled with examples of government policies that have succeeded because they have reinforced our most essential habits of liberty, or failed because they eroded those habits. The story of America itself is testament to the unprecedented success of liberty—as it had succeeded in no other time or place—simply due to a common commitment among an active and informed citizenry to the principles that undergird and sustain freedom. Part of America's great strength has been our ability to identify our own inconsistencies and to empower the right leadership that will replace failure with success, serfdom with liberty.

Lombardi and Reagan showed that real turnaround isn't just possible; it's available to anyone with the courage to challenge the status quo and the perseverance necessary to replace habits of failure with habits of success. Once you have both, it's not long before you're changing history.

CHAPTER TEN

THE BOWLING GREENS IN OUR BACKYARDS

I n the introduction to this book, we recalled one of the most stirring, defining moments in American history: the reading of the Declaration of Independence to the American army assembled in lower Manhattan, and the ensuing destruction of the statue of King George III on Bowling Green.

The American troops were mostly volunteers—farmers and shopkeepers with hardly any military training. They had little reason to think they stood much of a chance against the professional, battle-hardened force of nearly thirty thousand British soldiers that was wading ashore nearby.

But they *believed* in something. It was an idea crystallized in the words of the proclamation that rang out that day in lower Manhattan: there are self-evident truths that derive from our Creator. That simple idea, and those patriots' courage to fight for it against overwhelming odds, would shake the world.

Today we look to a future fraught with peril. Many Americans fear that our nation's best years might well be behind us. But if you are burdened by such thoughts, you can take inspiration from the courage and sacrifice of our founding generation, and the unwavering faith in a better future they showed even in their darkest hours.

In the months after American troops were informed of the Declaration of Independence, those same men were sent reeling back in defeat. Battle after battle was lost across the summer and into the winter of 1776. An army of more than twenty thousand would be whittled down to fewer than five thousand in November as they retreated across New Jersey back behind the Delaware. On Christmas night they undertook a final, desperate lunge, and at last achieved a small victory at Trenton. But the struggle had just begun. The following year that army would be pummeled again and again in front of Philadelphia, losing the capital of our revolution.

Then came the horrid winter at Valley Forge, where thousands died of disease, starvation, and exposure—yet still they believed. They believed as they struggled through years of terrible warfare. And they still believed when, having overcome impossible odds and emerged victorious, they were again assembled just outside of New York City, watching as the last of the invading fleet weighed anchor and fled.

Whether you can trace your bloodline back to our founding generation or you have just sworn your citizenship oath, you are the heir of those American patriots. We are all their heirs. And that binds us together in a promise to both past and future generations—we must pass to our children and those yet unborn an America that is free, strong, prosperous, and united by the promise of our Declaration.

This means we must remain vigilant against the escalating threats to our liberties. And while the U.S. military is defending us from foreign attack, we cannot neglect the threats within our own borders.

The founding generation faced down the threats of their day on the front line. But today the fight is taking place on a multitude of fronts, on a thousand Bowling Greens. The conflict is playing out not on isolated battlefields, but in our own backyards. And the force for liberty in these fights is not an army, but groups of concerned parents, churchgoers, small business owners, and individuals who unite in the struggle to preserve our way of life.

What follows are examples of the Bowling Greens of today, when ordinary Americans stood up for their rights and fought for their beliefs against powerful opponents. Some were victorious, some were not, and others are still fighting—but they all demonstrated the courage and conviction that is a hallmark of the American character.

DEFENDING FAITH AND FAMILY

LILA ROSE TAKES ON PLANNED PARENTHOOD

The nation's biggest abortion provider, Planned Parenthood receives more than $330 million a year from federal, state, and local governments.[1] While the amount of these subsidies has changed over the years, the point remains that since 1970 American taxpayers, regardless of whether they support abortion-on-demand services, have been subsidizing an organization that provides exactly those services.

But a new generation of young, pro-life activists like Lila Rose is leading the effort to end federal funding of abortions. Rose founded her pro-life organization—Live Action—when she was fifteen years old. In 2011, she released a series of undercover videos exposing Planned Parenthood clinics for, among other things, its willingness to help a purported pimp secure illegal abortions for underage girls.

Rose's activism revealed the seamy side of an organization that portrays itself as a champion of women's health. It also drew new support for a long-time effort by Congressman Mike Pence of Indiana to eliminate Planned Parenthood's federal funding. In February 2011, the U.S. House passed an amendment by a vote of 240–185 to eliminate $330 million in taxpayer subsidies for Planned Parenthood. Though the measure was defeated in the Senate, it is the closest the pro-life movement has come to stopping the flow of federal dollars to the nation's largest abortion provider.

DEFENDING THE CROSS

a. The Mojave Desert Cross

In southeastern California, deep within the Mojave National Preserve, a cross has stood atop a remote outcropping of rock for seventy-five years to commemorate Americans killed in World War I. In 2002, a nearby resident filed suit claiming the cross, because it was located on federal lands, was an unconstitutional religious display. The Supreme Court in 2010 vacated that ruling, but shortly after its decision, the cross was torn down and stolen. Since then, the National Park Service has refused to allow the cross to be replaced.[2]

The fight to defend the cross has been led by a couple, Wanda and Henry Sandoz, who had previously lived near the memorial and are regarded as its unofficial caretakers. They earned this role after they befriended the late John Riley Bembrey, a World War I veteran who was among the group of veterans that had originally erected the cross in 1934. Before he died, Bembrey asked Henry to look after the monument. Henry agreed, and he set the stage for this protracted battle when he refused an official's request to dismantle the cross. "I told her not 'no,' but 'hell, no,'" Sandoz recounts.[3]

The Sandozes' struggle led to an act of Congress calling for a land swap that would have given the Veterans of Foreign Wars control of the memorial's land in return for a nearby five-acre plot of land donated by the Sandozes. Despite this act, however, the Obama administration has failed to restore the cross. In cooperation with the Sandozes, the Veterans of Foreign Wars have now filed a lawsuit to force the Obama administration to carry out the congressionally mandated land swap, so that the group can finally restore the cross.

Wanda Sandoz explained the stakes of the case. "We realize this country wouldn't be what it was without the veterans," she said. "To me, I know it sounds corny, but that cross out there in the middle of nowhere is as important to me as the Vietnam memorial. All your memorials in Washington, D.C., they're beautiful, they're impressive, they're wonderful, but they say the same exact thing as that cross is saying."[4]

b. The Wren Cross at the College of William and Mary

Founded in 1693 by British royal charter, the College of William and Mary is the second oldest institute of higher learning in the United States. Known as the "Alma Mater of a Nation," it educated many of America's Founding Fathers, including Thomas Jefferson, James Monroe, and John Marshall.

Since 1732, the Wren Chapel has been a focal point of the William and Mary campus. Originally having served as a site for daily prayers and training for Anglican clergy, the chapel today remains a center of student life, hosting spiritual activities as well as major speakers, social events, and alumni weddings.

In the 1930s, a nearby Episcopal church donated its altar cross to the chapel, which the college permanently displayed on the altar beginning in 1932. In October 2006, the William and Mary president removed the cross from Wren Chapel, saying he wanted the chapel to be a "more welcoming place."

A group of students and alumni immediately rebelled. Students Joe Luppino-Esposito, Ben Locher, Matthew Beato, and Will Coggin, along with alumnus Vince Haley, organized SaveTheWrenCross.org, an online petition—eventually endorsed by more than twenty thousand people—dedicated to restoring the cross. The effort led to an avalanche of op-eds and editorials about the cross in student and local newspapers. Alumna Karen Hall started a companion SaveTheWren-Cross blog, which covered the growing backlash. With members of the Virginia General Assembly as well as then-governor Tim Kaine denouncing the college's actions, the school reversed course and restored the cross to the chapel permanently.

As the *Wall Street Journal* reported a few months later in June 2007, the campaign's effects reverberated even after the administration's capitulation: "This experience has emboldened what might be called the William and Mary electorate. A new organization is now asking if the governing Board of Visitors should renew the college president's contract. That's normally a rubber-stamp affair, but now college executives are being forced to defend themselves against charges of poor financial stewardship....The merits of these disputes seem less important than the fact that there is now earnest and public discussion about the performance of college administrators, who, like career government bureaucrats, are usually adept at avoiding accountability. Stakeholders are suddenly feeling empowered."[5]

c. On Mount Soledad

Similar to the Mojave Desert Cross, the Mount Soledad Cross is a 29-foot cross atop Mount Soledad in La Jolla, California. While a cross has been on the site since 1913, this specific cross was erected in 1954 as the centerpiece of a Korean War memorial. The cross has been at the center of an ongoing legal battle since 1989, when a California citizen sued the City of San Diego, alleging the cross violates the First Amendment and the California Constitution.

As the west coast regional director of the Thomas More Law Center, San Diego attorney Charles LiMandri has been in the forefront of the efforts to defend the cross since 2004. LiMandri's law office has donated more than $1 million in legal fees and other costs to the case.

In January 2011, the Ninth Circuit Court of Appeals ruled the cross unconstitutional, with Judge McKeown writing, "Overall, a reasonable observer viewing the Memorial would be confronted with an initial dedication for religious purposes, its long history of religious use, widespread public recognition of the Cross as a Christian symbol, and the history of religious discrimination in La Jolla." LaMindri commented afterward that he was disappointed but not surprised by the decision: "I read it as being very political and agenda-driven, as opposed to a real legal scholarly decision."[6]

The case is expected to be appealed to the U.S. Supreme Court.

RETURNING GOD TO THE CAPITOL VISITOR'S CENTER

Although ordinary American citizens stand at the forefront of the new Bowling Greens, politicians occasionally do their part. One instance is the dispute over the newly built, $621 million visitor center at the Capitol building in Washington, D.C., which became part of the radical secularists' campaign to remove faith from the public square.

As part of their anti-religious crusade, radical secularists whitewash the central role that religious faith has always played in American life, recasting our history as a noble struggle by secularists against the dark forces of religion. This was apparent in the attempt to remove God from the Capitol Visitors Center. Upon its completion in December 2008, the center drew widespread criticism for its multitude of historical inaccuracies, the most blatant of which was a stone engraving of the incorrect national motto: rather than "In God We Trust," the inscription read "E Pluribus Unum."

To correct this and other inaccuracies, Congressman J. Randy Forbes of Virginia led 108 members of Congress in drafting a letter of protest to the Architect of the Capitol.

Thanks to Forbes' leadership, along with that of Senator Jim DeMint of South Carolina, the engraving was corrected in late 2009. As Forbes wrote, "The efforts of the individuals that have joined in this issue have enabled those visitors to experience a more accurate depiction of our nation's heritage written in stone. This win should serve as an example to Americans all across the country that because we believe, we stand, and because we stand, we can make a difference."[7]

DEFENDING CIVIL SOCIETY

PLEDGE OF ALLEGIANCE IN WACO

Citizens of McLennan County, Texas, believed something was missing from the weekly meetings of their commissioners court; specifically, their elected officials needed to be reminded before every meeting whom they worked for. And so began a citizen-led effort to ensure that every weekly meeting began with a prayer and the Pledge of Allegiance.

The commissioners insisted they could not say a prayer or the Pledge until a new policy was adopted, and that would take time. So citizens took matters into their own hands—at one meeting, attendees spontaneously began leading the room in the Pledge of Allegiance. Soon, people like Toby Marie Walker of the Waco Tea Party began coming to the meetings every week to make sure that even without a new policy, the Pledge would be recited.

After two months of deliberation and debate, a new policy was finally approved. On July 13, 2010, for the first time ever, the McLennan County Commissioners Court officially opened its weekly meeting with a prayer and the Pledge of Allegiance.

RAISING THE NEXT GENERATION OF PATRIOTS

As American Exceptionalism comes under continued attack, now more than ever, America's youth need to be taught the values and the principles upon which our country was founded. Fortunately, local efforts are being organized around the country to make that happen.

Many of these efforts are led by the Vacation Liberty School, first started by Eric Wilson of the Kentucky 9/12 Project. The first Vacation Liberty School was held in Georgetown, Kentucky, where three dozen children, ages ten to fifteen, learned about the Constitution, the Founding Fathers, and the role of faith in our history.

According to the Associated Press, "The curriculum includes lessons like 'equal rights, not equal results,' 'recognize men don't create rights—only God,' and 'understanding falsehoods of separation of church and state.'" The report continues:

> On Monday, the first night of Vacation Liberty School, the basement of Gano Baptist church was converted into a tyrannical kingdom meant to resemble colonial England where students were told they must suppress their laughter, sit apart from their friends and flawlessly recite "Twinkle, Twinkle Little Star."
>
> Against the urgings of a mock king's representative, the brave ones ventured through the rugged terrain of a maze of upside-down tables discovered an adjoining room with all the luxuries of the New World. There they could play basketball, toss beanbags and ride a teeter-totter while being showered with confetti as Neil Diamond's "Coming To America" blared over the speakers.[8]

Through interactive games and other methods, the project aims to instill an understanding of free enterprise, the Constitution, the Founding Fathers, and the role of faith in American history. Said Tim Fairfield, one of the teachers, "If we're going to take our country back, we've got to remember where we came from—not only as adults, but we need to teach our children."[9]

Since the program's launch in Kentucky, other chapters have started up in Ohio, Colorado, New York, Florida, and Missouri. This summer, Vacation Liberty School will be run by the St. Louis chapter of "As a Mom," a nationwide network that describes itself as a "sisterhood of mommy patriots." Committed to transmitting the values of our Founding Fathers, these mothers believe that "just as the American colonists discovered the principles of liberty through a variety of experiences and experiments involving societies and human nature, our children will discover these principles for themselves through our activities."[10]

CITIZENS UNITED

The First Amendment to the U.S. Constitution prohibits Congress from making a law "abridging the freedom of speech." In 2008, Citizens United—a conservative non-profit corporation dedicated to restoring our government to citizen control—put to the test America's commitment to that prohibition.

At issue was Citizens United's effort to run TV ads and air a film critical of Hillary Clinton within thirty days of the 2008 Democratic primaries. The McCain-Feingold Act of 2002 banned such messages if they were corporate-funded, a law that Citizens United and many conservatives regarded as a clear violation of freedom of speech. As Citizens United president David Bossie explained, "The idea that the government must approve the content and timing of political speech upon threat of prison is inimical to America. Political speech, above all else, should be protected in this country."[11]

Citizens United's challenge to the law was ultimately settled by the Supreme Court in the landmark case *Citizens United v. Federal Election Commission*. In a 5–4 decision, the court sided with Citizens United and struck down part of the McCain-Feingold law. Writing for the majority, Justice Kennedy argued, "If the First Amendment has any force, it prohibits Congress from fining or jailing citizens, or associations of citizens, for simply engaging in political speech." In his concurring opinion, Justice Scalia powerfully argued for a broad interpretation of the First Amendment, insisting it was written in "terms of speech, not speakers," and "its text offers no foothold for excluding any category of speaker."

PROTECTING PRIVATE PROPERTY

At the time of America's founding, Americans distinguished themselves from other nations with their belief that individuals are personally sovereign and that power flows from the citizen up; it is not bestowed upon the people by any state, judge, or bureaucracy.

This principle was severely tarnished in the 2005 Supreme Court case *Kelo v. New London*, in which the court ruled 5–4 that the government could invoke eminent domain to seize the house of a private citizen,

Susette Kelo, and turn it over to a private developer who claimed he would generate more jobs and tax revenue.

In her subsequent testimony before the U.S. Senate Judiciary Committee, Kelo explained that she was fighting for something even more important than her home: "The battle against eminent domain abuse may have started as a way for me to save my little pink cottage. But it has rightfully grown into something much larger—the fight to restore the American Dream and the sacredness and security of each one of our homes."[12]

Susette Kelo was right, and her struggle inspired action throughout the country. Five years after the *Kelo* decision, the Institute for Justice issued a report on the backlash to *Kelo*, including the following points:

- "*Kelo* educated the public about eminent domain abuse, and polls consistently show that Americans are overwhelmingly opposed to *Kelo* and support efforts to change the law to better protect property rights."
- "Citizen activists defeated at least forty-four projects that sought to abuse eminent domain for private gain in the five-year period since *Kelo*."
- "Forty-three states improved their laws in response to *Kelo*, more than half of those providing strong protection against eminent domain abuse."
- "Nine state high courts restricted the use of eminent domain for private development since *Kelo* while only one (New York) has so far refused to do so."
- "The New London project for which the property was taken in *Kelo* has been a complete failure and is now Exhibit A in what happens when governments engage in massive corporate welfare and abuse eminent domain. Although the project failed, Susette Kelo's iconic little pink house has been moved to downtown New London and preserved. It stands as a monument in honor of the families who fought for their rights and inspired the nation to change its laws to better protect property owners."[13]

Although Susette was defeated in court, her case sparked a wave of citizen activism to defend private property and curb the abuse of eminent domain laws. She also earned the support of millions of Americans who understood her little home could just as easily have been theirs.

MISSOURI TO D.C.: BACK OFF

When the president signed ObamaCare into law in March 2009, citizens in Missouri were not content to sit back and allow this government power-grab—they decided to act.

Advocacy organizations, tea party groups, and Missouri legislators worked together to craft Proposition C, a ballot initiative to block the federal rule forcing all Americans to buy health insurance. To garner support for the measure, the St. Louis Tea Party instituted a "Block Captain" program that trained citizens in grassroots organizing and recruiting. A leader of the effort, Missouri lawyer Benjamin Evans, recalled how volunteers, with little financial backing, helped to cultivate a popular movement against the mandates of ObamaCare: "The Facebook page became a clearinghouse for low-cost solutions to the problem. Bumper stickers, homemade signs, and many other ideas were created at home by individuals, vetted by larger groups, and then distributed through personal social networks and e-mail chains."[14]

Appearing on the August 2010 primary ballot, Proposition C was approved by an overwhelming 71 percent of Missouri voters—even though the measure's supporters had been outspent 4-to-1 by its opponents. The day after the vote, Dwight Janson, who had first joined the effort after attending a tea party event, told the *St. Louis Post-Dispatch*, "It's the vote heard 'round the world." Explaining why he became involved in the issue, Janson said simply, "I was tired of sitting on the sidelines bouncing my gums."[15]

HAD ENOUGH IN BELL, CALIFORNIA

The term "public service" has historically been associated with sacrifice and selflessness for the public good. Residents of Bell, California, however, discovered one day that many of their own public servants had become extremely adept at serving themselves.

In July 2010, the *L.A. Times* revealed that Bell's local officials were helping themselves to exorbitant salaries, topped by the city manager's $787,637 annual income. Caught red-handed and shamelessly hoping to cling to power, the officials proffered ridiculous justifications for their self-generosity. But outraged taxpayers would have none of it. They staged rallies and stormed the city council chamber, demanding the thieves' immediate resignations.

Cristina Garcia, a resident of the mostly Hispanic city, helped to lead many of these protests on behalf of her new organization, the Bell Association to Stop the Abuse, or BASTA, which in Spanish means "enough." Unable to withstand the withering public censure, the town's top administrators resigned. Later, the city manager and several other officials were arrested and charged with misappropriating over $5.5 million of taxpayer money—in a town where one in six residents lives in poverty.[16]

A few tainted officials managed to retain their positions—but not for long. On March 8, 2011, Bell residents held a recall election and overwhelmingly voted to oust the mayor and three council members indicted in the scandal. And after that, BASTA made it clear that its work was not yet done. As it noted on its website soon after the recall election, the group now aims to fundamentally reform Bell's local government in order to prevent such abuses from recurring in the future:

> BASTA's work is just beginning. Our new focus will be charter reform and ensuring that transparency really does exist in Bell.
>
> The community came together and an overwhelming 95% of the voters, said "BASTA" to the old council members and their corrupt practices. In order to ensure our work was not in vain we must keep vigilant and involved.
>
> BASTA still has a lot of work. 35% of the voters participated yesterday, that's 3 times as much as past municipal elections, but still shy of where we should be. We made

progress, but a reminder that changing a culture and bringing about real change won't happen overnight and that we have a lot of work ahead for us.

Let's celebrate this new start and the victories we have experienced together over the last 8 months, but let's not forget that our work is not done and democracy only works if we stay involved and informed.[17]

WORK AND INNOVATION

THE DC SCHOLARSHIP OPPORTUNITY PROGRAM

Our Founders' emphasis on individual liberty and free enterprise helped to create the most innovative society in human history. But innovation suffers when competition is stifled and mediocrity is protected—and that's what is happening in our public education system today. Restrictive work rules and powerful teachers unions are preventing many public schools from experimenting with new approaches to education, leading to student failure. For example, in California's Los Angeles Unified School District, 50 percent of students are not graduating from high school, and a full 90 percent don't make it to college.[18]

But thanks to the hard work of concerned parents, things are beginning to change. A great example is the renewal of the DC Scholarship Opportunity Program. Begun in 1994, SOP was the first federally funded school-voucher program in the country. It provided nearly 2,000 children from low-income families in Washington, D.C. with scholarships of $7,500 a year to cover tuition and fees at participating private schools.

After a few years, the program showed tremendous results and had earned broad local support. Here are some of its accomplishments:

- Students who used their scholarships had graduation rates of 91 percent.
- The Department of Education's Institute for Education Sciences found that SOP had one of the largest achievement impacts of any of the programs studied.

- Four studies from Georgetown University and the University of Arkansas showed that parents of SOP recipients were becoming more active and astute educational consumers.
- A February 2011 Lester & Associates poll found that 74 percent of D.C. residents support reauthorizing the SOP program.[19]

Despite these stellar results, in spring 2009 congressional Democrats passed—and President Obama signed—a spending bill that failed to reauthorize the program. This decision, a clear gift to the teachers unions, provoked the anger of poor D.C.-area parents whose kids were deprived of a lifeline that had helped some students escape the city's disastrous public schools. These parents, led by Virginia Walden Ford of D.C. Parents for School Choice, then began a two-year campaign to renew the scholarship program.

The parents' activism kept the issue alive despite Congress' refusal to reconsider its decision. The tide turned after the 2010 midterm elections, when Republicans regained control of the House of Representatives and vowed to revive SOP. As a vote on the issue approached, Ford wrote, "Parents across the country are watching Congress right now to see if their members will do the right thing and stand courageously with children who only want a better future—or if they'll side with richly-funded special interest groups that place adults and the status quo above the needs of low-income families."[20]

On March 30, 2011, with the outspoken support of Speaker John Boehner, the House of Representatives passed the SOAR Act, which would reopen SOP and provide $20 million annually for five years for new scholarships, along with another $20 million apiece for D.C.-area charter schools and traditional public schools. At the Republicans' insistence, the bill was included in the budget deal of April 2011 and signed into law by President Obama.

Upon SOP's revival, *National Review*'s Kathryn Lopez remarked that "John Boehner just walked Barack Obama into being a civil-rights leader."[21] There's some truth to that, but the real architects of this victory were the people of Washington, D.C.—people like Virginia Walden Ford.

ANDREA WECK AND THE FIGHT FOR SCHOOL CHOICE

On May 29, 2009, Arizona governor Jan Brewer approved a bill known as "Lexie's Law," which saved private school scholarships for special needs and foster children from being eliminated by opponents of school choice. The law was named for Lexie Weck, a then-seven-year-old girl with autism, cerebral palsy, and mild mental retardation. Lexie's mother Andrea used an Arizona voucher program to transfer Lexie from a failing public school to Chrysalis Academy, a small, private school in Tempe for autistic children.

Lexie made great progress at Chrysalis, but her continuation there was jeopardized when the Arizona Supreme Court sided with teachers' unions, the ACLU, and various other organizations that had sued to shut down the voucher program. Nevertheless, the fight for school choice continued, as Arizona parents like Andrea Weck pressured lawmakers to find a substitute for the program. Ultimately, the legislature passed "Lexie's Law," which created a $5 million tax credit for businesses that help fund schooling for children with disabilities.[22]

Said Weck at the signing, "I am incredibly grateful that the legislature and governor moved so quickly to save the scholarships my daughter and hundreds of other children rely on.... Attending a school that meets her needs has changed Lexie's life, and I am honored that the legislature named this program after my beautiful little girl."[23]

FREE SPEECH IN OUR NATION'S CAPITAL

Bill Main and Tonia Edwards own a company in Washington, D.C. that provides tours of the city on Segways, two-wheeled electric vehicles. They thought they had created an innovative, successful little business for themselves—until they ran up against the D.C.-area bureaucracy.

Following the grand government tradition of issuing useless, stifling regulation, D.C. authorities adopted a rule requiring tour guides to pass a test and secure a government permit if they plan to describe people and places in the city. If they don't get the permit, they could face up to ninety days in jail. So Bill and Tonia sued the government to withdraw the regulations on free speech grounds. In February 2011, a federal judge upheld the permitting requirement.

Bill and Tonia lost their case, but they drew public attention to the growing problem of occupational licensing requirements, which are making it increasingly difficult and expensive for everyday people to start up and operate a small business. According to the Institute for Justice, which represented Bill and Tonia in their lawsuit, the percentage of the workforce required to obtain a government license has jumped from less than 5 percent in the 1950s to more than 30 percent today.

These kinds of onerous bureaucratic requirements not only suppress economic activity, they impinge on our freedom, as the Institute of Justice explained: "Particularly as the nation tries to recover from a massive recession—and as individuals who have lost their jobs try to start over, often by starting their own businesses—it is imperative that people be allowed to pursue their dreams without the government standing in their way imposing unnecessary barriers in the form of occupational-licensing requirements. Only by setting people free—to describe, to create, to *work*—can we truly create sustained economic growth."[24]

SAFETY AND PEACE

KEEPING TERRORISTS OUT OF THE BIG APPLE

The beginning of an NBC New York story on January 30, 2010 said it all:

> Democracy does work.
>
> After a growing number of regular people and powerful politicians alike had begged to move the 9/11 terror trials, Obama administration officials confirmed to NBC News that they will not hold the trials in New York City.[25]

Having repeatedly denounced his predecessor's prosecution of the War on Terror, President Obama took office vowing to do away with military tribunals for terrorism suspects and instead to try them in U.S. civilian courts.

But when the Obama administration announced its intention to transfer 9/11 mastermind Khalid Sheikh Mohammed and four other accused terrorists to civilian courts in New York City, near the site of the most devastating terrorist attack on America in our history, Americans rose up in protest. The backlash was most visible in New York City itself, where numerous demonstrations were staged by grassroots organizations such as the 9/11 Never Forget Coalition, a diverse group comprising families of 9/11 victims, first responders, military families, war veterans, and other concerned Americans.

In advance of its December 2010 rally, the coalition announced, "This Coalition was formed to fight the decision of President Barack Obama and Attorney General Eric Holder to try the 9/11 co-conspirators in New York City's federal court, effectively giving war criminals the same rights as American citizens while endangering the safety of all New Yorkers."[26]

As the public outcry intensified, local city leaders as well as national political figures began speaking out against the administration's plans to bring terrorists to the American mainland and treat them like ordinary criminals. Eventually, the administration was forced to back down and end its two-year-long moratorium on military tribunals for terror suspects. Thanks to the willingness of thousands of New Yorkers and many other Americans to take a public stand, today Khalid Sheikh Mohammed remains right where he belongs—in Guantanamo Bay.

★ ★ ★

In America we see protests all the time representing a galaxy of political perspectives. They used to be dominated by the Left, but in recent years, an energized, grassroots conservative movement has emerged whose adherents are unafraid to voice their objections to the constant encroachments of government. In tea parties and town hall meetings, from Bell, California, to New York City, Americans are speaking out like never before against over-reaching and irresponsible government on the local, state, and national levels.

As we make our voices heard, we must never forget how few nations enjoy the most basic rights—to speak freely, worship freely, and petition their leaders for a redress of grievances. People throughout the world are persecuted for speaking against their governments the way we do every day. As I write these words, Syrian army units and police forces are killing their own people in the streets. The victims' crime? They gathered together to seek changes to government policies.

Though we sometimes take them for granted, our rights are unusual in this world—and they existed almost nowhere else when our Founders enshrined them in our nation's founding documents. To not only have these rights, but to live in a country founded for the express purpose of securing them, is an exceptional privilege enjoyed by every American— and one we must guard with eternal vigilance.

CONCLUSION

JANUARY 20, 2021

The election of 2012 will bring us to an historic crossroads. The direction we choose will determine whether we will continue as an exceptional nation or follow a path of decline and fade into mediocrity, inadequacy, and failure.

In 1900 many people believed that the twentieth century would be dominated by Britain, just as the previous century had been. Yet two world wars and two generations of socialism laid waste to British prosperity, power, and global leadership. By 2000 no one could deny the twentieth century had, in fact, been the American century. What will be said of the United States in the year 2100, or even 2050? That choice will be made by the American people.

Let's be clear what this choice entails: we can cultivate an America that reaffirms and recommits to the self-evident truths of the Declaration of Independence that have made us a nation like no other in history. This choice leads to a future of even greater opportunities, a future that is freer, safer, healthier, and more prosperous.

Or we can reject these truths and surrender to a debt-ridden, government-centric system dominated by politicians and stultifying bureaucrats who will gladly manage our decline as long as they stay in charge. This choice will lead to economic ruin and an increasingly dangerous world.

Those are the stakes of the 2012 election.

A PEOPLE'S MOVEMENT TO REPLACE THE LEFT

While the election of 2012 is the first step toward a better future, I believe we must look further down the road than November 6, 2012; the key date is actually January 20, 2021.

If we are successful in replacing the Left and restoring American Exceptionalism, by January 20, 2021, eight years after the 2012 election, America will be stronger than at any time in our lifetimes. On that day, a new conservative president will be taking the oath of office. Looking on will be both houses of Congress, led by strong majorities that believe in American Exceptionalism and are working to strengthen and protect it every day. The federal government will have turned significant powers back to the states, local governments, and the people—including the more than 513,000 elected officials in the United States who serve as governors, state legislators, and as members of school boards, city councils, and county commissions. And our nation will be reaping the rewards that come from listening to the American people.

The hard, steady work of returning power to the people will be far more important than the decisions of any one person. No man or woman in the Oval Office can achieve change on this scale. It will require the active participation of millions of Americans.

Conservatives will need a long-term commitment and strategic vision to reverse the damage the Left has done to America. After all, in its quest to transform America into a radically secular, government-controlled utopia, the Left has spent a century building up a system dominated by bureaucrats and special interest groups. And the Left continues its crusade today despite the undeniable failure of its vision, as evident in the wreckage of so many countries that turned to socialism or other forms of central planning. Its own track record shows that the left-wing governing philosophy of class warfare, class envy, and the redistribution of wealth is incapable of meeting the challenges of the twenty-first century.

The system we are fighting for is the one established by our Founders, a republic that rewards work and merit, cultivates civil society and faith, confronts and defeats threats to our way of life, and returns power to the American people. Benjamin Franklin wondered whether Americans could keep such a republic. Abraham Lincoln answered this question for his generation at a battlefield at Gettysburg four score and seven years after the signing of the Declaration of Independence:

> It is for us the living, rather, to be dedicated here to the unfinished work which they who fought here have thus far so nobly advanced. It is rather for us to be here dedicated to the great task remaining before us—that from these honored dead we take increased devotion to that cause for which they gave the last full measure of devotion—that we here highly resolve that these dead shall not have died in vain—that this nation, under God, shall have a new birth of freedom—and that government of the people, by the people, for the people, shall not perish from the earth.

Now, we too must answer Franklin's question for our own generation.

It will not be enough to reject the Left's big government policies at the ballot box—the American people did that in 1972, 1980, 1994, and 2010, yet the Left carries on, seemingly undiminished. That's because its power stretches beyond public office to the commanding heights of our society—our academic institutions, newsrooms, courtrooms, and throughout the fields of arts and entertainment.

If we are to reclaim our Founders' republic, we must not merely *reject* the Left and its failed policies, but *replace* them. To do that, we need three things: a positive vision to offer the American people; the votes to implement it; and the will to carry it through. This effort should be propelled by a political movement that can communicate why we must change, how we can accomplish that change, and what responsibilities that change will require of every individual. In building this movement to replace the Left, we should take inspiration from the First Continental Congress, which in 1776, in the Declaration of Independence, made its own historic call for replacing the corrupt, abusive system of its day with a new model based on superior values.

The new conservative movement must be just as committed to freedom as were the revolutionary signers of the Declaration. Just as in their day, today's patriots are farmers, shopkeepers, doctors, entrepreneurs, coal miners, and workers from every corner of America. As the Left struggles to rend our traditional bonds of family, community, and country, and to dissolve the American nation into a collection of rival interest groups scrambling for their own piece of the government pie, it is the ideals of the Declaration which again must bind us together.

THE FOUNDERS' STRUGGLE BECOMES OUR OWN

In the hard winter of 1778, General George Washington committed the American colonists to victory by building up a well-trained professional army. He recruited new soldiers, steeled the will of veterans, and equipped them all for the fight ahead. It was not enough to declare independence; it had to be won on the battlefield. As Thomas Paine so rightly declared in 1776, "Heaven knows how to put a proper price upon its goods; and it would be strange indeed if so celestial an article as FREEDOM should not be highly rated."

After their improbable victory, the Founders had to ensure the principles they had fought for were embodied in their founding documents, realized in their own lives, and preserved for generations to come. When their first attempt to codify these values of liberty—the Articles of Confederation—proved inadequate, they acknowledged its flaws and worked out a replacement. The result was the United States Constitution, the greatest source and guarantor of the rule of law and human liberty in history.

The Founders succeeded in their task in one generation; they rejected tyranny, won their liberty, and secured it for themselves and future generations. They challenged subsequent generations to safeguard the republic and make it even stronger and freer. In their wisdom, they gave us the tools to accomplish that task. Generations of Americans since have accepted that challenge and proved themselves worthy of the Founders' bequest.

It is that endowment that gives us the means to restore American Exceptionalism. Our American Creed—that all men and women are created equal, possessed of a God-given dignity and personally sovereign—embodies truths that apply beyond America's borders; it is an invitation to *all* mankind to affirm its unalienable rights and pursue happiness. We must each live up to that Creed to keep faith with God and our forebears.

Countless Americans have struggled at great cost to ensure our country lives up to its ideals. Hundreds of thousands died fighting a wrenching Civil War that led to a new birth of freedom dedicated to the founding principles. In the following century, Americans extended our creed to millions in bondage when we defeated the tyrannies of fascism, Japanese militarism, and after a decades-long struggle, Soviet Communism. Back at home, civil rights activists pricked the nation's conscience with their dignified struggle to allow all Americans, regardless of race, to realize their unalienable rights.

The task of renewal now falls to us, to this generation of Americans. Our faith in a better future—one of the great features of the American character—is being shaken by ever-growing debt and deficits, broken bureaucratic systems, an increasingly intrusive government, rising hostility to God and traditional values, a sluggish economy, new economic and strategic challenges, and malevolent enemies bent on our destruction. For the first time in our lives, fully half of Americans believe that their children will be worse off than themselves. Only one in five Americans today believes that the future will be better.[1] Our challenge is to stand with those believers in an even greater America and prove them right.

A NEW AMERICAN CENTURY

If we are successful, America in the twenty-first century will be a land of liberty—a land where the natural rights and inherent dignity of every man, woman, and child are both protected by government and affirmed by fellow citizens. Risk-takers will reap their just rewards for their endeavors. Excellence, hard work, and merit will be honored and admired, not punished and scorned. Every citizen will have access to the tools of success and be encouraged to make use of them. Education—the best means of achieving social mobility—will no longer breed mediocrity for so many of our children, but will instead provide a path of upward mobility to all who seek it.

America will once again become the land of the never-ending "second chance." Americans will be free to try, fail, try again, and succeed. Experimentation and innovation will be encouraged through free competition. Anyone with a bigger and better idea will find the tools and the opportunity to achieve it. We will become more independent as technological progress and a thriving economy allow us to free ourselves of foreign energy suppliers and foreign holders of U.S. debt. We will out-compete, out-work, and out-innovate the world.

America will be a land of infinite possibility. We will tear down the walls that limit success and hamper opportunity. Government will stop tying down entrepreneurs, innovators, and adventurers with red tape and senseless hurdles. We will empower every American with a hand-up to rejoin the competition, not a handout to stand on the sidelines.

A successful twenty-first-century America will be a self-governing nation with a responsible, independent, sovereign citizenry. The people will rediscover their extraordinary ability to govern themselves and will demand that power and responsibility be returned to the states and to the American people. All forms of government will be of, by, and for the people—not the bureaucracy and the elites. Local control will empower individuals to take charge of their own healthcare and education, and generally to run their own lives as they see fit.

A richer, freer, and stronger America will be an even more generous and more virtuous America. For those in need, independent citizens will come together in common purpose to provide aid with more efficiency and dignity than any government bureaucracy could. Those who give their time, talents, and money to others will be held in the high regard they deserve.

The ties of nation, society, community, neighborhood, and family will be strengthened. Americans will be called to public service and civic engagement in the same spirit with which they pursue their own happiness. Engaged citizens will ensure that government maintains the consent of the governed and works in the public interest.

America will treasure the family as the center of human civilization and the means by which the habits of liberty are instilled in the next generation. Instead of attempting to assume parental responsibilities, government will empower parents to protect, teach, and support their own children, in faith and freedom.

God, as the endower of our great rights and responsibilities, will be recognized and honored as a crucial part of our history and culture. People of faith will be free to express their beliefs without government interference. Religion and morality will remain the indispensable supports of liberty for generations to come, giving our lives hope, inspiration, and meaning.

Americans in the twenty-first century will protect our liberty and dignity by defending ourselves against those who would do us harm. We will be willing to pay the high price necessary to secure a safe and peaceful world for ourselves, our children, our allies, and for all mankind. We will stand up for what is right and stand up to those who want to destroy our freedom. America will convey, to friend and foe alike, that we will boldly confront tyranny, as we have so many times in the past. We will reject appeasement and pleas for "peace at any price," knowing that peace is best attained through a nation's strength and its unwavering resolve to defend its safety and its people's rights.

America will open its heart to those who wish to join us in our pursuit of freedom and dignity. Those that wish to affirm our creed will be encouraged to do so by following our laws and embracing our traditions. We will work to help other nations that want to live in peace and liberty. And we shall work to remain as a city upon a hill, the bright beacon of opportunity, hope, and freedom, for all the world to see.

The fight to renew America begins in 2012. I ask you to join us in this effort to restore America as a nation like no other.

ACKNOWLEDGMENTS

America is an exceptional country. I have spent more than five decades learning what we need to do to survive and flourish as a nation. The conclusions I have reached are the result of much listening, learning, and collaborating with friends, colleagues, family, and experts, without whom none of this would be possible.

Vince Haley has played an especially important role through these last eight years. He has had a tremendous influence on my thinking about the role of our Creator in creating unalienable rights, the legitimacy of religion in American public life, and a host of other issues. He was the driving intellectual force behind our movie *Nine Days that Changed the World*, and here once again he is the thought leader in outlining a set of principles that are central to the survival of America.

Bethany Haley, Vince's wife, did a brilliant job of helping us think through chapter four on faith and family. She is a remarkable woman with a deep understanding of the role of faith and family in a healthy society. Callista and I are very fond of their daughter Alina, who has brightened all our lives in the last year.

Vince and I were helped by a number of very smart, hardworking people.

Sean Kennedy is my former intern at the American Enterprise Institute and did the lion's share of the research for several chapters. He contributed greatly to the chapters on the American Creed and civil society.

Bill Forstchen has been my coauthor for eight novels (including seven *New York Times* bestsellers). He helped bring to life the opening story of Bowling Green and the extraordinary story of the Battle of Midway.

Ken Hagerty is a leader at ReAL (Renewing American Leadership). He made significant contributions to the opening section of the book.

Brady Cassis has been my research director at the American Enterprise Institute (a job Vince Haley had years ago) and is a superb, conscientious, and remarkably capable researcher. Brady helped with the initial draft of the safety and peace chapter and was incredibly dependable on a number of research requests.

Caitlin Laverdiere, also a research associate at the American Enterprise Institute, was expedient and reliable on both research and fact checking.

Peter Ferrara, director of entitlement and budget policy at the Institute for Policy Innovation, is a brilliant economist who truly understands the importance of a free-market system in preserving and enhancing America as an exceptional nation. He is a colleague in the fight for a pro-jobs, pro-entrepreneurship government policy. Peter and I have been working together on projects since his days in the Reagan White House. He contributed greatly to the sections on economic activity and the work ethic.

Peter's new book, *America's Ticking Bankruptcy Bomb: How the Looming Debt Crisis Threatens the American Dream and How We Can Turn the Tide Before It's Too Late*, should be read by every citizen concerned about America's future.

Adam Waldeck is a remarkable coordinator of tea party activities at American Solutions and assisted with the vignettes in chapter ten about the Bowling Greens in our backyards. He has dedicated himself to listening and learning from America's grassroots activists.

Jack Langer at Regnery is a superb editor and helped not only with editing, but also some critical writing where needed. He is a real pleasure to work with.

AEI interns Danielle Fezouati and Alex Hilliker have provided invaluable support in putting together research for this book. Kevin Preskenis, an intern with Renewing American Leadership, also helped enormously with research and fact checking.

As a scholar at the American Enterprise Institute since 1999, I have had the privilege of learning from some of the most brilliants minds, including Michael Novak, Karlyn Bowman, Charles Murray, Alex Pollock, Steve Hayward, Kevin Hassett, Danielle Pletka, David Gerson, James Q. Wilson, Ambassador John Bolton, Sally Satel, Peter Wallison, and Michael Barone. Arthur Brooks, president of AEI, has shown tremendous leadership, inspiring others with his energy and enthusiasm. Former AEI president Chris DeMuth has also had a tremendous impact on my thinking about public policy. I'm also grateful for the generosity of Ken and Yvonne Hannan, who have helped support our efforts at AEI over the years.

Thanks also to experts Herman Pirchner, Walter Isaacson, John Goodman, Cliff May, Grover Norquist, Ed Feulner, Dave Bossie, Craig Shirley, Marc Rotterman, Brett Schaefer, David Barton, Attorney General Edwin Meese, Andrew McCarthy, and Anne Bayefsky for their advice and ideas.

As always, I consulted my dear friend and mentor, Dr. Steve Hanser, for his advice on this book. He pushed me to thoughtfully and effectively communicate the significance of American Exceptionalism throughout the entire writing process.

My longtime spokesman and press secretary, Rick Tyler, has improved and enhanced this book by reviewing and critiquing the text and offering his keen insight on how best to communicate our ideas. As founder of Renewing American Leadership, he has been a true leader in forging the bridge between religious liberty and free markets, uniting social and fiscally minded Americans under a common purpose in seeking freedom.

Our general advisor on research, Terry Balderson, sends me hundreds of news articles from around the world each day, allowing me to stay briefed and up to date on a wide variety of topics. I am grateful for his support.

Our team at American Solutions has led and supported a national movement of citizens in creating real change on the issues vital to American Exceptionalism. Joe Gaylord, CEO of American Solutions and my longtime adviser and co-designer of the Contract with America, contributed his vast political knowledge. Steve Everley is a proven expert on how to develop an American Energy plan. Dan Kotman, Tim Cameron, Ben Locher, and Sukamar Manduva have enhanced our ability to communicate online with citizens and bloggers. Paige Bray has done great work in running American Solutions, with the support of Whitney Smith and Lindsey Harvey. Finally, our intern Dustin Thompson has done great work in assisting the American Solutions team.

Our daughter, Kathy Lubbers, has been a true leader as president and CEO of Gingrich Communications up through this year, seeing us through twenty-three books and thirteen *New York Times* bestsellers. Her leadership was key in the development and execution of this book.

My thanks to the rest of the Gingrich Communications team, including Joe DeSantis, our communications director, who plays a key role in my weekly newsletter and nonfiction work; Michelle Selesky, our communications coordinator and talk radio expert; Christina Maruna and Ross Worthington, who lead our online effort at Newt.org and GingrichProductions.com; Sylvia Garcia, who runs The Americano, a Hispanic bilingual news and opinion site; Jorge Hurtado, who patiently teaches and assists me with my Spanish; and our communications intern, Catherine Butterworth, who has been a tremendous support for the entire team.

Our daughter, Jackie Cushman has become a talented writer, who inspired me by writing her own book, *The Essential American: 25 Documents and Speeches Every American Should Own,* which is a must-read for understanding the brilliant men and women who prove that America is exceptional.

The many projects we accomplish, including this book, are only possible with the support and dedication of my team at the Office of Speaker Newt Gingrich. Sonya Harrison does a brilliant job of managing and scheduling all our many projects. Her leadership, along with the support of the always-energetic Bess Kelly and Kate Pietkiewicz, are vital to our success.

Alicia Melvin, our special assistant, has enabled us to accomplish more than we could ever imagine. Her hard work, dedication, and enthusiasm are unmatched, and we are grateful for her support and friendship.

Anna Haberlein has taken our documentary, *Nine Days that Changed the World*, about Pope John Paul II's pilgrimage to Poland in 1979, to new heights by working with schools, organizations and churches to screen the film nationwide and share the Holy Father's message of freedom through faith—a belief that is also the foundation of American Exceptionalism.

At the Center for Health Transformation, Nancy Desmond, Dave Merritt, Vincent Frakes, Laura Linn, Melissa Ferguson, Wayne Oliver, and Amy Nyhuis have done great work in developing the principles of a twenty-first century healthcare system.

The team at Regnery Publishing has made writing and publishing books a true joy. Their president, Marji Ross, has proven time and again that she is truly an inspirational publisher. The aforementioned Jack Langer is a remarkable editor, and Jeff Carneal, president of Eagle Publishing, has been supportive in growing and enhancing my weekly *Human Events* newsletter.

Once again, Randy Evans and Stefan Passantino have guided and assisted us with their legal talents. Randy is my general advisor and strategist for all my wide-ranging activities, and Stefan is a leading expert on election law and counsel to our companies.

Finally, my wife Callista is an inspiration to me. Having her by my side has made this project a true joy. I marvel at her hard work, dedication, and unparalleled attention to detail. Whether she is golfing, producing one of our seven documentary films, or singing in the Choir of the Basilica of the National Shrine of the Immaculate Conception, Callista gives it her all and lives life to the fullest. Playing the piano, the French Horn, and singing, she possesses a range of talent and energy that are part of the American experience. Her journey from Whitehall, Wisconsin, to Luther College in Decorah, Iowa, to Washington, D.C. to serve as chief clerk of the House Committee on Agriculture, and then to lead Gingrich Productions as president and CEO, is a story of talent, diligence, and commitment that is classically American.

NOTES

INTRODUCTION

1. Matt Miller, "Ohhh, America, you're so strong," *Washington Post*, November 18, 2010, http://www.washingtonpost.com/wp-dyn/content/article/2010/11/17/AR2 010111703216_pf.html (accessed April 15, 2011).
2. Michael Kinsely, "U.S. is not greatest country ever," *Politico*, November 2, 2010, http://www.politico.com/news/stories/1110/44500.html (accessed April 15, 2011).
3. Neal Gabler, "One nation, under illusion," *Boston Globe*, October 13, 2009, http://www.boston.com/bostonglobe/editorial_opinion/oped/articles/2009/10/13/one_nation_under_illusion/ (accessed April 15, 2011).
4. See video of Obama's remark here: http://www.youtube.com/watch?v=ZEvH_f9VADA (accessed April 15, 2011).
5. Glenn Greenwald, "Obama and American Exceptionalism," Salon.com, March 29, 2011, http://www.salon.com/news/opinion/glenn_greenwald/2011/03/29/exceptionalism/index.html (accessed April 15, 2011).
6. "G.E.'s Strategies Let It Avoid Taxes Altogether," *New York Times*, March 24, 2011, http://www.nytimes.com/2011/03/25/business/economy/25tax.html (accessed April 15, 2011).
7. Joseph R. Fornieri, ed. *The Language of Liberty: The Political Speeches and Writings of Abraham Lincoln* (Washington, D.C.: Regnery, 2009), 576.

CHAPTER ONE

1. Michael Kammen, *The People of Paradox* (New York: Cornell University Press, 1972), 13.
2. Bernard Bailyn, *The Ideological Origins of the American Revolution* (Cambridge: Harvard University Press, 1992), 66.
3. Gordon S. Wood, *The Radicalism of the American Revolution* (Vintage Press, 1993), 13.

4.   John Adams, "Letter to Thomas Jefferson, 28 June 1813," in *The Works of John Adams: Second President of the United States*, ed. Charles Francis Adams (Boston: Little, Brown & Co., 1856), 45–46.

5.   Quoted in Gordon S. Wood, *The Radicalism of the American Revolution*.

6.   Bernard Bailyn, *The Ideological Origins of the American Revolution*.

7.   Paul Johnson, *A History of the American People* (New York: Harper Collins, 1997), 116.

8.   John Smith, as cited by Elisa Carbone, *Blood on the River: James Town 1607* (Viking Press, 2006).

9.   William Bradford, *Of Plymouth Plantation*.

10.   Paul Johnson, *A History of the American People*, 32.

11.   Michael Novak, *On Two Wings: Humble Faith and Common Sense at the American Founding* (Encounter Books, 2001), 6–7.

12.   Gordon S. Wood, *The Radicalism of the American Revolution*, 112.

13.   John Adams, letter to Hezekiah Niles, 1818, Bernard Bailyn, *The Ideological Origins of the American Revolution*, 1; cited by Dinesh D'Souza, *What's So Great About Christianity* (Washington, D.C.: Regnery Publishing, 2007), 72.

14.   Melanie Randolph Miller, *Envoy to the Terror: Gouverneur Morris and the French Revolution* (Dulles, VA: Potomac Books, 2005), 187.

15.   Paul Johnson, *A History of the American People*, 116.

CHAPTER TWO

1.   Taken from "America's Bill of Rights at 200 Years," by former Chief Justice Warren E. Burger, printed in *Presidential Studies Quarterly*, Vol. XXI, No. 3, Summer 1991, p. 457. This anecdote appears in numerous other works as well.

2.   Alexander Hamilton, John Jay, James Madison, *The Federalist on the New Constitution* (Philadelphia: Benjamin Warner, 1818), 53, #10, James Madison.

3.   John Adams, *The Works of John Adams, Second President of the United States*, ed. Charles Francis Adams (Boston: Charles C. Little and James Brown, 1850), Vol. VI, p. 484, to John Taylor on April 15, 1814.

4.   Bernard Bailyn, *The Ideological Origins of the American Revolution*, 60.

5.   Quoted in *The Future of Religion in American Politics*, ed. Charles W. Dunn (Lexington: The University Press of Kentucky, 2009), 105, in an 1811 letter to Benjamin Rush.

6.   Quoted in Gordon S. Wood, *The Creation of the American Public, 1776–1787* (Chapel Hill, N.C.: University of North Carolina Press, 1998), 95.

7.   Gordon S. Wood, *The Radicalism of the American Revolution*, 44.

8.   Paul Johnson, *A History of the American People*, 22.

9.   George Whitefield, "The Great Duty of Family Religion"; available at: http://www.biblebb.com/files/gw-006.htm (accessed April 20, 2011).

10.   Benjamin Franklin, *The Autobiography of Benjamin Franklin* (Dover Thrift Edition, 1996).

11.   Michael Novak, *The Spirit of Democratic Capitalism* (Madison Books, 1990), 41.

12.   Benjamin Franklin, "Information to Those Who Would Remove to America," written in 1794 and reprinted at Founding.com; available at: http://www.founding.com/founders_library/pageID.2148/default.asp (accessed April 20, 2011).

13.   Benjamin Franklin, *On the Price of Corn and Management of the Poor*, written in 1776 and reprinted at Founding.com; available at: http://www.founding.com/founders_library/pageID.2146/default.asp (accessed April 20, 2011).

14.   Howard S. Miller, "Legal Foundation of American Philanthropy, 1776–1844," The State Historical Society of Wisconsin, Madison 1961; available at: http://www.hks.harvard.edu/hauser/philanthropyclassics/pdf_files/Miller.pdf (accessed April 20, 2011).

15.   Alexis de Tocqueville, *Democracy in America* (Chicago: University of Chicago Press, 2000), Chapter 12.

16.   Gordon S. Wood, *The Creation of the American Public*, 293.

17.   Alexander Hamilton, John Jay, James Madison, *The Federalist on the New Constitution* (Philadelphia: Benjamin Warner, 1818), 53, #57.

18.   Paul Johnson, *A History of the American People*, 151.

CHAPTER THREE

1.   "Speech By President Sarkozy Before Congress," November 7, 2007, *New York Sun*; available at: http://www.nysun.com/national/speech-by-president-sarkozy-before-congress/66054/ (accessed April 19, 2011).

2.   Real American Stories, One Nation United, "Alp Gurpinar"; video available at: http://www.realamericanstories.com/alp-gurpinar/?curpage=12 (accessed April 19, 2011).

3.   "Full Transcript of Julia Gillard's Speech to U.S. Congress," March 10, 2011, *Herald Sun*; available at: http://www.heraldsun.com.au/news/world/full-transcript-of-julia-gillards-speech-to-us-congress/story-e6fr-f7lf-1226018899482 (accessed April 19, 2011).

4.   "Citizenship: The Pursuit of Happiness," ReasonTV; available at: http://reason.tv/video/show/the-pursuit-of-happiness (accessed April 19, 2011).

5.   Ibid.

6.   Tony Blair, "Tony Blair on Clinton, Bush, and the American Character," *Time,* September 2, 2010; available at: http://www.time.com/time/world/article/0,8599,2015409-3,00.html (accessed April 19, 2011).

7.   Real American Stories, One Nation United, "Alp Gurpinar"; video available at: http://www.realamericanstories.com/alp-gurpinar/?curpage=13 (accessed April 19, 2011).

8.   Apostolic Journey To the United States of America and Visit to the United Nations Organization Headquarters, Welcoming Ceremony, Address of His Holiness Benedict XVI, April 16, 2008; available at: http://www.vatican.va/holy_father/benedict_xvi/speeches/2008/april/documents/hf_ben-xvi_spe_20080416_welcome-washington_en.html (accessed April 19, 2011).

9.   ABCNews "ABC's Jeffrey Kofman on Becoming an American Citizen," February 25, 2010, The World Newser [blog]; available at: http://blogs.abcnews.com/theworldnewser/2010/02/abcs-jeffrey-kofman-on-becoming-an-american-citizen.html (accessed April 19, 2011).

10. Posted by FFree Thinker2, "Christopher Hitchens: America—The Greatest Country in the World?" May 2, 2009; video available at: http://www.youtube.com/watch?v=t-cQZNcaujs&feature=related (accessed April 19, 2011).

11. Posted by chosun79, "Anthony Kim—The American Dream," October 1, 2008; video available at: http://www.youtube.com/watch?v=CNhuowMs9-0 (accessed April 19, 2011).

12. Posted by NETNebraska, "I Am an American—Nebraska Stories," November 4, 2009; video available at: http://www.youtube.com/watch?v=klX9aRvpO7A (accessed April 19, 2011).

13. Real American Stories, One Nation United, "Giuliana Rancic"; video available at: http://www.realamericanstories.com/giuliana-rancic/?curpage=7 (accessed April 19, 2011).

14. Real American Stories, "Teuta Dedvukaj"; video available at: http://www.realamericanstories.com/teuta-dedvukaj-new/?curpage=8 (accessed April 19, 2011).

15. Real American Stories, "A Perfect Fit—NEW"; available at: http://www.realamericanstories.com/a-perfect-fit/ (accessed April 19, 2011).

16. Real American Stories "George Padavil"; video available at: http://www.realamericanstories.com/george-padavil/?curpage=14 (accessed April 19, 2011).

17. Real American Stories, One Nation United, "Oleg Haskel"; video available at: http://www.realamericanstories.com/oleg-haskel/?curpage=14 (accessed April 19, 2011).

18. Real American Stories, One Nation United, "Tova Friedman"; video available at: http://www.realamericanstories.com/tova-friedman-new/?curpage=5 (accessed April 19, 2011).

19. Real American Stories, One Nation United, "NEW Global Soap Project"; video available at: http://www.realamericanstories.com/global-soap-project-new/?curpage=1 (accessed April 19, 2011).

CHAPTER FOUR

1. "The Christian Religion by David Barton," David Barton Blog, August 10, 2010; available at http://www.davidbarton.org/2010/08/17/the-christian-religion-by-david-barton/ (accessed April 26, 2011).

2. Carl Pearlston, "Is America a Christian Nation?" *Connecticut Jewish Ledger*, April, 2001; available at: http://www.catholiceducation.org/articles/politics/pg0040.html (accessed April 26, 2011).

3. Charles W. Dunn, *The Conservative Tradition in America* (Lanham, MD: Rowman & Littlefield, 2000), 134.

4. "The Moral Basis of a Free Society," The Hoover Institution, November 1, 1997; available at: http://www.hoover.org/publications/policy-review/article/6486.

5. Revelation 3:20.

6. Paul Johnson, *A History of the American People,* 39.

7. Albert Enoch Pillsbury, *Lincoln and Slavery* (Boston: Houghton Mifflin, 1913), 30.

8. The Constitution and Declaration of Independence as Issues in the Lincoln-Douglas Debates, Willard L. King and Allan Nevins, *Journal of the Illinois State Historical Society (1908-1984)*, Vol. 52, No. 1, Lincoln Sesquicentennial (Spring, 1959), 21.

9. Alexandra Stern, *Eugenic Nation: Faults and Frontiers of Better Breeding in Modern America* (American Crossroads), 210.

10. Leila Zenderland, *Measuring Minds: Henry Herbert Goddard and the Origins of American Intelligence Testing* (Cambridge Studies in the History of Psychology), 274.

11. "Eugenics and the Nazis – the California connection," *San Francisco Chronicle* (9 November 2003).

12. African Studies Center, University of Pennsylvania, "Letter from a Birmingham Jail [King, Jr.]"; available at: http://www.africa.upenn.edu/Articles_Gen/Letter_Birmingham.html (accessed April 26, 2011).

13. Ibid.

14. Remarks on East-West Relations at the Brandenburg Gate in West Berlin, June 12, 1987, Ronald Reagan Presidential Library; available at: http://www.reagan.utexas.edu/archives/speeches/1987/061287d.htm (accessed April 26, 2011).

15. Ibid.

16. Address at Commencement Exercises at the University of Notre Dame, May 17, 1981, Ronald Reagan Presidential Library; available at: http://www.reagan.utexas.edu/archives/speeches/1981/51781a.htm (accessed April 26, 2011).

17. Remarks at the Annual Convention of the National Association of Evangelicals in Orlando, Florida, March 8, 1983 Ronald Reagan Presidential Library; available at: http://www.reagan.utexas.edu/archives/speeches/1983/30883b.htm (accessed April 26, 2011).

18. "Dissenting Opinion of Wallace v. Jeffree," Justice William Renquist, June 4, 1985; available at: http://www.belcherfoundation.org/wallace_v_jaffree_dissent.htm (accessed April 26, 2011).

19. *Engel v. Vitale*, 370 U.S. 421 (1962).

20. *Abingdon School District v. Schempp*, 374 U.S. 203 (1963).

21. *Stone v. Graham*, 449 U.S. 39 (1980).

22. *Wallace v. Jaffree*, 472 U.S. 38 (1985).

23. *Allegheny County v. ACLU*, 492 U.S. 573 (1989).

24. *Lee v. Weisman*, 505 U.S. 577 (1992).

25. *Lamb's Chapel v. Center Moriches Union Free School District*, 508 U.S. 384 (1993).

26. *Locke v. Davey*, 540 U.S. 712 (2004).

27. *McCreary County v. ACLU*, 545 U.S. 844 (2005).

28. For more instances of the assault on religious liberty, see www.alliancedefensefund.org.

29. "Defending Religious Freedom in America," ADF; available at: http://www.alliancedefensefund.org/ReligiousFreedom (accessed April 26, 2011).

30. *Barton v. City of Balch Springs;* more information available at: http://www.law.com/jsp/law/LawArticleFriendly.jsp?id=900005543320 (accessed April 26, 2011).

31. "Report Documents Attacks on Religious Freedom," North Carolina Family Policy Council, October, 2004; available at: http://www.ncfamily.org/stories/041025s1.html (accessed April 26, 2011).

32. Vince Haley, "Save the Wren Chapel," National Review Online, November 17, 2006; available at: http://www.nationalreview.com/articles/219285/save-wren-chapel/vince-haley (accessed April 26, 2011).

33. "Missouri school sued by student who refused to support gay adoptions," *USA Today*, November 2, 2006; available at: http://www.usatoday.com/news/nation/2006-11-02-gay-adoption_x.htm (accessed April 26, 2011).

34. *Catherina Lorenza Cenzon-Decarlo v. The Mount Sinai Hospital*; available at: http://oldsite.alliancedefensefund.org/userdocs/Cenzon-DeCarloComplaint.pdf (accessed April 26, 2011).

35. "Religious Speech and Hate Crimes," ADF; available at: www.alliancedefensefund.org/UserDocs/ChurchHateCrimes.pdf (accessed April 26, 2011).

36. "'How he linked abortion and slavery,'" *California Catholic Daily*, News Release from Marin Catholic High School, January 12, 2010; available at: http://www.calcatholic.com/news/newsArticle.aspx?id=6f41c695-55f9-489c-b1ec-7ffe90022e94 (April 26, 2011).

37. "Christians threatened with arrest in Richmond for sharing Gospel, lawsuit filed," ADF News Release, February 1, 2010; available at: http://www.adfmedia.org/News/PRDetail/3696 (accessed April 26, 2011).

38. "Group Loses Tax Break Over Gay Union Issue," *New York Times*, September 18, 2007; available at: http://www.nytimes.com/2007/09/18/nyregion/18grove.html (accessed April 26, 2011).

39. "The Homosexual Agenda: The Principal Threat to Your Religious Freedom," ADF; available at: http://www.alliancedefensefund.org/Marriage (accessed April 26, 2011).

40. "Public Schools Intolerant of Religious Expression," ADF; available at: http://www.alliancedefensefund.org/PublicSchools (accessed April 26, 2011).

41. Ibid.

42. George Washington's Inaugural Address, April 30, 1789, National Archives; available at: http://www.archives.gov/legislative/features/gw-inauguration/ (accessed April 26, 2011).

43. William J. Bennett, *The De-Valuing of America* (CO: Focus on the Family Pub, 1994), 255.

44. "Proposition 8 Cases," California State Supreme Court, May 26, 2009; available at: http://www.courtinfo.ca.gov/opinions/archive/S168047.PDF

(accessed April 26, 2011), and Lisa Leff, "Court halts Calif. gay marriages pending appeal," *The Washington Times*, August 16, 2010; available at: http://www.washingtontimes.com/news/2010/aug/16/court-halts-calif-gay-marriages-pending-appeal/ (accessed April 26, 2011).

45. Steven Ertelt, "New Planned Parenthood Report: Record Abortions Done in 2009," LifeNews.com, February 23, 2011; available at: http://www.life-news.com/2011/02/23/new-planned-parenthood-report-record-abor-tions-done-in-2009/ (accessed April 28, 2011).

46. *Pierce v. Society of Sisters*, US Supreme Court, June 1, 1925; available at: http://supreme.justia.com/us/268/510/case.html (accessed April 26, 2011).

47. *Wisconsin v. Yoder*, US Supreme Court, May 15, 1972; available at: http://supreme.justia.com/us/406/205/case.html (accessed April 26, 2011).

48. IN RE: VISITATION AND CUSTODY OF SENTURI N.S.V. (October 25, 2007); available at: http://www.state.wv.us/wvsca/docs/fall07/33334.htm (accessed April 26, 2011).

49. ParentalRights.org, from footnote 2 to article, http://www.parentalrights. org/index.asp?Type=B_BASIC&SEC={571D1CA7-1BA8-4E61-A55A-EE75EAD37DCE}: "This was not a reported decision and personal names are withheld in such cases as a matter of course. Our source for this information was Michael Farris, J.D., who advised the parents relative to this case."

50. *In Re: Sumey*, 94 Wn. 2d 757, 621 P. 2d 108 (1980); available at: http://www.nymatlaw.com/sumey-621-p2d-108/ (accessed April 26, 2011).

51. "Homeschooling: Helping Children Achieve Academic and Personal Success," Calvert School, 2010; available at: http://homeschool.calvertschool. org/downloads/Calvert_Homeschooling_Academic_Success.pdf (accessed April 26, 2011).

52. Brian Ray, Ph.D., "Research Facts on Homeschooling," The National Home Education Research Institute, January 11, 2011; available at: http://www. nheri.org/Research-Facts-on-Homeschooling.html (accessed April 26, 2011).

53. Charles Dexter Cleveland, *A Compendium of American Literature* (Philadelphia, 1859), 273–74.

CHAPTER FIVE

1. Corinne Maier, *Hello Laziness: Why Hard Work Doesn't Pay*, trans. David Watson (London: Orion, 2005).

2. Rebecca Leung, "France: Less Work, More Time Off," CBS News *60 Minutes*, June 29, 2005, http://www.cbsnews.com/stories/2005/06/27/60II/

main704571.shtml?tag=contentMain;contentBody (accessed April 25, 2011).

3. Michael Novak, *The Spirit of Democratic Capitalism* (Lanham, MD: Madison Books, 1991).

4. Ibid., 39–40.

5. Os Guinness, *The Call: Finding and Fulfilling the Central Purpose of Your Life* (Nashville: Thomas Nelson, 2003), 40.

6. Michael Novak, *The Spirit of Democratic Capitalism*, 91.

7. From Ken Burns, *Brooklyn Bridge*, PBS Documentary, 1981.

8. George Washington, Letter to Benjamin Harrison, October 10, 1784.

9. Daniel J. Boorstin, *The Americans: The Colonial Experience* (New York: Vintage Books, 1958), 10.

10. Frederick Jackson Turner, *Rereading Frederick Jackson Turner* (New Haven, CT: Yale University Press, 1998), 31.

11. Ibid., 59.

12. Ron Chernow, *Alexander Hamilton* (New York: Penguin, 2004).

13. Alex Hutchinson, "The Top 50 Inventions of Past 50 Years," *Popular Mechanics*, December 1, 2005, http://www.popularmechanics.com/technology/gadgets/news/2078467 (accessed April 18, 2011).

14. Michael Novak, *The Spirit of Democratic Capitalism*, 99–100.

15. Robert Rector, Katherine Bradley, and Rachel Sheffield, "Obama to Spend $10.3 Trillion on Welfare: Uncovering the Full Cost of Means-Tested Welfare or Aid to the Poor," The Heritage Foundation, Special Report #67, 2009.

16. Peter Ferrara, *America's Ticking Bankruptcy Bomb* (New York: HarperCollins, 2011).

17. U.S. Bureau of the Census, Current Population Reports, Series P-60, No. 80, "Income in 1970 of Families and Persons in the United States," p. 26.

18. U.S. Bureau of the Census, Current Population Reports, Series P-60, No. 180, "Money Income of Households, Families, and Persons in the United States: 1991," p. 7.

19. Peter J. Ferrara, "It's Time To Block Grant Welfare To The States," Forbes.com, February 23, 2011; available at: http://www.forbes.com/2011/02/23/welfare-poverty-economics-opinions-contributors-peter-ferrara.html (accessed April 28, 2011).

20. Ron Haskins, "Welfare Reform: Success or Failure? It Worked," Brookings Institution, March 15, 2006, http://www.brookings.edu/articles/2006/0315welfare_haskins.aspx (accessed April 25, 2011).

CHAPTER SIX

1. "Five Years After Katrina: Progress Report on Recovery, Rebuilding and Renewal," Office of Governor Haley Barbour, August 29, 2010; available at: http://www.governorbarbour.com/news/2010/aug/Katrina5years.pdf (accessed April 25, 2011).
2. Michael Novak, *The Spirit of Democratic Capitalism* (Lanham, MD: Madison Books, 1991), 135.
3. Ibid., 135.
4. Gordon Wood, *The Americanization of Benjamin Franklin* (New York: Penguin, 2004), 42, 49.
5. Charles Morris, *American Catholic* (New York: Times Books, 1997), 17–18.
6. Alexis de Tocquevile, *Democracy in America*, Part I, ch. 12.
7. Gordon Wood, *The Radicalism of the American Revolution*, 328–29.
8. Burke, *Reflections on the Revolution in France*, para 75.
9. Tocqueville, *Democracy in America*, Part II, ch. 5.
10. Ibid., II, 4.6
11. Arthur Brooks, *Gross National Happiness* (New York: Basic Books, 2008), 190; and Brooks, "Philanthropy and the Non-Profit Sector," in *Understanding America*, ed. James Wilson and Peter Schuck (PublicAffairs, 2008), 542. Brooks says that giving remains steady at between 1.5 and 2% of GDP annually. 2010 GDP exceeded $14 trillion.
12. Brooks, *Who Really Cares* (New York: Basic Books, 2006), 117–18.
13. "About Our Founder," Carnegie Corporation of New York, http://carnegie.org/about-us/foundation-history/about-andrew-carnegie/ (accessed April 28, 2011); and "A Tribute: Colonel James Anderson," Carnegie Library of Pittsburgh, http://www.clpgh.org/exhibit/anderson.html (accessed April 28, 2011).
14. Gordon Wood, *The Creation of the American Republic: 1776-1787* (Chapel Hill: University of North Carolina Press, 1998), 120.
15. Martin Luther King Jr., "Letter from the Birmingham Jail," April 16, 1963.
16. United States Foreign-Born Population, Data Tables, http://www.census.gov/population/www/socdemo/foreign/datatbls.html (accessed April 28, 2011).
17. Marisa Schor, "A Comparative Study of Russian Jewish Immigrants Based on Absorption Strategies," Dissertation American Jewish University, 2005; available at: http://academics.ajula.edu/Content/ContentUnit.asp?CID=1639&u=5971&t=0 (accessed April 25, 2011).
18. Ibid.

19. George Rupp, "1975: The Largest Refugee Resettlement in American History," *International Rescue Committee*, June 27, 2008; available at: http://www.rescue.org/blog/1975-largest-refugee-resettlement-effort-american-history-irc-75 (accessed April 25, 2011).

20. Joseph Cao, "Interview with Brian Lamb," C-SPAN Q and A, January 11, 2009; available at: http://www.q-and-a.org/Transcript/?ProgramID=1213 (accessed April 28, 2011).

21. The hallmark legislative accomplishment that addressed welfare reform was H.R.3734, Personal Responsibility and Work Opportunity Reconciliation Act of 1996; available at: http://thomas.loc.gov/cgi-bin/query/z?c104:H.R.3734.ENR: (accessed April 28, 2011).

22. Yuval Levin, "Beyond the Welfare State," *National Affairs* No. 7, Spring 2011; available at: http://www.nationalaffairs.com/publications/detail/beyond-the-welfare-state (accessed April 25, 2011).

23. Ibid.

24. Charles Murray, *The Happiness of the American People*, Irving Kristol Lecture, AEI, March 2009; text of speech available at: http://www.aei.org/speech/100023 (accessed April 25, 2011).

25. Ibid.

26. Howard S. Miller, *The Legal Foundations of American Philanthropy, 1776–1844* (Madison: State Historical Society of Wisconsin, 1961).

27. Patrick Fagan, "How the Death Tax Kills Small Businesses, Communities, and Civil Society," Heritage Foundation Backgrounder, No. 2438, July 26, 2010; available at: http://www.heritage.org/research/reports/2010/07/how-the-death-tax-kills-small-businesses-communities-and-civil-society (accessed April 25, 2011).

28. Heather Higgins, "The 'Diversity' Threat to California Charity," *Wall Street Journal*, May 30, 2008; available at: http://online.wsj.com/article/SB121210971023331419.html (accessed April 25, 2011).

29. Katherine Mangu-Ward, "The Politics of Giving," Reason Foundation, February 23, 2010; available at: http://reason.org/news/show/the-politics-of-giving (accessed April 25, 2011).

30. Caroline Preston, "Fla. Adopts Legislation to Protect Foundations' Autonomy," *Chronicle of Philanthropy*, Philanthropy.org, June 1, 2010; available at: http://philanthropy.com/blogs/government-and-politics/fla-adopts-legislation-to-protect-foundations-autonomy/24434 (accessed April 25, 2011).

31. Bradley Olson, "City puts a stop to homeless outreach," *Houston Chronicle*, January 13, 2011; available at: http://www.chron.com/disp/story.mpl/metropolitan/7381016.html (accessed April 25, 2011).

32. Thomas Korosec, "Dallas law cracks down on feeding the homeless," *Houston Chronicle*, August 7, 2005; available at: http://www.chron.com/disp/story.mpl/metropolitan/3299402.html (accessed April 25, 2011).

33. Talking Points of Ryan Messmore, "Obama's Latest Proposal to Reduce Charitable Deductions Would Crowd Out Civil Society," Heritage Foundation Backgrounder #2538, March 29, 2011; available at: http://www.heritage.org/research/reports/2011/03/obamas-latest-proposal-to-reduce -charitable-deductions-would-crowd-out-civil-society (accessed April 25, 2011).

34. "Diploma Count: 2009," *Education Week*, June 11, 2009; available at: http://www.edweek.org/ew/toc/2009/06/11/index.html (accessed April 28, 2011).

35. RiShawn Liddle, "Return of the One-Room Schoolhouse," *The American Spectator*, March 28, 2011; available at: http://spectator.org/archives/2011/03/29/return-of-the-one-room-schoolh (accessed April 25, 2011).

36. Jennifer Medina, "At California School, Parents Force an Overhaul," *New York Times*, December 10, 2010; available at: http://www.nytimes.com/2010/12/08/education/08teacher.html (accessed April 25, 2011).

37. Jim Newton, "Education Battle at Compton Unified School," *LA Times*, April 18, 2011; available at: http://www.latimes.com/news/opinion/commentary/la-oe-newton-compton-20110418,0,5430463.column (accessed April 25, 2011).

38. Ohio Liberty Council and Ohio Project, "2011 Ballot Initiative on Healthcare passes 300,000 Signatures," April 22, 2011; available at: http://www.ohiolibertycouncil.org/?p=3440 (accessed April 28, 2011).

CHAPTER SEVEN

1. Marc Fisher, "In Tunisia, act of one fruit vendor unleashes wave of revolution through Arab world," *Washington Post*, March 26, 2011; available at: http://www.washingtonpost.com/world/in-tunisia-act-of-one-fruit-vendor-sparks-wave-of-revolution-through-arab-world/2011/03/16/AFjfsueB_print.html (accessed April 26, 2011).

2. Ibid.

3. Hernando de Soto, "Egypt's Economic Apartheid," *Wall Street Journal*, February 3, 2011; available at: http://online.wsj.com/article/SB10001424052748704358704576118683913032882.html (accessed April 28, 2011).

4. Hernando de Soto, "Assessing the Success of Capitalism," Commanding Heights; available at: http://www.pbs.org/wgbh/commandingheights/shared/minitext/int_hernandodesoto.html#6 (accessed April 26, 2011).

5. Gordon S. Wood, *The Creation of the American Republic* (NC: University of North Carolina Press, 1969), 33.

6. Ibid., 32.

7. John J. Wallis, "The Concept of Systematic Corruption in American History," University of Maryland & National Bureau of Economic Research, April 2005; available at: http://www.bsos.umd.edu/gvpt/apworkshop/wallis05.pdf (accessed April 26, 2011).

8. Ibid.

9. Center for Health Transformation, Wall Charts – 2010 Health Reform Law, http://www.healthtransformation.net/cs/wallcharts (accessed April 28, 2011).

10. Richard Epstein, "Government By Waiver: The Breakdown Of Public Administration," *Forbes*, November 23, 2010; available at: http://blogs.forbes.com/richardepstein/2010/11/23/government-by-waiver-the-breakdown-of-public-administration/?boxes=opinionschannellatest (accessed April 26, 2011).

11. Thomas Jefferson, letter to Mr. Jarvis, September 1820.

12. *Barnes v. Glen Theatre, Inc.*, 501 U.S. 560, 569 (1991).

13. *Romer v. Evans*, 517 U.S. 620, 635 (1996).

14. Ibid., 578.

15. *Lawrence v. Texas*, 539 U.S. 582 (O'Connor, J., concurring).

16. Ibid., 599.

17. *Williams v. Morgan*, 478 F.3d 1316, 1322 (11th Cir. 2007).

18. *United States v. Extreme Associates, Inc.*, 352 F.Supp.2d 578 (W.D. Pa. 2005), rev'd 431 F.3d 150 (3d Cir. 2005), and *Reliable Consultants, Inc. v. Earle*, 517 F.3d 738 (5th Cir. 2008).

19. *Reliable Consultants, Inc. v. Earle*, 538 F.3d 355, 362 (5th Cir. 2008) (Garza, J., dissenting from denial of rehearing).

20. See the letter here: http://www.justice.gov/opa/pr/2011/February/11-ag-223.html (accessed April 26, 2011).

21. Ibid.

22. Barack Obama, *The Audacity of Hope* (New York: Random House, 2006), 223.

CHAPTER EIGHT

1.   Franklin D. Roosevelt, Fireside Chat 17, "On an Unlimited National Emergency," May 27, 1941.

2.   Ronald Reagan, First Inaugural Address, January 20, 1981.

3.   Nikita Khrushchev, *Khrushchev Remembers* (Boston: Little, Brown, and Company, 1974).

4.   Ronald Reagan, Acceptance of the Republican Nomination for President, July 17, 1980.

5.   Ibid.

6.   Office of Management and Budget, "Table 3.1—Outlays by Superfunction and Function: 1940–2016," Historical Tables, Budget of the United States Government, Fiscal Year 2012, Washington, D.C.: U.S. Government Printing Office, 2011; available at: http://www.whitehouse.gov/sites/default/files/omb/budget/fy2012/assets/hist.pdf (accessed April 28, 2011).

7.   Ronald Reagan, "Evil Empire Speech," March 8, 1983.

8.   Bruce Parrott, "The Soviet Debate on Missile Defense," *Bullet of the Atomic Scientists*, April 1987, pg. 9.

9.   Erick Stakelbeck, *The Terrorist Next Door* (Washington, D.C.: Regnery Publishing, 2011), 57–58, 197.

10. Kerry Picket, "(Audio) CBC Congressman: KKK bigger threat than Muslims," *Washington Times*, March 10, 2011; available at: http://www.washingtontimes.com/blog/watercooler/2011/mar/10/audio-cbc-congressman-twt-terror-hearing-your-pape/ (accessed April 27, 2011).

11. Representative Benny Thompson, quoted in Robert Spencer, "Congressman says King hearings should be scrapped because they will provoke jihadists," JihadWatch.org, March 11, 2011; available at: http://www.jihadwatch.org/2011/03/congressman-says-king-hearings-should-be-scrapped-because-they-will-provoke-jihadists.html (accessed April 27, 2011).

12. Statement by Press Secretary Robert Gibbs on the Iranian Election, WhiteHouse.gov, June 13, 2009; available at: http://www.whitehouse.gov/the_press_office/Statement-by-Press-Secretary-Robert-Gibbs-on-the-Iranian-Election/ (accessed April 27, 2011).

13. "Obama Refuses to 'Meddle' in Iran," BBC, June 19, 2009; available at: http://news.bbc.co.uk/2/hi/8104362.stm (accessed April 27, 2011).

14. Ryan Lizza, "The Consequentialist," *The New Yorker*, May 2, 2011, http://www.newyorker.com/reporting/2011/05/02/110502fa_fact_lizza?printable=true&currentPage=all (accessed April 27, 2011).

15. Charles Krauthammer, "Obama's New Start," National Review Online, December 24, 2010; available at: http://www.nationalreview.com/arti-

cles/255914/obama-s-new-start-charles-krauthammer (accessed April 27, 2011).

16. "Allies Are Split on Goal and Exit Strategy in Libya," *New York Times*, March 24, 2011; available at: http://www.nytimes.com/2011/03/25/world/africa/25policy.html?_r=1&pagewanted=all (accessed April 27, 2011).

17. Ibid.

18. "NATO takes command of part of Libya operation," FOXNews.com, March 24, 2011; available at: http://www.foxnews.com/world/2011/03/24/france-libya-operation-weeks-months (accessed April 27, 2011).

19. Ryan Lizza, "The Consequentialist," *The New Yorker*.

CHAPTER NINE

1. See the video here: http://www.realclearpolitics.com/video/2010/09/20/cnbc_town_hall_questioner_to_obama_im_exhausted_of_defending_you.html (accessed May 2, 2011).

2. Jon Meacham, "We Are All Socialists Now," *Newsweek*, February 7, 2009; available at: http://www.newsweek.com/2009/02/06/we-are-all-socialists-now.html (accessed May 2, 2011).

3. Stephen Dinan, "Social Security in the red this year," *Washington Times*, August 5, 2010; available at: http://www.washingtontimes.com/news/2010/aug/5/social-security-red-first-time-ever/ (accessed May 3, 2011).

4. The Prowler, "Nullification Nancy," *American Spectator*, July 5, 2005; available at: http://spectator.org/archives/2005/07/05/nullification-nancy (accessed May 2, 2011).

5. Ben Geman, "Energy Department official highlights 'resilience' in oil markets amid Libyan unrest," *E² Wire*, February 22, 2011; available at: http://thehill.com/blogs/e2-wire/677-e2-wire/145551-energy-department-official-cites-resilience-in-oil-markets-amid-libyan-unrest?utm_campaign=E2 Wire&utm_source=twitterfeed&utm_medium=twitter (accessed May 2, 2011).

6. Arthur B. Laffer, Stephen Moore, and Peter Tanous, *The End of Prosperity: How Higher Taxes Will Doom the Economy—If We Let It Happen* (New York: Simon & Schuster, 2008), 88.

CHAPTER TEN

1. Matthew Jaffe and John R. Parkinson, "House Votes to Strip Planned Parenthood of Federal Funding," ABC News, February 18, 2011; available at: http://abcnews.go.com/Politics/house-votes-strip-planned-parenthood-federal-funding/story?id=12951080 (accessed May 2, 2011).

2.   "Caretakers of Stolen Mojave Desert Cross Vow to Replace It," FoxNews.
      com, May 11, 2010; available at: http://www.foxnews.com/us/2010/05/11/
      thieves-steal-mojave-desert-memorial-cross-nighttime-heist/#ixzz1KI99Ch54
      (accessed May 2, 2011).

3.   Robert Barnes, "For Couple, Memorial Became a Mission," *Washington
      Post*, September 28, 2009; available at: http://www.washingtonpost.com/
      wp-dyn/content/article/2009/09/28/AR2009092803125.html (accessed May
      2, 2011).

4.   Ibid.

5.   The article can be read here: "A College Education," originally published in
      the *Wall Street Journal* Review & Outlook, June 16, 2007; available at
      GoACTA.org, http://www.goacta.org/press/Articles/2007Articles/07-06-
      16WSJ.cfm (accessed May 2, 2011).

6.   "Appeals Court: Mt. Soledad Cross Is Unconstitutional," 10News.com,
      January 4, 2011; available at: http://www.10news.com/news/26366967/
      detail.html (accessed May 2, 2011).

7.   "Victory: 'In God We Trust' Unveiled in Capitol Visitors Center," Congress-
      man Randy J. Forbes, September 30, 2009; available at: http://forbes.house.
      gov/News/DocumentSingle.aspx?DocumentID=147350 (accessed May 2,
      2011).

8.   "At Vacation Liberty School, Kentucky kids get civic lessons with a Christian
      twist," FOX News, July 15, 2010; available at: http://www.foxnews.com/
      us/2010/07/15/vacation-liberty-school-kentucky-kids-civics-lessons-chris-
      tian-twist/ (accessed May 2, 2011).

9.   Ibid.

10.   St. Louis Vacation Liberty School, http://stlvls.webs.com/index.htm (accessed
      May 2, 2011).

11.   David Bossie, "Hypocrisy in Citizens United Chatter," *Politico*, February 2,
      2010; available at: http://www.politico.com/news/stories/0210/32331.html
      (accessed May 2, 2011).

12.   Jeff Benedict, *Little Pink House: A True Story of Defiance and Courage*
      (New York: Grand Central Publishing, 2009).

13.   "Five Years After *Kelo*: The Sweeping Backlash Against One of the Supreme
      Court's Most-Despised Decisions," Institute for Justice; available at: http://
      ij.org/index.php?option=com_content&task=view&id=3392&Itemid=165
      (accessed May 2, 2011).

14. Benjamin Evans, "Replicating the Success of Prop C," National Review Online, August 12, 2010; available at: http://www.nationalreview.com/articles/print/243657 (accessed May 2, 2011).

15. Tony Messenger, "Prop C passes overwhelmingly," stltoday.com, August 4, 2010; available at: http://www.stltoday.com/news/local/govt-and-politics/article_c847dc7c-564c-5c70-8d90-dfd25ae6de56.html (accessed May 2, 2011).

16. Dan Whitcomb, "Mayor, officials arrested in California pay scandal," Reuters, September 22, 2010; available at: http://www.reuters.com/article/2010/09/22/us-california-payscandal-arrests-idUSTRE68K40N20100922 (accessed May 2, 2011); and "Voters in California's corruption-bit Bell make clean sweep," Reuters, March 9, 2011; available at: http://www.reuters.com/article/2011/03/09/us-corruption-bell-election-idUSTRE7286GZ20110309 (accessed May 2, 2011).

17. BASTA, http://basta4bell.com/ (accessed May 2, 2011).

18. "California's Parent Revolution," *Wall Street Journal* Review & Outlook, December 7, 2010; available at: http://parentrevolution.org/wp-content/uploads/2010/12/Wall-Street-Journal-Opinion-12-7-10.pdf (accessed May 2, 2011).

19. "The D.C. Opportunity Scholarship Program is Making a Difference," D.C. Parents for School Choice; available at: http://www.saveschoolchoice.com/pdf/Facts.pdf (accessed May 2, 2011).

20. "D.C. Parents Call on Congress to Put the needs of Kids Ahead of Special Interest Politics," PRNewsWire.com, March 24, 2011; available at: http://www.prnewswire.com/news-releases/dc-parents-call-on-congress-to-put-the-needs-of-kids-ahead-of-special-interest-politics-118588989.html (accessed May 2, 2011).

21. Kathryn Jean Lopez, "Icing on the Cake," National Review Online *The Corner*, April 9, 2011; available at: http://www.nationalreview.com/corner/264305/icing-cake-kathryn-jean-lopez (accessed May 2, 2011).

22. Matthew Ladner, "Arizona Legislature passes 'Lexie's Law' to replace vouchers," Goldwater Institute, June 1, 2009; available at: http://www.goldwater-institute.org/article/2826 (accessed May 2, 2011).

23. "Arizona Governor to Sign Lexie's Law To Save Scholarships for Special Needs and Foster Children," Institute for Justice, May 29, 2009; available at: http://www.ij.org/index.php?option=com_content&task=view&id=2735&Itemid=165 (accessed May 2, 2011).

24. "License to Describe: Challenging Washington D.C.'s Tour-Guide Licensing Scheme," Institute for Justice; available at: http://www.ij.org/about/3491 (accessed May 2, 2011); and video; available at: http://www.ij.org/freedomflix/16-licensetodescribe (accessed May 2, 2011).

25. Jonathan Dienst and Hasani Gittens, "9/11 Terror Trials Will Not Be Held in New York City," NBC, January 30, 2010; available at: http://www.nbc-newyork.com/news/local/911-Terror-Trials-Will-Not-Be-Held-in-NYC-83083662.html (accessed May 2, 2011).

26. Andrew C. McCarthy, "Never Forgot Coalition Plans Rally Against Civilian Trials for 9/11 Terrorists," National Review Online *The Corner*, November 23, 2009; available at: http://www.nationalreview.com/corner/190768/never-forget-coalition-plans-rally-against-civilian-trials-911-terrorists-andrew-c-mcc (accessed May 2, 2011).

CONCULSION

1. CBS News Poll, May 26, 2010, http://www.cbsnews.com/htdocs/pdf/poll_052510.pdf (accessed May 2, 2011).

INDEX